DIETRICH BONH▮▮▮▮▮

his *Ethics* and its value for Christian Ethics today

Harold Lockley

The Phoenix Press
(Swansea)

Typeset by CBS Felixstowe
Printed by Intype, London

Published by the Phoenix Press (Swansea)

ISBN 1 858650 20 8

A CIP catalogue record for this book is available from the
British Library.

To

ANDREW, SIMON AND PETER

Semper fideles

CONTENTS

Frontispiece: Dietrich Bonhoeffer

PREFACE

The origins of this study of Dietrich Bonhoeffer's *Ethics* stem from a conviction that Western society continually needs to examine the roots of its ethical and moral thinking, and at no time is this more true than the present. Bonhoeffer's *Ethics*, although incomplete and unrevised by its author, is nevertheless generally acknowledged among students of ethics to be one such attempt.

The importance of the work is amply attested. Not only did Bonhoeffer himself regard it as the culmination of his academic endeavours – a child by which he wished to be remembered – but many Bonhoeffer scholars have also thought the same. Ronald Gregor Smith, for example, a pioneer among such scholars, described it as a rich treasury containing the finest of Bonhoeffer's ideas still awaiting discovery; sadly among his compatriots, at least, his suggestions for the most part, have gone unheeded. *Ethics* continues still to be the least known of all Bonhoeffer's works in English theological circles.

By a curious irony it seems to have been Bonhoeffer's intention to use an invitation from Dr. John Baillie to lecture in Edinburgh in the summer of 1939 on a theme which would provide a basis for his book on ethics. The war intervened and British ethical students missed the opportunity of a privileged introduction to this remarkable work. Unfortunately, too, little or nothing of a serious nature has been done in this country, since, to come to grips with the somewhat complex and daunting ideas which the *Ethics* contains.

It has been otherwise elsewhere. Both on the Continent and the United States of America Bonhoeffer's *Ethics* have for some time now been the subject of serious study and enquiry and my chief indebtedness is therefore to scholars living and working in these parts of the world. In this study, wherever appropriate, this indebtedness has (I hope) been suitably acknowledged either in the text or in the footnotes appended to each chapter. Newcomers to the *Ethics* should, I believe, find the straightforward exposition and interpretation of Bonhoeffer's ethical ideas in my earlier chapters helpful. Others may perhaps find my attempt to evaluate their significance for christian moral and ethical thinking today in the later chapters of greater interest. Needless to say, this attempt has been prompted by my own personal belief that ethical and moral behaviour, at their best, must be based on the acceptance of belief in the christian revelation of God in Jesus Christ.

The work was first submitted in the form of a dissertation for the research degree of M.Litt, in the University of Cambridge, and I am grateful to the authorities there, including particularly the Reverend Canon Brian Hebblethwaite, Fellow and Dean of Chapel in Queens' College, Cambridge, who supervised my studies, and the Reverend Don Cuppitt, Fellow and formerly Dean of Emmanuel College who supplied me with initial advice and encouragement: due acknowledgement must also be made of the help given by the Reverend Canon S. W. Sykes, Regius Professor of Divinity in the University of Cambridge, now Bishop of Ely, and the Reverend O. O'Donovan, Regius Professor of Moral and Pastoral Theology in the University of Oxford, and to Emmanuel College for providing hospitality during my time in residence. To my late wife I owe more than I can say, not only for the privilege of introducing me into the Bonhoeffer family but also for her willing cooperation in the venture, as well as for her help with German translations. Finally, thanks are due to Miss Juliet Atkins and Mrs. Judith Loades of the Phoenix Press who prepared the manuscript for publication and saw it through the press.

Quorn, Leicestershire
1993

CHAPTER 1

BACKGROUND

In the opening chapter of his book *Ethics and the Limits of Philosophy*, (1) which sets out to describe the present state of moral philosophy, Bernard Williams reminds his readers of Socrates' remark in Plato's *Republic* that discussing morality is no trivial matter since a whole way of life is at stake. Socrates is arguing against Thrasymachus that morality makes for happiness and that the just man is happier than the unjust, (2). Few serious-minded people would wish to plead that moral inquiry is a waste of time; indeed in the present climate of opinion the state of morality rates high as a popular subject for discussion. However, while Plato was undoubtedly convinced that philosophy could successfully deal with the basic questions affecting moral behaviour, others have not been quite so certain. Williams himself admits to being sceptical about the powers of philosophy in this respect, and even to being sceptical about morality itself.

Christian thinkers throughout history have been at one in attaching importance to questions relating to the moral life, and in this matter Jerusalem has agreed with Athens; but, like Bernard Williams, they have often shown less confidence in the capacity of philosophers as such to answer them. (3) St. Bernard of Clairvaux, for example, in the twelfth century asked: 'What do the apostles teach us? Not to read Plato, nor to turn and return to the subtleties of Aristotle... they have taught me to live. Do you believe it is a little thing to know how to live? It is a great thing and indeed the greatest'. (4)

English Christianity - with the notable exception of the Roman Catholic Church - has largely been reluctant to apply the resources of rigorous thought to questions of moral and ethical conduct. Even the Church of England, with its justifiable reputation for pastoral concern, has generally been content to point to the example of Jesus Christ as providing sufficient guidance to the good life without having recourse to the reasonings of moral philosophers. Seventeenth century Caroline divines and twentieth century moral theologians of the stature of bishops Kirk and Mortimer have enriched but scarcely determined the main direction of Anglican moral thinking. Those responsible for the training of Anglican ordinands in the early 1960s are only too well aware of the problems created by the decision to drop the 'Ethics papers' from the General Ordination Examination of that time - a situation only remedied by the publication of suitable handbooks on christian ethics by the official body responsible for training for the ministry, and by the restoration

of the examination in 1975. (5) Yet the 1960s are now generally
acknowledged to be the decade in which 'permissive' attitudes first began to
manifest themselves in British society, and to influence moral, cultural and
intellectual behaviour for good or ill according to one's particular point of
view.

The situation in which the theological colleges found themselves at this
time reflected the position of many people in the country at large, which was
one of moral confusion. It is fair to say that, in spite of growing pressures
from 'moral majorities', the present position (1993) remains much the same.
If the question is asked: how has this state of moral confusion come about?,
the answer on the practical level is: through the breakdown of moral standards;
or more philosophically speaking: through the disappearance of moral and
metaphysical absolutes. It is not our purpose here to delve into the deeper
reasons for this - simply to state what is universally accepted as an established
fact. Writers on the subject are many and varied and their views very well
known. Among the most important in recent years to merit quotation are
Basil Mitchell, a committed Christian, and Alasdair MacIntyre, who is more
of a rationalist in his approach; the opinions of both command more than the
usual amount of respect.

Mitchell, in the published form of his Gifford Lectures, *Morality: Religious
and Secular*, gives an account of 'our contemporary moral confusion' in an
introductory chapter, in the course of which he pinpoints three basic questions
underlying the confusion, about which he believes there is disagreement.

> 'There are differences', he writes, 'as to what is right or wrong,
> good or bad; and hence as to what moral concepts to employ.
> There are differences as to whether there is such a thing as
> morality. And there are differences as to what, if morality does
> exist, is the point or purpose of it. Disagreements as to what is
> right or wrong, good or bad are often not settled, or even made
> explicit enough to be discussed, because of disagreements on the
> other questions.' (6)

MacIntyre, whose impressive book *After Virtue* has points in common
with Mitchell's, similarly attributes much of today's confusion to the absence
of any clear consensus as to the meaning of moral concepts. These, MacIntyre
believes, are no longer able to function in an overall framework or context
such as supplied them with their original meaning and significance. In a
frequently quoted passage he declares:

> What we possess... are the fragments of a conceptual scheme,
> parts which now lack those contexts from which their significance

derived. We possess indeed simulacra of morality, we continue
to use many of the key expressions, both theoretical and practical,
of morality.' (7)

Later in the book MacIntyre explains that this state of affairs 'is the
outcome of a long history from the later middle ages until the present during
which the dominant lists of the virtues have changed, the conception of
individual virtues has changed and the concept of a virtue itself has become
other than what it was.' (8)

Both these writers point to a linguistic confusion which reflects the
underlying moral disorder and which makes conversation in a common
language of ethical discourse well nigh impossible. Our principal purpose in
drawing attention to this confusion however is (as we have already stated)
only to establish it as a fact of modern life. Seldom, if ever before, in history
has the public been made aware of such a number and variety of moral
standards on offer. That this is in some way associated with a similar
diversity of views and practices in the religious sphere is of course not
accidental. Today's religious spectrum ranges from a narrow, dogmatic
fundamentalism, such as we see in Northern Ireland and in some Islamic
sects in this country, through conventional denominational Christianity to a
multifarious collection of eastern mystical and occult groups which defy
classification. Such diversity is not new in human society; what is new is the
official recognition that in Britain we now live in a multi-cultural and
religiously pluralist country.

It is tempting for Christians lamenting these two phenomena, namely, the
diversity of moral views and the diversity of religious views, to link the two,
and to attribute the failure of the one to the failure of the other. Religious
belief and moral practice have been seen to be closely allied since time
immemorial, and the decline in church attendance is frequently cited as the
chief reason for the loss of moral certainty within the nation. This explanation
is altogether too simplistic; church-going no longer has the hold upon large
numbers of people that it once had, but the necessary link between better
church attendance and moral conduct has yet to be established; other factors
- growth in affluence, weakening of family ties, egalitarianism - also have to
be considered. Moreover the failure of those who advocate a purely secular
approach, in order to produce a coherent set of moral values acceptable to
all, suggests that the alternative of rational persuasion by itself cannot provide
an answer. Religion, morality and reason are clearly interrelated, and it
would seem the problem has to do more with the deeper reaches of human
nature and with the overall make-up of man himself.

Basil Mitchell is very much convinced of the importance of considering
the relationship between morality and religion, in addition to examining the

extent to which morality is bound up with human needs. His basic assertion is that in Western Europe moral beliefs and practices have been radically affected by the christian doctrine of man, his creation and redemption, and that this, along with the influence of classical philosophers, has ensured the acceptance of a continuous ethical tradition among christian and secular moral philosophers alike. Traditional values in the West are therefore intimately associated with christian belief. Agreement however between religious and non-religious thinkers on this score (Mitchell believes) is no longer possible; he continues:

> 'that tradition is now visibly disintegrating. Nothing is more striking than our present confusion and perplexity about morality. We find ourselves in the situation in which, with Socrates and Plato, moral philosophy first came into existence. When the customary foundations of morality are sufficiently shaken, there is no alternative but to examine them carefully and then replace or restore them.' (9)

The disintegration to which Mitchell refers is perhaps less conspicuously evident among those intellectuals who dissociate morality from religion than among those who influence popular culture and motivate the day-to-day behaviour of ordinary folk. Two features tend to be prominent in mass culture as unspoken assumptions of a working morality; the first is ethical relativism, which derives from the apparent lack of any solid ground in modern society upon which to base moral or ethical decisions. People's lives appear to be at the mercy of the shifting sands of human needs and social conditions, so that moral actions are subject to circumstances. The second feature is ethical egoism, which relates moral decisions mainly to individual or collective self-interest and is daily nurtured by commercial pressures and human greed. In the absence of agreed normative standards reinforced by strong religious or civic sanctions individualism reigns and confusion follows. Hence what MacIntyre has described as 'the interminable and unsettlable character of so much contemporary moral debate. (10)

Even so the debate continues. Mitchell's conclusion that we have no alternative but to examine the customary foundations of morality still holds, not least for the practical reason that we live in a 'functional' age in which the acid test for many people of what is worthwhile is whether or not 'it works'. Clearly much of what has come to be commonly accepted in private or public morality nowadays does not 'work', since there is no manifest increase in happiness accruing to the individual or society observable compared with former times - there are those who would even claim that the reverse is true. In addition both Christianity and secular humanism would attach considerable importance to providing a 'better world' for future generations, a rallying-cry which helped to unite the nation in two world wars. Curiously enough the threat of nuclear war, influential as it is in determining the moral climate today, does not seem to have inhibited serious ethical thinking about the future as one might perhaps have expected. Indeed a leading moralist, R. W. Hare, chose to dedicate his book *Freedom and Reason* to his children in the hope that 'through the discussion of the problems of ethics, the world in which they have to live may be one in which these matters are better understood.' (11)

For committed Christians, willing to engage in the task of re-examining the foundations of morality, a number of approaches seem to be available - this in itself must be accounted gain when set against the more limited christian approaches of the past. Four such approaches may be selected by way of example, the first being that of Basil Mitchell whose academic liberalism accords well with scholarly opinion. In the final chapter of *Morality: Religious and Secular*, while making no claim that morality cannot exist without religion, nor that religious people are necessarily more moral than non-religious, Mitchell concludes nevertheless that there is a certain congruency between secular moral values and christian values and that exponents of the two should continue in close dialogue and discussion. What will result he is unable to say - there might be a movement back in the direction of traditional ethics, or conceivably away from it; the important thing for moral persons is the overcoming of inertia. Religion and morality for Christians, consequently, should become more and more a matter of conscious choice, based upon deliberate reflection and faith. (12)

Another approach is represented by the Roman Catholic philosopher G. E. M. Anscombe who, failing to find a basis for moral obligation in a secular ethic, settles for locating the 'ought' in the divine will; obligation is in fact imposed by divine law. This view of the relationship of morality and religion has biblical warrant, and renders the dependence of morality upon religion analogous to that of a flower upon a root. Anscombe thus writes:

> 'Naturally it is not possible to have such a conception unless you believe in God as a lawgiver.... But if such a conception is dominant for many centuries, and then is given up, it is a natural result that the concepts of obligation, of being bound or required by law, should remain though they had lost their root.' (13)

The implication presumably is that these 'concepts of obligation', without their root, become disparate fragments of morality which will eventually wither and die.

A third approach is that referred to by an American scholar, Stanley

Hauerwas, in a recent work *The Peaceable Kingdom*. Here the 'doing of ethics', particularly in a community context, receives considerable attention. This he compares with the traditional catholic and protestant approaches which start from theological positions - the one from a theology of nature, the other from a theology of grace - and which he believes distorts the whole ethical enterprise. Christian ethics is not to be primarily understood as following on after systematic theology, but (In Hauerwas's own words)

> 'rather it is at the heart of the theological task. For theology is a practical activity concerned to display how Christian convictions construe the self and world. Therefore theological claims concerning the relation of creation and redemption are already ethical claims'. (14)

Elsewhere Hauerwas makes it clear that ethics as a form of theological reflection takes place 'in service to a community, and it derives its character from the nature of that community's convictions.' (15) The distinctive feature of this approach, therefore, is the emphasis upon christian ethics and morality as living out theology within the life of the christian community.

These summarised statements from Anglican, Roman Catholic and Methodist writers are recognizably traditional, however different they may be in their approach. A fourth way of examining the foundations of morality and exploring the connection between religion and morals is to be found in the writing of the radical Don Cupitt. Cupitt's writings however may be thought of as directed less to the traditional christian believer than to the modern equivalent of what Friedrich Schleiermacher called 'cultured despisers' of religion, that is, the body of thinking people put off by 'the dogmas and propositions of religion.' The position set out by Cupitt in his book *The World to Come* (1982), for example, is, in effect, that Nietzsche's prediction that nihilism would be upon us by the twentieth and twenty-first centuries must be taken seriously, and that this is indeed now happening. As with Nietzsche, Cupitt believes that a return to the christian certainties is no longer possible. Unlike Nietzsche, however, he sees 'the possibility of salvation on the far side of (nihilism)' if we are prepared to follow 'the way of negation to the very end.' This, Cupitt suggests, involves the continuance of critical questioning to the point where any recognisable structuring of the world and the self breaks down and nothing conceivable is left, not even one's own interests and concerns. To engage in such radical questioning (Cupitt believes) is much the same as to practise traditional meditation, which by means of the purgative way arrives eventually at a higher level of being and morality. Instead, therefore, of the old morality, whether private or social, which was the product of egoism, anxiety and the will-to-power, values will be spontaneously generated which allow 'simple sociality, disinterestedness and altruism' to emerge. Such is identifiable as the ethics of the Kingdom. (16) Cupitt's approach has the merit of meeting modern nihilistic tendencies head-on and is based on the view that equally radical questioning of traditional Christianity leaves us with no other possible alternative. Whether this is so, or whether another approach, based on a less radical view of Christianity, (such as one of the three we have just outlined) is more likely to provide us with the answer to the present state of moral confusion, is not for us at this stage to decide. Our principal purpose is to examine in some detail the approach of another christian writer, Dietrich Bonhoeffer, whose *Ethics* represents a similar attempt to confront the moral problems of his time and to suggest possible answers to them.

Bonhoeffer was writing some fifty years ago under the pressures of an alien and evil political regime, and it was against this background that his thinking in *Ethics* developed. For the present, however, it is necessary to look first at Bonhoeffer's own personal background - to which he himself attached importance - particularly as we see it reflected in the *Ethics* itself before turning to consider the Germany of his day. We begin by drawing attention to three features in Bonhoeffer's personal life which need to be mentioned in this connection. The first concerns the remarkable consistency between his life and his thought, that is to say between his ethical thinking and the way he lived. His life embodied his thought. Consequently there can be no real understanding of what Bonhoeffer wrote in *Ethics* about 'concrete' action (for example) without some knowledge of his life as a Lutheran pastor, theologian, ecumenist, resistance leader and conspirator, activities which eventually resulted in his death on a scaffold. Concrete action shaped the man and the man in turn shaped the action.

A specific example of the way in which Bonhoeffer's ethical thinking influenced his action is to be found in the prison essay 'What is Meant by "Telling the Truth"?', which is included in the *Ethics*, (17) and which can only be properly understood against the background of interrogation which he was then undergoing. Many months' experience as a conspirator, planning the death of Hitler, had taught Bonhoeffer that truthfulness need not always mean exact correspondence between thought and speech; account must also be taken of the particular situation, or set of relationships, in which one stands at a given time. As a result he and his friends had been forced to learn the ways of deceitfulness and deception which were alien to them. Writing only a few months before his interrogations, he had reminded other members of the conspiracy - 'we have learnt the arts of equivocation and pretence; experience has made us suspicious of others and kept us from being truthful and open'. (18) It was this experience which led Bonhoeffer to conclude in his prison essay that:

'If any utterance is to be truthful it must in each case be different
according to whom I am addressing, who is questioning me, and
what I am speaking about. The truthful word is not in itself
constant; it is as much alive as life itself.' (19)

By this means Bonhoeffer was able to delay discovery of the plot to
dispose of Hitler and to protect himself and the lives of his friends, at least
for the time being.

There can be little doubt therefore that the poem 'Stations on the Road to
Freedom', written on receipt of the news of the failure of the July 20 plot
against Hitler's life in 1944, summarises Bonhoeffer's view of his own life.
The four 'stations' referred to in the poem - Discipline, Action, Suffering,
Death - were for him stages on a road which he himself had chosen to follow
and which now he believed himself predestined to complete:

'Freedom, we sought you long in discipline, action, suffering.
Now as we die we see you and know you at last, fact to face.'
(20)

Commenting on this in a letter a week later, Bonhoeffer makes the
important ethical point that suffering should be regarded 'as an extension of
our action and a completion of freedom' - the reason being that faith is an
essential ingredient of ethical action and is exercised to the full in suffering
and death. Thus, 'in suffering, the deliverance consists in our being allowed
to put the matter out of our own hands into God's hands. In this sense death
is the crowning of human freedom.' (21)

The second feature of Bonhoeffer's life which needs to be highlighted in
connection with his ethical thinking relates to his home background and to
the lasting effect it had upon him. Karl Jaspers has written of 'the tranquillity
of the cultured, bourgeois Christian world that spoiled its own freedom and
lost touch with its origin', (22) a description which aptly fits the world of
the Weimar Republic and the social class into which Bonhoeffer was born.
In spite of the devastating upheavals of his time, following upon the take-
over of Germany by the National Socialists in 1933, Bonhoeffer continued
to retain his hold upon the bourgeois values he had acquired at home.
However, along with this, there went a remarkable capacity for change in
order to adapt to the godlessness of the society which the National Socialists
introduced. In a prison letter dated 22 April 1944 Bonhoeffer declares:

'I've certainly learnt a great deal, but I don't think I have changed
very much.... Self-development is... a different matter.... Of course,

> we have deliberately broken with a good deal, but that again is something quite different.... Everything seems to have taken its natural course, and to be determined necessarily and straightforwardly by a higher providence.' (23)

Even so Bonhoeffer was well aware of the differences which separated his own adult life from that of his parents; by comparison it was much more 'fragmentary', and it was this which provided the impetus for a new radical look at ethical issues. While continuity with one's past was a gift for which one had cause to be grateful, the challenge of change was inescapable and had to be met. (24)

These two elements interwoven in Bonhoeffer's life, namely, continuity and change, are well illustrated by characters in fragments of a drama and a novel which he attempted to write during his prison period. In the drama, Christoph, of bourgeois stock and clearly speaking for Bonhoeffer, is taken to task by the young Heinrich, of working-class origins, who complains about the lack of solid ground under his feet which he and the working-class need to help them to live and to enable them to die. 'Don't you see the difference?', Heinrich cries out, 'You have a foundation, you have ground under your feet, you have a place in the world. For you there are self-evident values, for which you stand and for which you would gladly lay down your lives, because you know your roots are so deep that they will continue to sustain you. You are only concerned with one thing, to keep your feet on the ground.'

The fragment of a novel contains a conversation between Christoph (who again is Bonhoeffer) and the Major (representing a humane older generation) which takes place against the background of misuse of power and authority. The Major is less concerned with theoretical ideas, statements of faith and moral principles than with actual meeting and living with other people in a positive and human way. Christoph in reply denounces this attitude as one of compromise which is completely useless in combatting the forces he believes to be the 'incarnation of evil itself'. The Major's weapons, according to Christoph, belong to the past; now 'it's a question of the content of life, of man's ultimate convictions, values and standards, and consequently of that "all or nothing" which you so condemn... people look for men who dare to put a firm standard in their hands, who have the courage to live in accordance with it and to fight for it.' (26) It would appear to be not accidental that these two positions taken by Christoph reflect two aspects of the thinking of the author himself. Christoph in the drama is Bonhoeffer with 'ground under his feet', epitomizing the need for continuity, while Christoph in the novel is Bonhoeffer adapting to change, contending against evil with weapons which are no longer out-moded.

The third feature arising from Bonhoeffer's personal background, which has a bearing upon his ethical thinking, has to do with his attitude to authority. Both his middle-class upbringing and the Lutheran Church to which he belonged bred in him a predilection for order and authority. Hence the urgent need for him in adulthood to come to terms with the wholesale disintegration of the established society in which his early life had been spent. Ethically speaking, this was an ordered society in which the moral absolutes were clearly discernible and relationships and roles unquestionably fixed. Even in the *Ethics*, where Bonhoeffer seeks to work out an ethic applicable to the changed situation, he retains his belief in the 'unalterable relation of superiority and inferiority'. (27) It was a belief which only circumstances compelled him to change.

The theological warrant for the belief was the Lutheran Church's attachment to the Pauline injunction of Romans 13:1 about subjection to governing authorities. From this followed a doctrine of creation which designated specific 'orders', 'offices' and 'estates' through which God's commandment made itself known. The fundamental weakness of such a doctrine is well set out by Karl Barth in an early collection of addresses published under the title *The Word of God and the Word of Man.*

> 'One of the dangers of Lutheranism, old and new' (Barth declares) 'is the teaching that there is a hierarchy of so-called offices, or sacred functions, from that of the father and mother through that of the pastor to that of the God- sent king - a hierarchy which is supposed to be part of the actual order of creation and within which the conduct of man is justified in a special way. Now what is this but an evasion of the question, What ought we to do?' (28)

Bonhoeffer was indeed to discover in such 'orders of creation' an Achilles' heel when faced by Nazi misuse of the doctrine to support perverted teachings about the state, race and family. His attempt however to replace this with the alternative concepts, first of 'orders of preservation', then in *Ethics* of 'divine mandates' could hardly be described as successful. By the time of his death Bonhoeffer's taste for a doctrine of orders and offices had well-nigh disappeared. In spite of his indebtedness to church and family for 'ground under his feet', understandably in prison he was not enamoured with the concept of authority as such. *Letters and Papers from Prison* show Bonhoeffer distinguishing between the office and the person who holds it (preferring the latter), seeking no official authority for himself or for the church, but anxious to be identified with the religionless of the world and to be caught up into the suffering of God.

We have now reached the stage where it is necessary to look closer at the condition of Germany itself, particularly as we find it reflected in the writing of the *Ethics* to which it undoubtedly gave rise. The National Socialist clouds were already on the horizon when in 1929 Bonhoeffer in his Barcelona address 'What is a Christian Ethic?' began to search for a concrete ethic which was fully in touch with 'mother earth'. (29) The search continued and when the Finkenwalde seminary, which he then ran, was forcibly closed in 1937 Bonhoeffer was able to confide to a colleague that this meant that 'he would at last get down to writing his *Ethics*.' (30) The work was put in hand in 1939 and, as we know, was interrupted by his arrest four years later and remained unfinished. Eberhard Bethge, Bonhoeffer's friend and collaborator, who edited the surviving material has testified to the inevitability of its writing from the ethical, political and theological points of view. (31) Ethically, Bethge tells us (and as we have seen) the subject had been with Bonhoeffer for most of his ministry; politically, Bonhoeffer had in 1939 begun to commit himself to the conspiracy to overthrow Hitler; and theologically, for Bonhoeffer, according to Bethge, 'the emphasis now had to be shifted from the theology of creation to eschatology. (Bonhoeffer) regarded a preoccupation with the theology of creation as anything but concrete. The hour might come again, he thought, when such a preoccupation would be admissible, but not until the hour of the theology of the *eschaton* was past.' (32)

The *Ethics* then was born in times which Bonhoeffer himself describes as apocalyptic, both as regards Germany and western civilisation as a whole. 'Everything established', he records in *Ethics*, 'is threatened with annihilation. This is not a crisis among other crises. It is a decisive struggle of the last days.... As an apostasy from all that is established it is the supreme manifestation of all the powers which are opposed to God. It is the void made god'. (33) It is fear of the void, Bonhoeffer continues, that results in a loss of the sense of both past and future and leads people to live only for the present moment; so that unspeakable crimes leave no permanent impression and lotteries and games of chance become men's main preoccupation. The effect of all this on personal integrity, Bonhoeffer believes, is to inhibit any kind of inner self-development and to prevent any growth towards individual maturity. In addition, the Machiavellian tactics of unscrupulous politicians ensure that expediency replaces justice, and that inordinate fear breeds suspicion between a man and his neighbour. (34) This and similar passages in the opening chapters of *Ethics*, 'The Love of God and the Decay of the World' and 'The Church and the World', supply us with ample evidence of the disastrous impact which the disintegration of moral and ethical standards had upon Bonhoeffer at this time.

Equally important however for our purpose is some consideration of the attitude of the Lutheran Church to this critical situation. For Bonhoeffer of course, as a pastor and theologian, its attitude was crucial. In his earliest writings he had pinned his hopes on the church as the place where Christ was to be found, where faith was aroused and reconciliation made possible. In the passage previously quoted, where Bonhoeffer identifies the deteriorating situation in Germany and the West with the advent of the Apocalypse, (35) he goes on to remind his readers of the two hopes on which alone man could rely; one is the miracle of faith which is proclaimed and awakened in the church; the other is the 'restrainer' (mentioned in 2 Thessalonians 2:7) identified as the power of the state which, with God's approval, sets limits to evil and maintains order. So, upon the church (in Bonhoeffer's eyes) much depended if the descent into the abyss was to be halted.

Relevant to this was Bonhoeffer's interest in the 'unchurched'; in normal times, he believed, the gospel spoke clearly to the outcasts, the publicans and sinners; when the times were out of joint, however, his experience was that the honest and the good tended to respond to the gospel and to return'to the church, while the wicked remained obstinately apart. (36) Accordingly Bonhoeffer attached considerable importance to this class of uncommitted men and women of goodwill, whose support for the church, he judged, would be decisive for the future of the West. During a course of lectures on spiritual care (*Seelsorge*) given to his ordinands at Finkenwalde 1935-1937 the composition of this unchurched class was broken down into three groups. The first group distinguished by Bonhoeffer consisted of those whom he described as living *alongside* the church i.e., those finding fulfilment in their family and vocation and who attended church when it happened to suit them. The second group was made up of the educated and cultured (*Gebildete*) who, although often close to the church, stood over it, despising its narrow-mindedness and the educational limitations of its clergy. The third were the discontented and disappointed whom Bonhoeffer described as *against* the church, opposing it on every conceivable occasion. The seminarians were given helpful advice on how to deal with each of these groups in turn. (37)

When the battle between church and state began in earnest in 1934 it was chiefly to the *Gebildete*, his own social class, that Bonhoeffer turned for help in supporting the Confessing Church. His conviction (as we have seen) was that there were not a few of them 'who in their struggle for justice, humanity and freedom have learnt once again to speak the name of Jesus Christ, even though it is often with hesitation and with genuine fear'. On the principle therefore that 'he that is not against us is for us' Bonhoeffer was prepared to welcome their support. (38)

Nevertheless the creation of the Confessing Church had the effect of splitting the Lutheran and other evangelical churches of Germany and of leaving the *Reichskirche*, supported by the 'German Christians' (*deutsche*

Christen), in possession of the field. Its main attractions for many lay in its support for Hitler's nationalistic demands (particularly the repeal of the penalties of the Versailles treaty of 1919), and in its theological conservatism with regard to the 'two kingdoms' doctrine and the authority of the state. Even reputable scholars such as Adolf Schlatter (Bonhoeffer's teacher), Paul Althaus and Gerhard Kittel were of the side of Nazi authoritarianism and the cult of the divinely-appointed Führer. This loyalty to the state ran deep and all the churches were affected by it, so that when the break came and the Confessing Church was formed, the Barmen Declaration which set it up denounced the *Reichskirche* not the state, pronouncing its 'more and more clearly evident style of teaching and action' to be theologically unsound. (39)

The attitude of the German churches to some of the ethical problems thrown up by National Socialist policies was not as unequivocal as some would have wished. James Richmond in an interesting contribution to the John Macquarrie *Festschrift, Being and Truth*, while recognising the complexity of the German situation during the Church-Struggle, notes an apparent lack of ethical sensitivity on the part of the churches to the inhumane policies of the Nazis from the beginning. Richmond goes along with the view that the German churches became involved in an ecclesiastical struggle with the state when it was probably already too late; he also accepts the allegation that 'the *Kirchenkampf* was an excessively, not to say vexatiously, churchy, biblical and administrative wrangle which too late or only superficially confronted the ethical issues with appropriate seriousness.' (40) If this is true, and a good case can be made out for it, it is greatly to Bonhoeffer's credit that he was among the first to speak out against the persecution of the Jews, on the grounds that they were fellow human beings, well before the 'Aryan Clause' became applicable to Jewish Christians in the church. (41) Later, on at least two occasions, Karl Barth was to confess that during his years in Germany he had been too preoccupied with his 'churchly and theological task' to give a public warning, along with Bonhoeffer, about the persecutions, to his abiding shame. (42)

In spite therefore of Bonhoeffer's own preoccupation with similar 'churchly and theological' tasks it is clear that earlier than most (although probably not as early as he would have wished) he saw in the Nazi threat something grotesquely evil, and realised that what was at stake was not simply the survival of the church. Bonhoeffer's later disillusionment with the self-preservation tactics of the Confessing Church shows this indeed to be the case; his decision to press on with the writing of the *Ethics* was the logical result. For this reason too the failure of the church to stem the tide of apostasy from Christ, as well as to master the social, economic, sexual and educational problems of the day, looms large as a significant theme in

Ethics. (43) The church by her own guilt 'has given offence', Bonhoeffer writes, 'so that men are prevented from believing her message.... The dogmatically correct delivery of the Christian proclamation is not enough; nor are general ethical principles; what is needed is concrete instruction in the concrete situation'. (44)

Thus for Bonhoeffer the political situation under the National Socialist regime was one in which ethical and moral attitudes assumed prime importance from the beginning. They were not divorced from theological interests, as with some of his fellow-churchmen, but arose out of his commitment to the search for God's concrete word to men; consequently in addressing the German situation Bonhoeffer's theology took on a predominantly ethical flavour. One of his main regrets was that in a situation which was so patently evil few of his contemporaries showed any taste for ethics. At a period in history 'oppressed by a superabounding reality of concrete ethical problems', he writes, little interest is being shown 'in any kind of theoretical or systematic ethics'. (45) Herein then lies the key to an understanding of Bonhoeffer's *Ethics* it is the product of a firm conviction that the West, and Germany in particular, was living in the last days. Eschatological thinking therefore provided the basic theology, and concrete ethics the practical application. Bonhoeffer's distinctive approach, accordingly, to all this was to throw himself into the thick of events, and by thought and action endeavour to re-shape them.

In the first five chapters which follow we shall examine the principal ideas which underlie the thinking of the *Ethics*, against the background of Bonhoeffer's ongoing theological and political development. These deal with his concepts of reality, the church, Jesus Christ, the divine commandment and the natural. These then lead into a chapter summarizing and assessing the strengths and weaknesses of the *Ethics* as a whole. A final chapter offers specific insights from the *Ethics* of value for christian ethics today.

FOOTNOTES

(1)   Collins 1985, p.1.
(2)   *The Republic* I, 352 d. Penguin 2nd. ed. rev. 1974, p.98.
(3)   *Op. cit.*, p.3.
(4)   Cited by G. Leff in *Medieval Thought*, Penguin, 1958, p.135.
(5)   E.g., *A Handbook for Teachers of Christian Ethics in Theological Colleges*, 1964 and *Teaching Christian Ethics*, 1974.
(6)   Clarendon Press, 1980, p.6.
(7)   Duckworth, 1981, p.2.
(8)   *Ibid.*, p.210.
(9)   *Morality: Religious and Secular*, 1985, pp.1-2. See also D. Cupitt, *Life Lines*, 1986, p.12.
(10) In *After Virtue*, 1981, p.210.
(11) Oxford University Press, 1965, p.vii.
(12) See pp. 160 ff.
(13) 'Modern Moral Philosophy' in *Philosophy*, 33 (1958) 1-19, p.6. Cited by A. E. Holmes, *Ethics. Approaching Moral Decisions*, 1984, p.74.
(14) *The Peaceable Kingdom*, 1984, p.55.
(15) *Ibid.*, p.54.
(16) *The World to Come*, 1982 especially Chapter 8 and pp.136f.
(17) *E*, pp.363-71.
(18) 'After Ten Years', *Letters and Papers from Prison*, 3rd. ed. rev. 1971, p.16.
(19) *Ibid.*, p.365.
(20) *LPP*, p.15.
(21) Letter of 28:7:44, *LPP.* p.375.
(22) *Philosophical Faith and Revelation*, translated by E. B. Ashton, New York, 1967, p.310. Cited by J. Macquarrie, *Extentialism*, 1973, p.214.
(23) *LPP*, pp.275-6.
(24) See especially letters 23:2:44 and 22:4:44, *ibid* pp.219 and 275-6.
(25) *True Patriotism*, ed. E. H. Robertson, 1973, p.214. (*GS*111, p.494. The complete German text is in *Fragmente aus Tegel*, eds. R & E Bethge, Christian Kaiser Verlag, 1978, pp.21-64. E.T. *Fiction from Prison*, R & E Bethge with C. Green, Philadelphia: Fortress Press, 1981).
(26) *T.P.*, pp.230-2 (GS111, pp.507-9).
(27) p.289.
(28) Translated by D. Horton, Hodder and Stoughton, 1928, p.171.
(29) *No Rusty Swords*, ed. E. H. Robertson, 1965, pp.39-48. (GS111, pp.48-58).
(30) In *I Knew Dietrich Bonhoeffer*. eds. Wolf-Dieter Zimmermann and R.

G. Smith, 1966, p.161.

(31) *Dietrich Bonhoeffer. Theologian, Christian, Contemporary.* London: Collins, 1970, p. 379

(32) *Ibid*, p.378.

(33) *E*, pp.105-6.

(34) *Ibid.*, pp.107f.

(35) For the view that apocalyptic was an important element in Luther's thinking, see G. Rupp 'The Turk, The Pope, And the Devil' in *Seven-Headed Luther*, 1983, pp.256ff.

(36) *E*, pp.60f.

(37) *Spiritual Care*, 1985, pp.48ff.

(38) *E*, p.57.

(39) The English text on the Barmen Declaration is printed in E.H. Robertson, *Christians Against Hitler*, 1962, pp.48-52.

(40) 'God and the Natural Orders' in *Being and Truth*, 1986, p.405.

(41) See Bethge, *D.B.* pp.234ff.

(42) 1945 addressing German theologians in P.O.W. Camps see Bethge, *D.B.*, p.92. 1967 in letter to Bethge, cited by A. Dumas in *Dietrich Bonhoeffer, Theologian of Reality*, 1971, p.240.

(43) See especially section 'Guilt, Justification and Renewal', pp.110-19, and pp.354ff.

(44) *E.*, p.354.

(45) *Ibid.*, p.64.

CHAPTER 2

BONHOEFFER AND REALITY

Early in 1928, soon after graduating, Bonhoeffer made an important decision, namely, to opt for an active ministry in the Church rather than, as expected, for a life of purely academic teaching and research. It is possible to see in this a foreshadowing of his later concern for reality as a whole, but whether it is or not, it was during his year as an assistant pastor in Barcelona that he read *Don Quixote*, that masterly satire on reality, for the first time. He was to return to it time and time again, especially in preparation for his *Ethics*. (1) In it Bonhoeffer's basic themes of reality and the good were conjoined:

> 'Good is not in itself an independent theme for life; if it were so
> it would be the craziest kind of quixotry. Only if we share in
> reality can we share in good.' (2)

For Bonhoeffer, Don Quixote and Sancho Panza represent two opposing views of reality - Don Quixote the idealist, living in a fantasy world, 'who takes a barber's dish for a helmet and a miserable hack for a charger and who rides into endless battles for the love of a lady who does not exist', (3) and Sancho Panza the positivist, living in an empirical world of 'brute facts', who typifies 'complacent and artful accommodation to things as they are.' (4)

Under the Nazi regime Bonhoeffer saw that what he believed to be satanic forces were playing havoc with traditional ethical and moral concepts, (3) and that the old weapons of reason, conscience, duty and the like were, as was Quixote's sword, blunt and rusty. Even polished and sharpened they were only fit for tilting at windmills. A radically new approach to a world no longer ethically grounded was urgently required. Bonhoeffer sought it in an attempt to investigate the true nature of reality.

A closer examination of the meaning of the word 'reality' is needed at this point. In English it has to serve to cover a wide range of meanings from the metaphysical to the actual. In German Bonhoeffer follows Hegel's use of *Wirklichkeit* (with its root *werken* - 'to bring about' or 'effect') to suggest something 'realized' or 'being realized'. It is therefore to be contrasted with *Reality* which carries with it more the meaning of factual reality as such. R. McAfee Brown, in the introduction to his translation of André Dumas's *Dietrich Bonhoeffer, Theologian of Reality*, points to a somewhat similar distinction in French between la *réalité* and le *réel*. (6) The exceptionally rich and special way, however, in which Bonhoeffer employs this Hegelian term will become more apparent as the discussion develops.

It is important also to bear in mind the extent to which F. W. Nietzsche, with his insistence on the primacy of the concrete, influenced Bonhoeffer in his understanding of reality. This influence however did not extend to the nihilistic implications drawn by Nietzsche. In this respect their views on the nature of reality differed fundamentally. Nazi nihilistic attitudes, too, possibly contributed (in a reactionary way) to Bonhoeffer's thinking in this respect, even if some positive traces of them are discernible in his later penchant for conspiratorial techniques. (7)

But Bonhoeffer, as we shall see, was himself firmly convinced that his view of reality was bible-based, not only because scripture provided the necessary warrant for the fact of the Incarnation, but also because it rooted the presence of God in worldly life itself. Israel's encounter with God in the reality of this world had produced a religion of 'this-worldly transcendence', giving the ultimate meaning and significance to earthly existence and human activity. This 'earthliness' as an ethical theme, appears first in an address on ethics, in 1929, when, like Nietzsche, Bonhoeffer drew attention to the myth of Antaeus, the giant who remained invincible only so long as his feet remained firmly planted on the ground. (8) It was further developed in his University lectures *Creation and Fall* (1932-3), and fully formulated as a 'genuine worldliness' in *Ethics* and the prison letters.

We must now take a closer look at the background to the development of Bonhoeffer's concept of reality, since its full flowering in *Ethics* and *Letters and Papers* emerged only after a period of prolonged thought and action. It was in *Sanctorum Communio*, his doctoral thesis presented in 1927, that Bonhoeffer first challenged the concept of reality which 'idealism has failed to think through exhaustively but has identified with self-knowing and self-active mind', as he put it. Instead he insisted on its ethical character and on its origin in the reality of God and his revelation. (9) This reality, Bonhoeffer declared, can therefore only be apprehended as something 'given' and is to be found in the reality of the church. The church is not man-made but God-given as a revelation of reality. It stakes its claim to be the church of God on this fact and Christians accept this claim as a matter of faith.

So then reality is to be seen embodied in the church which Jesus Christ has established. Reality is there made actual and 'it is a matter merely of believing in that revealed reality in its empirical form.' (10) The break with Troeltsch's sociological idea of the church, as well as with that of Bonhoeffer's 'liberal' teachers is evident. The overtones may be those of Hegel, but the voice is authentic Bonhoeffer. To quote Dumas:

'The church is thus at the heart of reality. It is not an intimate circle where people cultivate the memory of Jesus' personality (Troeltsch); it is not a scolding pulpit from which sin and salvation are proclaimed to the outside world (the early Barth); nor is it a sacred institution serving as a repository of the means of grace (Roman Catholicism)..... It is the realization - fragmentary and hidden but also objective and empirical - of God's reunification of everyday life, of the human community, in Jesus Christ.' (11)

Act and Being, Bonhoeffer's habilitation thesis, completed in 1929, marks a further stage in the ongoing development of his view of reality. The problem of the relationship between the two concepts of revelation, transcendental act and ontological being (according to Bonhoeffer) lay behind the latest developments in theology; the protestant Karl Barth over-emphasizing the importance of the transcendental act, and the catholic E. Przymwara the importance of being. For his own solution Bonhoeffer turns again to the church as the place where revelation is located and where both act and being meet. This coming together is the work of God's revelatory act in Jesus Christ which by constituting the church provides a structure for revelation. The church can thus be described (in Bonhoeffer's phrase) as '*Christus als Gemeinde existierend*' (12) - Christ existing as community or congregation' (either word is possible) - the stress being placed upon God's revelation in terms of community rather than in terms of the individual. In Bonhoeffer's words:

'When the social category is thus introduced, the problem of act and being ... is presented in a wholly fresh light.' (13)

In view of this Bonhoeffer insists that 'revelation's mode of being... is definable only with reference to persons' and that God's freedom, visible in Christ the Word of his freedom, 'is most strongly attested in his having freely bound himself to historical man, having placed himself at man's disposal. God is not free *of* man but *for* man.' (14) To this extent Bonhoeffer is able to associate reality with the experience of 'being for others'. So the link between reality and ethics is made. Thus:

'Theory is unable to form a concept of reality. Reality is "experienced" in the contingent fact of the claim of "others". Only what comes from "outside" can show man the way to his reality, his existence. In "sustaining" the "claim of my neighbour" I exist in reality, 'I act ethically; that is the sense of an ethics not of timeless truths but of the "present".' (15)

Hence, for Bonhoeffer, the church becomes concretely visible not only when the Word is preached and heard, and the sacrament administered and faithfully received, but also when its conduct is loving - 'The Word of this community is preaching and sacrament, its conduct is believing and loving. It is in this concretion that one must think of the being of revelation, in "Christ existing as community".' (16)

This growing emphasis upon the foundation of ethics in reality appears frequently in lectures and addresses from now on as Bonhoeffer sought to find an authoritative basis for a 'concrete commandment'. For example, in his 1932 lecture *A Theological Basis for World Alliance*, he declares:

> 'What the sacrament is for the preaching of the Gospel, the knowledge of firm reality is for the preaching of the command. Reality is the sacrament of command.' (*Die Wirklichkeit ist das Sakrament des Gebotes*) (17)

Bonhoeffer's meaning here appears to be that knowledge of the situation as it truly is in reality is capable of producing a concrete command, which can be deemed to be sacramental in the sense of communicating God's revelation, as do the sacraments of baptism and holy communion.

Within a year the Nazi menace had become a terrible reality and a shift in Bonhoeffer's christological thinking begins to be discernible. His unfinished set of lectures on Christology, given in the summer of 1933, presents us with a Christ no longer identified wholly with the church, as before, but with a transcendent Christ, the centre of human existence, the centre of history and the mediator between nature and God.

This promising development of Christ's lordship over the world marks an extension of Bonhoeffer's thinking about reality; it is however interrupted by the rapid pace of political events and the beginning of the Church Struggle. Current theological debates about 'orders of creation' and 'orders of preservation' no longer seemed to be relevant to Bonhoeffer during the period of *The Cost of Discipleship* and *Life Together*, so instead he turned to the concept of discipleship to express his faith in reality. Concentration on the lordship of Christ accordingly gives way to the narrower concern for discipleship in the church.

The final phase in Bonhoeffer's development of the concept of reality begins with his commitment to direct political involvement sometime between 1939 and 1940. This provided the occasion for the writing of *Ethics* and for the prison correspondence. Here reality becomes all-embracing and the ends of the circle meet. To quote the authoritative Eberhard Bethge, close friend and biographer of Bonhoeffer:

'It is the time in which Bonhoeffer read with new fascination *Don Quixote*, the story of the honourable knight who became isolated from reality fighting for a principle. In 1932 reality was the dimension to preach to. In 1935 reality was the transit station. Reality is now full partner for man shaping his deeds.... Bonhoeffer no longer wants to have the world or the reality of the world without the reality of God.... Reality always is that which is entered into and accepted by Christ. By Christ's entering there is an ontological coherence of God's reality with the reality of the world. There are not two realities, but the one already entered by Christ and in the process of being judged and renewed.' (18)

We must now consider in more detail this full-blown concept of reality which, in spite of increasing concentration upon 'worldliness', provides the philosophical and theological background to Bonhoeffer's thinking from now on.

Determinative for any attempt to find a metaphysical basis for Bonhoeffer's ethics is the chapter in *Ethics*, 'Christ, Reality and Good', the opening section of which is headed 'The Concept of Reality' The whole chapter has been described as containing the very heart of *Ethics*. (19) In an important passage in his biography of Bonhoeffer, Eberhard Bethge explains Bonhoeffer's understanding of the concept of reality, as outlined in this chapter, in the following words:

'Reality is always the acceptance of the world by the one who has become man. Here Bonhoeffer seeks to avoid the positivist and idealistic understanding of reality, as he regards both as abstractions. He would like to by-pass the rocks of an actualistic situation ethic and yet hold to its validity. He would like to surmount the dim remoteness of a norm-ethic and yet accept its interest in continuity.' (20)

In this passage of Bethge's, we suggest, are to be found the three principal constituents of Bonhoeffer's mature concept of reality - first, the rejection of duality, next, the centrality of Christ, and third, concern for a concrete ethic. Each of these will now be considered in turn.

The rejection of duality is necessary in the interest of affirming the unity and ultimacy of the divine reality. This is fundamental and rightly the section 'The Concept of Reality' in the *Ethics* begins here:

'What is of ultimate importance', writes Bonhoeffer, 'is now no

longer that I should become good, or that the condition of the
world should be made better by my action, but that the reality of
God should show itself everywhere to be the ultimate reality....All
things appear distorted if they are not seen and recognised in
God.... But when we say that God is the ultimate reality, this is
not an idea, through which the world as we have it is to be
sublimated. It is not the religious rounding-off of a profane
conception of the universe. It is the acceptance in faith of God's
showing forth of Himself, the acceptance of His revelation.' (21)

This notion thus disposes of the accepted western view of reality as
consisting of two levels or two spheres, God and the world, nature and
supernature, the sacred and profane. According to Bonhoeffer, this was a
view which first became dominant in the Middle Ages, was later reinforced
in the period following the Reformation, and was now ripe for disposal.
Almost from the beginning Bonhoeffer had shown a distaste for anything
resembling a divided reality. In *Sanctorum Communio* he had attempted to
grapple with the division between opposing 'liberal' and 'conservative'
view of the church. In *Act and Being* the opposing 'ontological' and 'actual'
approaches to knowledge had been subjected to similar critical scrutiny and
replaced by knowledge of a different reality. But it was in his winter lectures
of 1932-33 on Genesis 1-3, later published as *Creation and Fall*, that
Bonhoeffer essayed a theological interpretation of creation which made sense
of reality as a whole.
    Ignoring any historical-critical considerations relating to the origins of
creation he concentrated on discerning the hand of God 'in the "middle" of
beginning' (in Bonhoeffer's words) as he creates and sustains the world in
which we live. According to Bonhoeffer, we have no knowledge of the
beginning or end of creation, only of the creator God as he meets us 'in the
middle'. (22) Faith alone enables us to see and obey its structure and shape.
God's creation is good because his Word has imposed this structure and
shape upon and within it and he is to be found, therefore, in the centre as
well as on the fringes of life. The Word reveals, however, not God's inner
nature or being but his commandment, and his writ runs through the whole
of reality. Thus the decisive effect of the Word is to bring about structure or
form (*Gestalt*), whose shape and pattern is that of the incarnate, crucified
and risen Lord. So - as a later comment in *Ethics* puts it - 'there are,
therefore, not two spheres, but only the one sphere of the realization of
Christ, in which the reality of God and the reality of the world are united.'
(23)
    The history and significance of this radical break with western traditional
thought is spelled out in the section of *Ethics*. 'Thinking in Terms of Two

Spheres.' Soon after New Testament times, Bonhoeffer claims, 'the conception of a juxtaposition and conflict of two spheres, the one divine, holy, supernatural and Christian, and the other worldly, profane, natural and un-Christian', began to dominate the West. It reached a climax for the first time during the medieval period, and then again during the period of 'pseudo-Lutheran' thought which followed the Reformation. The Middle Ages was characterized by the subordination of the natural realm to the realm of grace. The reverse tended to be the case in the pseudo-Lutheran scheme of things. Here, according to Bonhoeffer, 'the autonomy of the orders of this world is proclaimed in opposition to the law of Christ, and in the scheme of the Enthusiasts the congregation of the Elect takes up the struggle with a hostile world for the establishment of God's kingdom on earth.' (24)

This division of total reality, Bonhoeffer continues, is completely contrary to the teaching of the Bible and the Reformation, and carries with it unfortunate consequences. Chief among these is the relegation of Christ to a sphere of reality outside other realities, which have their own means of access other than through Christ. Existence therefore becomes either sacred or secular and the possibility opens up of living in either one or the other of these two autonomous spheres. The medieval monk and the nineteenth century protestant secularist are typical of these possibilities. Worse still, man is placed in a dilemma; if, instead of trying to seek Christ without the world, or the world without Christ, he tries to occupy both the *regnum gratiae* and the *regnum naturae* at one and the same time, man becomes subject to perpetual conflict. This in fact is true of most Christians since the Reformation, who believe this kind of existence to be the only way of living which is true to reality.

In attacking this duality Bonhoeffer was firmly convinced that he was returning both to the New Testament and to Luther. For him the New Testament was 'concerned solely with the manner in which the reality of Christ assumes reality in the present world, which it has already encompassed, seized and possessed.' (25) Martin Luther in his turn was motivated by the need to draw attention to the divine and cosmic reality - Jesus Christ. For this reason he was prepared to protest on behalf of the secular authority against the extension of ecclesiastical power by the Roman Church and against a Christianity which sought to be independent of the reality of Christ. In other words Luther's 'secular' protest was 'in the name of a better Christianity'. For the same reason (Bonhoeffer argues), if today Christianity is involved in a protest against the secular authority, it must be done 'in the name of a better secularity' rather than in the interests of preserving the spiritual as an end in itself. Bonhoeffer concludes:

'It is only in this sense, as a polemical unity, that Luther's

doctrine of the two kingdoms is to be accepted, and it was no
doubt in this sense that it was originally intended.' (26)

A further consequence of two-sphere thinking, according to Bonhoeffer,
is that it creates a static situation, as between the spheres, each becoming an
enclave with its own separate laws, and operating independently. There is
always then the possibility of a 'take-over bid' by one side or the other, but
no real chance of any progress towards genuine reconciliation in Christ.
Hence where the world is allowed to operate on its own, free from interference
from the law of Christ, it will soon become subject to licentiousness and
self-will. Where Christianity attempts to withdraw from the world, ignoring
its particular forms of life and activities, it too will become a victim of
presumption and give way to the irrational and unnatural. (27)

Bonhoeffer's remedy for this is well summarized by Jürgen Weissbach in
Two Studies in the Theology of Bonhoeffer, himself quoting from *Ethics*:

'The world is "always seen in the movement of being accepted
and becoming accepted by God in Christ". On the other hand, it
does not mean the identity of God and his world; unity is "but
solely from the reality of Christ, that is to say solely from faith in
this ultimate reality"'. (28)

The second constituent in Bethge's summary of Bonhoeffer's understanding
of reality has to do with 'the one who has become man'. It is in effect an
affirmation of the centrality of Christ. The pivotal position of Jesus Christ in
all that has been discussed so far will have become evident by now. It relates
not simply to the unifying of reality but to the disclosure of the nature of
reality itself. The key passage in *Ethics* needs to be quoted in full:

'Christian belief deduces that the reality of God is not in itself
merely an idea from the fact (*Tatsache*) that this reality of God
has manifested and revealed itself in the midst of the real world.
In Jesus Christ the reality of God entered into the reality of this
world. The place where the answer is given, both to the question
concerning the reality of God and to the question concerning the
reality of the world, is designated solely and alone by the name
Jesus Christ. God and the world are comprised in this name. In
Him all things consist (Col.1,17). Henceforward one can speak
neither of God nor of the world without speaking of Jesus Christ.
All concepts of reality which do not take account of Him are
abstractions.' (29)

The statement is comprehensive and, theologically speaking, there is little more that needs to be said - it is largely a question now of drawing out the implications. Heinrich Ott, writing of the theological legacy of Bonhoeffer in his book, *Reality and Faith*, makes two important points apropos this particular passage. One point is that Bonhoeffer has finally arrived here at the conclusion that Jesus Christ equals reality, 'that he is not only real, that he is not only one reality besides others, *but that he is that reality itself, which or who is the truly real in all that is real.*' (Ott's italics) The other point is that in it Bonhoeffer is answering his own question, 'Who Christ really is for us today?' Whenever, according to Ott, we come face to face with reality it could be Christ meeting us unawares. He is the same yesterday, today and for ever and is therefore ever-present, but 'it is the especial promise of this religionless epoch of ours, when the "metaphysical" transcendent divinity of God is disappearing, that Jesus Christ comes anew into sight for us in this universality and living reality of his.' (30)

What is also true, as Ott himself admits, is that we look to Bonhoeffer in vain for *specific* and *detailed* answers to the question of who Jesus Christ really is for us, and for practical solutions to the individual ethical problems which confront us today (31) - questions which continued to nag Bonhoeffer to the end of his life. What is important however is that in his equation of Jesus Christ with total reality, Bonhoeffer had found an anchorage for his faith which for him remained steadfast and sure.

Bonhoeffer's earliest sustained attempt to describe the christocentric nature of reality is to be found in *Christology*, an incomplete set of lectures delivered in 1933 and first published in 1960. Here the idea of the *Christus praesens* at work in our existence, in the sweep of history and in the structure of creation is systematically developed. The original intention was to deal with the subject in three parts - the 'Present Christ', the 'Historical Christ' and the 'Eternal Christ', but the third part was not begun. Basic to Bonhoeffer's approach is his belief that 'Jesus is the Christ present as the Crucified and Risen One', and that this presence is to be found personally, and embodied in the church. (32) Because Jesus Christ is God he is present eternally everywhere; because he is man he can be located in time and space. Thus when we speak of the presence of Jesus Christ in the church we are speaking of the whole person, that is to say, of the God-man. (33)

Using traditional terminology Bonhoeffer speaks of preaching as the form in which the Logos reaches the human Logos, the sacrament the form in which the Logos reaches man in his nature, and the community the form in which the Logos has extension in space and time. So that the church becomes 'the concrete place where the human existence received its form and structure in Christ, where the everyday world rediscovers its true reality, and where nature becomes redirected toward the One who is neither at its far reaches, nor its negation, but is its hidden centre.' Dumas, from whom this quotation is taken, goes on to say that:

> 'In this way, Bonhoeffer hopes to overcome the fatal divorce between objective meaning outside of man and an existential meaning confined to man, between a transcendent object and an individual subject, between objective nature and subjective history, between speculation focused on another world and a speculation reduced simply to a consideration of man. His formal principle... is a third way, along with Barth's objective revelation and Bultmann's existential interpretation, to speak of *God* while *speaking* about the reality in which God is already present.' (34)

The tension between 'act' and 'being', 'event' and 'existence' was one of which Bonhoeffer was acutely aware. For reality to become concrete, and revelation to become commandment, the tension had to be resolved. By associating the presence of Jesus Christ, the God-man, in the church as both its form and structure, and by locating the church at the centre of reality, he believed he had found the answer. Bonhoeffer's concept of the unity of reality hinges on this and the rest follows from it.

Fully to appreciate the grandeur of Bonhoeffer's christocratic (not just 'christocentric') conception it is necessary to bear in mind his emphasis upon the eschatological dimension as we have it in his later writings. Not only is the '*geschichtliche*' Christ the same person as the '*historische*' Jesus of Nazareth, totally present as exalted and humiliated in the church and the world, and indeed ontologically in all reality, he is the one who will restore all things in the fullness of time. In an Advent letter in the prison correspondence (published as *Letters and Papers from Prison*) Bonhoeffer refers to a line in a Christmas hymn of Paul Gerhardt's, 'I will restore everything' ('I*ch bring alles wieder*') and makes the comment:

> 'What does this "I'll bring again" mean? It means that nothing is lost, that everything is taken up in Christ, although it is transformed, made transparent, clear and free from all selfish desire. Christ restores all this as God originally intended it to be, without the distortion resulting from our sins. The doctrine derived from Eph.1,10 - that of the restoration of all things, *anakephalaiôsis, recapitulatio* (Irenaeus) - is a magnificent conception, full of comfort. This is how the promise "God seeks what has been driven away" is fulfilled.' (35)

Heinrich Ott observes:

> 'Jesus Christ appears... as he who "brings again", that is to say, sums up in himself and brings to view and to fulfilment the real and refined meaning of *all* reality.' (36)

It is perhaps noteworthy as indicating the direction in which Bonhoeffer's mind was moving at this late stage that he was also beginning to be concerned about 'unconscious' or 'anonymous' Christianity, that is, with a presence of Christ outside the church, active in the world and apprehended by non-Christians in the form of a 'natural piety' He was inclined to link this with an implicit faith along the lines of the Lutheran dogmatists' distinction between a *fides directa* and a *fides reflexa*, but this was not followed up. (37) It was however a logical consequence of his belief in Jesus Christ as the all-embracing reality, present in worldly life and experience, no longer confined to the visible church and still available in the absence of formal religion.

The third constituent in Bethge's statement about Bonhoeffer and reality relates to his search for a concrete ethic which is capable of incorporating the advantages of situationist ethic on the one hand and a normative ethic on the other. This ethic must be based fairly and squarely upon the reality of God as he manifests himself in Jesus Christ. So Bonhoeffer writes in *Ethics* - 'Christian ethics enquires about the realization in our world of this divine and cosmic reality which is given in Christ.' (38)

As a result the problem of ethics is no longer bound up with such questions as, 'How can I be good?' or 'How can I do good?', but with the quite different question 'What is the will of God?' Ethical enquiry also has as its objective another purpose. Instead, (to quote another passage from *Ethics*):

> 'The question of good becomes the question of participation in the divine reality which is revealed in Christ. Good is now no longer a valuation of what is, a valuation, for example, of my own being, my outlook or my actions, or of some condition or state in the world. It is no longer a predicate that is assigned to something which is in itself in being. Good is the real itself. It is not the real in the abstract, the real which is detached from the reality of God, but the real which possesses reality only in God.... The wish to be good consists solely in the longing for what is real in God.' (39)

Thus there arises the possibility of unified (and therefore 'good') man comparable with the unity of God and the world in Christ. Other ethical systems are characterized by conflict, but by sharing in the total reality which is Christ the Christian is himself an undivided whole. Because he belongs completely to Christ, who is in the world, he belongs at the same time also to the world. Here lies the guarantee of ethical formation in the thinking of Bonhoeffer; it is wholly concrete. The Incarnation (according to Bonhoeffer) had the effect of re-structuring reality with the 'form', 'structure', 'figure' or 'shape' (all are legitimate renderings of Bonhoeffer's use of '*Gestalt*') of Jesus Christ, making possible the realization of true manhood as well as true creation. The fall of Adam had resulted in re-structuring the world and de-humanizing humanity. The Second Adam's reconciling activity now offers the opportunity of 'conformation' (*Gleichgestaltung*) with the new reality, that is, Jesus Christ, both in an individual and collective sense.

Conformation is not a question of 'trying to be like Jesus', as commonly understood, nor of treating him simply as a teacher of the good life and seeking to apply his precepts to the world. It means allowing the form of the incarnate, crucified and risen Christ to take hold of us and to shape our form after his likeness - as indicated by St. Paul in Galatians 4:19. It also means the kind of transformation into the image of Jesus Christ mentioned by Paul in Romans 8:29., 12:2., 2 Corinthians 3:18., and Philippians 3:10. There is nothing un-scriptural in all this, Bonhoeffer believes; it is in full accordance with what the bible has to say about christian formation. In short, conformation with Christ means becoming a real man. (40)

Conformation thus makes it possible - where there is a genuine acceptance of participation in the reality of Jesus Christ's birth, death and resurrection - for the Word of God to take on concrete form. Conformation in fact begins in the church, which embodies the structure of Christ without being wholly and completely identical with him. Bonhoeffer is thus able to define the church as a 'section of humanity in which Christ has really taken form', and to declare that 'what takes place in her takes place as an example and substitute for all men'. (41) So the unique nature and position of the church is made plain; on the one hand, its visible, concrete character prevents it from being regarded as a spiritual force only; on the other, its public worship, organizations and parish life which testify to the reality of Jesus Christ, contain (as Bonhoeffer puts it) 'the whole reality of the world at once and reveals the ultimate basis of this reality'. (42) The first duty therefore laid upon members of the church is not to be concerned with themselves, nor with religious organization as such, not even with cultivating piety, but with manifesting the form of the crucified and risen Christ in the world. For this they will be equipped with the power of the holy spirit which impels both the church and individual members to witness before the world. (43)

By the summer of 1944, following (as he saw it) the steady retreat of the Confessing Church into a ghetto of theological opposition rather than open engagement with the real world of political resistance, Bonhoeffer was again expressing concern about the 'form' of the church - this time in an even more radical way. On 16th July he confided to Bethge that one has to live for some time in a community to understand how Christ is formed in it, (44) and a month later in *Outline for a Book* he was insisting that 'the church is the church only when it exists for others'. The disposal of all church property to those in need, the maintenance of the clergy on free-will offerings, or by engagement in a secular calling, and a sharing on a serving basis in the problems of secular life, are just a few of the implications, Bonhoeffer declares, of what it means for the church to have the 'form of Christ'. (45)

It was the search for concreteness in moral and ethical behaviour also which led Bonhoeffer to formulate his well-known distinction between the 'ultimate' and the 'penultimate'. Earlier references to this distinction are to be found in his 'Leadership Principle' address (1933), (46) and in *The Cost of Discipleship* (1937). In the latter, Bonhoeffer insists on the importance of taking a preliminary step of obedience before it is possible to believe. This means obeying a concrete command ('Come to church!') which, if it manifests the right disposition, can prove to be an act of faith in the ultimate word of Christ. (47) Bethge believes accordingly that even during this period of withdrawal from worldly activity at Finkenwalde, when Bonhoeffer is concentrating his eyes on the ultimate, his concern is still with the penultimate in the interests of concreteness. (48)

The situation had changed to one of deep political involvement by 1940-1, when the sections in *Ethics* fully developing this distinction came to be written. Acutely conscious of the conflicting demands of worldly and spiritual interests Bonhoeffer was looking for a middle way between the catholic treatment of the natural, which required the supernatural to perfect it, and the protestant attitude which tended to depreciate the natural when confronted with supernatural grace. The catholic way seemed to lead inevitably to naturalism, and the protestant to pietism - both of which Bonhoeffer rejected - so another way had to be found.

On the basis of his earlier thinking Bonhoeffer was able in *Ethics* to clarify the 'ultimate - penultimate' distinction in the light of his doctrine of justification by faith and christology. For Bonhoeffer the ultimate word of justification is seen in the cross of Christ which meets the penultimate both in mercy and judgement. Here, in Jesus Christ, God's reality meets the reality of the world and enables Christians to share in the same encounter. For this reason, christian living means neither destroying human reality, nor sanctioning it, but accepting it as a penultimate - that which is before the last - which preserves the way for the ultimate word by which the sinner is justified. The penultimate therefore must be taken seriously for the sake of the ultimate but not for its own sake alone. (49)

Nature and culture (one way of speaking of the penultimate) are then brought into the discussion and are shown to be given divine meaning and significance by the ultimate, thus enabling man to meet with God here and now as a necessary preliminary to salvation. 'Natural' and 'unnatural' accordingly acquire other meanings dependent on whether or not they are seen to be open to the coming of Christ for 'it is only through the incarnation of Christ that the natural life becomes the penultimate which is directed towards the ultimate'. (50) Bonhoeffer was convinced that the concept of the natural, which had fallen into discredit in protestant ethics and had been perverted by Nazi ideology, could only be recovered on this basis. His treatment of the natural in *Ethics* follows these lines, but unfortunately remains unfinished. (51)

This is the point at which Bonhoeffer's contribution to the world out of a concrete ethic would have been most helpful and illuminating. He whets our appetite by insisting that the 'ethical' must be thought of as tied to a concrete time and place, while discouraging us from thinking that human beings are continually (or exclusively) concerned with ethical problems. Bonhoeffer also believed that help was needed, not so much in the great moments of moral conflict as in the sphere of everyday happenings, for this is where the enunciation of general moral principles alone usually proves to be entirely inadequate. If we are to avoid 'a pathological overburdening of life by the ethical', he writes, it must not be assumed that we must always be busy taking high-minded decisions or discharging some lofty duty. As Ecclesiastes 3 reminds us, in human existence every thing has its time and season, 'eating, drinking and sleeping as well as deliberate resolve and action, rest as well as work, purposelessness as well as the fulfilment of purpose, inclination as well as duty, play as well as earnest endeavour, joy as well as renunciation.' (52) This theme is repeated in *Letters and Papers* - indeed intensified - but it is clear that Bonhoeffer's quest for concreteness in terms of ethical reality ends here. There is little more that is added to enable us to come to grips with specific moral problems, or with the wide-ranging ethical issues which confront us today. His life was cut short at the point at which he was beginning to work out the practical implications of his ethical thought. It is for others to apply themselves to this task.

There remains the task of touching briefly upon three areas in which Bonhoeffer's concept of reality seems to call for further discussion, bearing in mind the incomplete nature of his *Ethics*. It will be helpful to relate them to the three constituents in Bethge's description of Bonhoeffer's concept which have already been mentioned.

The first (it will be remembered) concerns the rejection of duality. The movement of Bonhoeffer's thought with regard to the *regnum Christi* does not disclose its full implications until 1939-40 when it is seen to be the dominating *motif* behind all his ethical thinking. Here for the first time in *Ethics* the classic texts referring to the cosmic and universal dominion of

Christ from Colossians and Ephesians are brought together and powerfully interpreted. (53) Earlier addresses, such as the public address Dein Reich komme! of 1932, had drawn attention to the importance of Christ's message for the world, but not in the context of cosmic reality. Here the categories were those of the Lutheran twofold division between church and state, where partnership between these two aspects of God's kingdom is stressed rather than their unity; so Christ's re-creating role is mainly confined to the church. The extension of Christ's dominion, when it came, was linked with Bonhoeffer's increasing interest in 'worldliness', as a later statement in *Ethics* makes clear:

> 'The purpose and aim of the dominion of Christ is not to make
> the worldly order godly or to subordinate it to the Church but to
> set it free for true worldliness'. (54)

Inevitably (it would seem) this all-embracing and exclusive dominion of Christ, particularly as later developed in *Letters and Papers*, runs the risk of obliterating any distinction whatsoever between nature and grace. Theologically the risk no doubt can be accepted, but in the world of practical affairs some account must be taken of the way in which the church and the world, the spiritual and the material, are in practice to be related, It is perhaps significant that Bonhoeffer seems to be least happy when dealing with Luther's doctrine of the two kingdoms, which he explains as being originally intended by Luther as a 'polemical unity'. No mention is made of the political, as well as the spiritual, considerations involved in Luther's views about reality itself. The *Ethics* sheds little light on this difference; nor does it take us very far, in practical terms, in working out the precise relationship between the *regnum gratiae* and the *regnum naturae*.

With regard to the second constituent in Bethge's statement - the centrality of Jesus Christ - what appears to be lacking is a more precise and practical explanation of the way in which the ontological Christ 'gears into' harsh worldly reality. In the prison letters faith-commitment (*metanoia* - as Bonhoeffer describes it) is the key, and we are assured that if we participate 'in the suffering of God in the secular life' and so allow ourselves 'to be caught up into the way of Jesus Christ', we shall be participating in reality. (55) But in *Ethics* the linking of the way in which Jesus Christ has brought reality into being with the everyday world is through 'the structures of responsible life', of which the concept of 'deputyship' (*Stellvertretung*) is perhaps the most important. This is the way, Bonhoeffer suggests in *Ethics*, that Jesus binds himself to things as well as to humankind. (56)

This ontological link-up, seen as part of the structure of reality, nevertheless lacks the incisiveness of the Pauline presentation in Romans 8 where the individual-creation connection is one of 'groaning and travailing in pain together' for their mutual redemption and liberation. Paul's conception is equally grandiose but has the merit of a greater appeal to the imagination than does Bonhoeffer's. Furthermore (following the lines of Teilhard de Chardin's adventurous thinking) one looks in vain for a detailed account of the manner in which Bonhoeffer sees the most intimate connection of all, between the spiritual and material, namely in the eucharist. One passage in *Christology* raises expectations:

'In the sacrament (Christ) is the penetration of fallen creation at a particular point. He is the new creation. He is the restored creation of our spiritual and bodily existence.' (57)

But in *Ethics*, except for an isolated reference to the doctrine of *anakephalaiôsis*, (58) the Teilhard de Chardin line is not pursued. A Bonhoefferian version of the 'omega point' remains un-articulated, giving way instead to his prime interest and consideration - the making real of the will of God through the reality of his self-revelation in Jesus Christ, who invites all men to share in the same reality and be saved.

Lastly, this leads into the third constituent of what Bethge understands by Bonhoeffer's concept of reality - concern for a concrete ethic. It has already been shown that this hinges not upon facing up to the question of doing or being good, in the traditional way, but of asking what is the will of God. Bonhoeffer's answer to this was touched upon in the closing words of the previous paragraph, namely, that the will of God is to be found in the making real of his self-revelation in Jesus Christ in the world and among men. In the first of three lectures on 'The Challenge of Dietrich Bonhoeffer's Life and Theology', delivered in Chicago in the early 1960s, (59) Eberhard Bethge refers to Bonhoeffer's early quest for the concrete nature of the divine revelation. Apropos this, Bethge in his lecture makes two important points; first, that for Bonhoeffer concreteness is the attribute of the revelation itself; and second, that divine authority attaches itself only to the command which is concrete and specific. Bonhoeffer, according to Bethge, was concerned less with *making* God's message concrete in time and space than with the fact that concreteness is inherent in the nature of revelation itself. In Bethge's view, for Bonhoeffer, concern with establishing the truth of this came before any attempt to indicate where and how the concrete revelatory word can be recognized and applied. So, continues Bethge, 'When (Bonhoeffer) is most certainly and passionately longing and looking for the concrete nature of the message, he turns his eyes... entirely on the revelation in Christ, in order to discover and describe its concreteness. Much later he calls it "this-worldliness". (60)

What this apparently means is that Bonhoeffer's search for concreteness does not go very far beyond affirming it as a fact of revelation; he did not survive long enough to be able to apply what was revealed, in all its authority and concreteness, to detailed and specific problems and situations. What is clear is that the absence of this kind of 'concreteness' is a genuine loss. As Heinrich Ott expresses it in *Reality and Faith*:

> '(Bonhoeffer) was not yet in a position to say precisely what it means that God himself is present in reality.... That he was not yet able to describe more precisely the real presence of God in the ethical situation, that he only gave an indication of it, does not imply that nobody can go on to give a more precise intellectual description of what he saw, as a visionary so to speak in the ethical realm.' (61)

FOOTNOTES

(1)   According to Bethge, Bonhoeffer 'thought he learnt more from *Don Quixote* than from many books on ethics.' *DB*. p.620.
(2)   *E.*, p.191.
(3)   *Ibid.*, pp.67-8.
(4)   *LPP.*, 21:2:44, p.217.
(5)   'After Ten Years', *LPP.*, p.4. This paper was produced by Bonhoeffer for private distribution at the beginning of 1943 and assesses the effects of a decade of Nazi rule. It has been described by Otto Dudzus, a pupil of Bonhoeffer, as 'the most valuable key to the fragments on *Ethics*' in *Bonhoeffer for a New Generation*, 1986, p.150. J. De Gruchy likewise sees it as 'a bridging text which links Bonhoeffer's ethical reflections with those theological explorations which are expressed in his prison writings.' See *Dietrich Bonhoeffer, Witness to Jesus Christ*, 1988, p.255.
(6)   p. ix, cf., pp.141 fn.2, 209 fn.82, 233 fn.32.
(7)   *Op.cit.*, *LPP.*, p.16.
(8)   *NRS.*, p.47. (*GS*111, pp.57f).
(9)   pp.29, 89.
(10) *Ibid.*, p.105.
(11) *Dietrich Bonhoeffer: Theologian of Reality*, p.93, a book which has greatly influenced the thinking of this and subsequent chapters.
(12) *AB.*, p.120. For fuller discussion on Bonhoeffer's use of 'Gemeinde' see below Chapter 4, fn.10.
(13) *Ibid.*,pp.122-3.
(14) *Ibid.*, p.90.
(15) *Ibid.*,p.86.
(16) *Ibid.*,p.125.
(17) *GS*1, p.147 (cf. NRS., p.164, where 'die Verkundigung des Gebotes' is mistranslated 'the preaching of the sacrament'). See also letter to Erwin Sutz, *GS*1, p.34 and 'Dein Reich komme!', *GS*111, p.273, and Moltmann, *Two Studies*, p.170.
(18) 'Bonhoeffer's Life and Theology' in *World Come of Age*, pp. 73-4.
(19) Dumas, op.cit., p.155.
(20) *DB.*, p.621.
(21) *E.*, pp.188-9.
(22) *CF.*, pp.9ff.
(23) p.197.
(24) *Ibid.*, p.196
(25) *Ibid.*, p.198.
(26) *Ibid.*, p.199.

(27) *Ibid.*, pp.199f.

(28) p.117.

(29) p.194. Bonhoeffer is here stressing the 'factual' nature of this particular reality (*'Tatsache'* - derivation, latin *res facti*, indicates 'matter-of-factness').

(30) *Reality and Faith*, p.168.

(31) See *ibid.*, p.276.

(32) p.43.

(33) *Ibid.*, p.45.

(34) *Dietrich Bonhoeffer: Theologian of Reality*, pp.33-4.

(35) p.170.

(36) *Reality and Faith*, p.179 fn.7.

(37) See *LPP.*, 27:7:44, p.373.

(38) *E.*, p.195.

(39) *Ibid.*, pp.190-1

(40) See *ibid.*, pp.80f.

(41) *Ibid.*, p.83.

(42) *Ibid.*, p.202.

(43) See *ibid.*, p.203.

(44) *LPP.*, p.359.

(45) Ibid., pp.282f. 'Outline for a Book' is no more than an outline. cf., attempts by E. Bethge in *Bonhoeffer: Exile and Martyr*, pp.137-54, and E. Robertson in *Bonhoeffer's Heritage* to fill out the 'Outline'.

(46) *NRS.*, pp.203f. (*GS*11, pp.37f.).

(47) p.55.

(48) *DB.*, p.375.

(49) *E.*, pp.130ff.

(50) *Ibid.*, p.145.

(51) *Ibid.*, pp.143ff.

(52) See *E,*, pp.264f.

(53) *E.g.*, pp.213,322.

(54) *Ibid.*, p.329.

(55) *LPP.*, 18:7:44, p.361.

(56) See pp.224 ff.

(57) p.59.

(58) p.322.

(59) In *World Come of Age*, pp.22-88.

(60) *Ibid.*, pp.32-3.

(61) p.181.

CHAPTER 3

BONHOEFFER AND THE CHURCH

'There is a word that when a Catholic hears it kindles all his
feelings of love and bliss; that stirs all the depths of his religious
sensibility, from dread and awe of the Last Judgement to the
sweetness of God's presence; and that certainly awakens in him
the feeling of home....
'And there is a word that to Protestants has the sound of
something infinitely more commonplace, more or less indifferent
and superfluous, that does not make their hearts beat faster;
something with which a sense of boredom is so often associated,
or which at any rate does not lend wings to our religious
feelings....
'Yes, the word to which I am referring is "Church", the meaning
of which we have forgotten'.

These words of Dietrich Bonhoeffer occur in a sermon preached in
Barcelona in 1928 to a German-speaking congregation surrounded by all the
sights and sounds of historic Catholicism. (1) Five years earlier, on a visit to
Rome, he had been immensely attracted by the Holy Week ceremonies in the
various churches, especially in St. Peter's. The general air of self-confidence
and universality, coupled with the genuine piety of its worshippers, seemed
to him to give the Catholic Church an authority all of its own. This impression
was profound and left a permanent mark upon him. (2) Henceforward
Bonhoeffer's interest, both from an academic and practical point of view,
began to centre less on the protestant tradition in which he had been brought
up (and which he still cherished) than upon the phenomenon of the church as
such. By the time of the Barcelona sermon this interest was sufficiently acute
for him to warn his protestant listeners that the word 'church' must have 'a
new or perhaps a very old meaning' attached to it. 'Woe to us', he added, 'if
that word does not become important in our lives.' (3)

A beginning had in fact been made when Bonhoeffer presented his doctoral
thesis, *Sanctorum Communio*, to the authorities of Berlin University in
1927. Here, endeavouring to find an authoritative and concrete base for the
church's existence, he broke away from the popular liberal view, (fashionable
in protestant circles during the 19th century) that the church was in essence
a collection of individuals regenerated by Christ, or a mere religious
association. While Bonhoeffer's family and cultured friends continued to

hold to this view, Bonhoeffer's own mind as a theological student came heavily under the influence of Karl Holl, a formidable Lutheran scholar, whose understanding of the church, like Martin Luther's, was much more influenced by St. Paul. In *Sanctorum Communio*, therefore, Bonhoeffer adopts the much more sophisticated Pauline doctrine of the church as the Body of Christ, present both in the local congregation of Christian believers and universally as a mystical reality. (4)

Alongside this, however, Bonhoeffer in his thesis makes full use of current sociological and theological views of the nature of community, and (more important) the new and radical teaching regarding revelation associated with Karl Barth. Both were vital to his study since it was to revelation that Bonhoeffer looked for the church's authority, as he looked to history and sociology for its concreteness. Equipped with these tools he set out as a matter of urgency in *Sanctorum Communio* to clarify the concept of the church, believing, as he did, that its failure had much to do with the apathy of Protestants as well as with their shallow interest in its purpose and mission.

It is possible, therefore, to find in *Sanctorum Communio* certain principles with regard to Bonhoeffer's understanding of the church which basically remained unaltered for the rest of his life. As will become clear, some changes were later to occur in the way in which these principles were applied, but, in general, the foundations laid down in this first book remained firm and stable. Summarized, the principles are these: first, the church is more than a mere religious fellowship or collection of well-intentioned individuals - it is a divinely-given reality created by God's revelatory action in Jesus Christ. There can be no uncertainty about this, according to Bonhoeffer, since the church has been established in history by the activity of the Holy Spirit, and has a visible and concrete existence in time and space.

Next, since the church, being founded on revelation, takes on empirical form and is concretely visible, it is to be accepted or rejected according to faith. Empirically it takes on the sociological character both of a community (*Gemeinshaft*) and of an association (*Gessellschaft*) and so, in Bonhoeffer's view, is unique in the sense of being both a historical human fellowship as well as a reality which is created by the Spirit.

Again, the empirical and the metaphysical meet in the reality of Christ's presence 'existing as community' (*Christus als Gemeinde existierend*) which establishes three distinct sets of relationships - that of the individual with Jesus Christ, that of fellowship with each other in Christ, and that of the 'collective person' or the new humanity of Christ. Thus the church is in being not simply as an instrument to serve the will of God but is seen to embody the actual will of God itself.

Lastly, the church is seen by Bonhoeffer as an exclusive body with a visible congregation whose membership qualification for belonging is belief not in some invisible reality but in the presence of Christ as an incarnate fact. It is the evidence of eyes and ears which matters - that is to say participation in the visible congregation where Word and sacrament are administered, rather than blind faith which Bonhoeffer believes has no concrete basis in every-day fact. So Bonhoeffer sums up his conviction:

> 'we believe that God has made the actual empirical church, in which the Word and the sacraments are administered, into his community, that it is the Body of Christ, that is, the presence of Christ in the world, and that according to the promise God's Spirit becomes effective in it.' (5)

Even so, within *Sanctorum Communio* Bonhoeffer found it necessary to make the same kind of distinction which Luther had made between a folk-church (*Volkskirch*) and a gathered-church (*Freiwilligkeitskirche*). Much as Luther regretted breaking away from the Church of Rome, in spite of being attracted by its historic and empirical character, he found in the folk-church of the German princes the concreteness which he needed. On the other hand, accepting as he did the doctrine of justification by faith as the sole means of salvation, the idea of a gathered-church was an essential concomitant of his thinking. So Bonhoeffer, while recognising that the strength of the Lutheran Church lay in its visible form and in its availability to all for the preaching of the Word, admitted too that the inner nature of the church was that of a gathered congregation. (6) Thus he was later able to claim Luther's support for the concept of the Confessing Church when the national church had obviously for him become Anti-Christ. For the present, however, Bonhoeffer was willing to concede that the *sanctorum communio* could be present both in the Roman Catholic Church and in the christian sect, since only God ultimately could recognize his own. Nevertheless Bonhoeffer firmly believed that the Protestant Church was the 'true' one and that it had been chosen by God as 'an especially pure instrument for his work'. (7)

Such in the main were Bonhoeffer's ideas in *Sanctorum Communio* at the early age of twenty-one in which he reveals his readiness to examine afresh his protestant preconceptions of the church. While Bonhoeffer himself would have claimed that by so doing he was simply drawing upon the teachings of Luther, in reality (as we shall see) the seeds of a new meaning were already being sown.

Bonhoeffer's *Act and Being*, written three years later, adds little or nothing to the views put forward in *Sanctorum Communio*. His main theme in this second book is the nature of the location of revelation, and clearly special attention is given to the contingent character of revelation manifested in Jesus Christ existing as community. Revelation, defined as both act and being, is thus identified with the church in which Jesus Christ proclaims and is proclaimed in his new humanity as both crucified and risen. In addition there is the same emphasis, as in the earlier book, on the exclusiveness of revelation within the church, and the same insistence on concreteness and on entrance into the community by belief and faith. Because of the personal nature of God's revelation in Christ the personal character of the church's activity, both individual and corporate, is developed to the point at which Bonhoeffer is prepared to insist (for example) that the word of forgiveness entrusted to the community is also bestowed on each member. Responsibility, therefore, for forgiving each other entails 'becoming a Christ' to one another as part of the individual's share in the proclamation of the gospel.

It is against the background of these two academic works that one can best understand such writings as *Life Together* and *Spiritual Care* which were the products of Bonhoeffer's teaching and pastoral experience in the Finkenwalde seminary during the years 1935-1937. Although many of his protestant contemporaries were affronted by what they thought of as 'monkish' and catholicising practices in the community-house (Brüderhaus) and seminary, the notion of a *collegium pietatis*, given to regular confession, recitation of the psalter, meditation and periods of organized silence stemmed logically from Bonhoeffer's concept of the church. 'Christian brotherhood', he wrote in *Life Together* 'is not an ideal which we must realize, it is rather a reality created by God in Jesus Christ in which we may participate'. (8) One suspects that Martin Luther himself, of whom Bonhoeffer once said (quoting Kierkegaard) that Luther would say the opposite today of what he said in his own day, (9), would in this case have approved of the *Brüderhaus* in view of the purpose for which it was created. Luther's departure from the monastery, as Bonhoeffer maintained, was not a rejection of monasticism as such; it was prompted by his wish to inject religious meaning and significance into the secular life. (10) Consequently Bonhoeffer no doubt believed that the training of ordinands for the Confessing Church in this particular way, in order to come to grips with the secular world of National Socialism, would have unquestionably met with Luther's approval and support. The Finkenwalde experiment can thus be seen as the practical working out of the ideas of christian community - a community based on fraternal love and the meeting of Christ in one another - which were first given expression in *Sanctorum Communio* and *Act and Being*.

It is generally agreed that the publication of these two academic works on the church marks the first phase of Bonhoeffer's theological activity. In 1932 a new phase opened in which political events were to have a profound effect on the way in which he conceived the church and its place in the purpose of God. About the same time Bonhoeffer found himself more and more involved in ecumenical discussions, both within and outside Germany, and these too further stimulated his thinking about the church.

The political influence came from the Nazi threat which could not be overlooked. Hitler took over the reins of government on 30 January, 1933 and immediately steps were taken to assume control of the German Evangelical Church. (11) On 6 April the promulgation of the so- called 'Aryan Clauses' inhibited any person of Jewish origin from holding public office in church or state.

Although Bonhoeffer was among the first to react in print, by producing a paper in the same month on 'The Church and the Jewish Question', (12) his approach was diplomatic and theological rather than political. He was of course aware that Luther himself had had no great love for the Jews as a race - and Bonhoeffer's own views were coloured by the fact that the Jews had 'nailed the redeemer of the world to a cross', (13) - but in his paper he unequivocally condemns the persecution of Jewish Christians within the church itself. 'What is at stake', Bonhoeffer writes, '.... is rather the task of Christian preaching to say: here is the church, where Jew and Christian stand together under the Word of God; here is the proof whether the church is still the church or not'. (14) In this position Bonhoeffer was encouraged in his correspondence with Karl Barth, who in like manner advocated (if anything more strongly) resistance to the Aryan Clauses based on theology rather than on politics. (15)

This paper, and the correspondence with Karl Barth, illustrate well the kind of political situation which was compelling Bonhoeffer to re-think his position with regard to the church. By this time he was prepared to admit to Barth that he was attracted to the idea of a Free Church and that he 'had no doubt at all that the *status confessionis* had arrived'. In this, too, Bonhoeffer received the support of Barth who, nevertheless, advised waiting to see which way the German Christian cat jumped. (16) The theological agonizing that lay behind all this is reflected in several lectures and papers which Bonhoeffer gave from 1932 onwards. For example, his lecture 'Dein Reich komme!', dated November the same year, gives us Bonhoeffer's first important statement on church-state relations. (17) It followed the capture by the National Socialists of enough seats to control parliament. The lecture repeats Luther's views about the separation and tension which must always exist between the two forms of God's Kingdom represented by church and state. Only at the end of the world will the twain become one. The Lutheran tradition of submission to the 'powers that be' is also implied, although it was to be only a matter of months before Bonhoeffer was criticising Luther's doctrine of 'orders of creation' because of its misuse by the Nazis, and seeking to replace it with the more Christ-centred doctrine of 'orders of preservation'.

(18) So the rapidly changing political scene begins to determine the shape of Bonhoeffer's theology of church-state relations.

It was against this kind of background also that Bonhoeffer was led to prepare two sets of university lectures for the summer term of 1932 - one on 'The Nature of the Church' and the other on 'Christian Ethics'. Together they reflect Bonhoeffer's undoubted concern for a 'relevant' church capable of speaking a 'concrete word' to a nation clearly heading for the abyss. In a paper, written about the same time as the first set of lectures, under the title 'What is the Church?', Bonhoeffer, in the Lutheran tradition, depicts a church which is simultaneously under sin and grace.

He begins by taking up the question of its relation to the world as a matter of urgency:

> 'The church is a bit of the world, a lost, godless world, under the curse, a complacent, evil world. And the church is the evil world to the highest degree because, in it, the name of God is misused, because in it God is made a plaything, man's idol.... But the church is a bit of the qualified world, qualified by God's revealing, gracious Word, which, completely surrendered and handed over to the world, secures the world for God and does not give up. The church is the presence of God in the world. Really in the world, really the presence of God.' (19)

It is this involvement in the world which enables a concrete word to be heard from the church in a given 'political' situation, but which at the same time fixes the boundaries for the Word. Thus it is not for the church to try to make politics christian, nor for it to pursue a political programme. Its responsibility is simply one of concrete command within the limits of finitude. If the occasion demands it, that command must be given, otherwise the state must be left to get on with its divinely appointed functions in peace. The responsibility is reciprocal - the state limits the church as the church limits the state.

The second influence which began to affect Bonhoeffer's thinking about the church in the second stage of development is the ecumenical. Bonhoeffer met this more positively and with less reluctance than he did the political. His introduction to the ecumenical movement came with an invitation to attend a meeting of the 'World Alliance for Promoting International Friendship through the Churches' (to give it its full title) in Cambridge in 1931. This was a body associated with the growing movement towards a World Council of Churches, which also included other influential international bodies such as the Councils for Faith and Order, and for Life and Work. Bonhoeffer was to become a youth co- secretary for Germany and Central Europe of the

World Alliance, and through this to become involved also with Faith and Order as well as Life and Work.

Reporting on the Cambridge meeting, which was chiefly concerned with the subject of disarmament, Bonhoeffer struck two notes which continued to resound throughout the length of his ecumenical activity. Both relate to his two dominant interests at this time - the theological and the ethical. The first note was outspokenly critical and had the support of some of the younger members present when Bonhoeffer was referring to 'the lack of a great basic theological understanding of our work (for which the hitherto almost universally accepted Anglo-Saxon basis is not sufficient)' - this reference was to the English and American predilection for conference resolutions based on broad christian principles. The second, equally emphatic, stressed the need for concrete action (in this case common action) for a real positive peace which would be based on Christianity saying 'the right word at the right time'. (20)

From Bonhoeffer's reports of subsequent ecumenical gatherings, as well as from papers presented to them, it becomes clear that the motivating force behind his interest in ecumenical affairs came from his search for an adequate theology, based on the Word of God, able to cope with the new phenomenon of a 'world-church', and from his belief in the need for concrete pronouncements from the church which would be capable of matching the grave situations now confronting the world. Thus a paper, given to the Youth Peace Conference in Czechoslovakia in 1932, (21) opens with the bald statement, 'There is still no theology of the ecumenical movement', and goes on to add that every time there is a new understanding of the nature of the church of Christ a new theology is produced to accompany it. The ecumenical movement is such a new self-understanding and 'it must and will produce a theology.' (22) Foremost among the questions which this raises (Bonhoeffer continues) is the problem of authority. This can have only one source, namely, that of Jesus Christ living and present in his church, and since his claim is total over the whole world the task of the churches in the World Alliance, which have come together the better to express this claim, is to proclaim the Word of God 'in the most concrete way possible, from the knowledge of the situation.' Hence the preaching of timeless principles is not good enough; from a detailed and full knowledge of the situation and circumstances prevailing the Church 'should be able to say quite definitely: "Engage in this war" or "Do not engage in this war".... A commandment must be definite, otherwise it is not a commandment.' (23)

It does not seem to have occurred to Bonhoeffer at this stage that the 'world-church' might ever be divided within itself as to the truth and applicability of the Word of God in a given situation. Given sufficient humility and study in the quest for a concrete commandment it probably seemed to him unthinkable that a word would not be forthcoming. Accordingly there was some substance in the criticism by some of Bonhoeffer's ecumenical colleagues that his main interest in these matters was not that of church unity, in any organizational sense, but that of establishing a doctrinal basis in the light of which the problems of the world could be discussed and concrete pronouncements could be made.

There followed a series of similar meetings within a relatively short period in which Bonhoeffer continued to hammer home his two principal concerns - a world-church theology, and an authoritative word for the world. His abiding hope that the ecumenical movement would eventually succeed in these efforts ensured that the concept of the church remained a constant preoccupation during this period and was kept in the forefront of his mind. This was especially true of the conferences which he attended in Gland (Switzerland) in the same year and at Fanö (Denmark) in 1934. (24) However, by the date of the Fanö Conference events in Germany had begun to produce the kind of changes which not only raised doubts in Bonhoeffer's mind about the effectiveness of the ecumenical movement, but also brought about a major development in his concept of the church. The changes related to the virtual take-over of the Evangelical Church by the German Christians and the consequent formation of the dissenting Confessing Church at Barmen in the same year. The claims of the German Christians, with their false theology, had to be resisted and, as Luther himself would have allowed in a situation of extremity, those churches which held to the gospel of Jesus Christ, revealed in scripture and restated at the Reformation, had no alternative (in Bonhoeffer's view) but to stand together as a single church on the basis of their confession.

Almost immediately, as one of the leaders of the Confessing Church, Bonhoeffer found himself justifying in theory what for all practical purposes was a new church. His work at Finkenwalde (training ministers for the Confessing Church) provided him with both the opportunity and the stimulus for working out the practical and theological implications of these momentous decisions. An early indication of his theological position is to be found in a sermon preached soon after the German Christians had secured a majority in the church elections of 1933. Predictably his text was Matthew 16, 13-18 and the theme the rock-like nature of the church built by Christ on Peter's confession of faith in him as Lord. This set the scene for the flowering of Bonhoeffer's concept of the church at this stage. That church was to be identified with the Confessing Church - now no longer an academic aspiration but a living, vibrant reality.

The manifesto of the Confessing Church was, in effect, *The Cost of Discipleship*, a book based upon teaching given by Bonhoeffer at Finkenwalde between 1935 and 1937. (25) The Confessing Church was now a fact, and its form and character could best be protected by the kind of discipleship and obedience which its Lord demanded in the Sermon on the Mount. Thus is comes about that in *The Cost of Discipleship* christology begins to assume at least an equal prominence with ecclesiology - fed no doubt by Bonhoeffer's preparation for his christology lectures of 1935. The paramount need now, however, is for discipline within the church and this is the subject of other lectures at Finkenwalde, later published under the titles of *Life Together* and *Spiritual Care*. Eberhard Bethge has shown how the idea of a *vita communis* (described in *Life Together*) had been gathering momentum for several years in Bonhoeffer's mind. (26) Training for the Lutheran ministry seemed to him to be lacking in spirituality as well as too much under the domination of university faculties. In England Bonhoeffer had come into contact with the monastic-type of ministerial training favoured by the Anglican colleges of Mirfield and Kelham; he had also expressed a keen interest in visiting Mahatma Gandhi's *ashrama* in India. Even so, Bonhoeffer was at pains to reassure his Lutheran critics that 'not monastic seclusion, but concentration for the life outside, this is the goal.' (27)

One further task occupied Bonhoeffer's attention during this second phase of working out his concept of the church - a task which he regarded as vital, as far as other ecumenical leaders were concerned. It was the question of the precise boundaries of the church, where they began and where they came to an end. An article written for the journal *Evangelische Kirche* in June 1936 took up this task, (28) and was immediately attacked for its 'legalism', 'enthusiasm' and 'Romanism'. Few Confessing theologians could be found to give it their approval, with the notable exception of Helmut Gollwitzer who entered the lists on Bonhoeffer's behalf. The article was provoked by a debate among Confessing Church leaders as to whether their provincial Councils of Brethren should co-operate with the governing committees of the German Reich Church or not. (29) Bonhoeffer, in the spirit of the Barmen Declaration, maintained that the boundaries of the Confessing Church set themselves; they were determined by the Word of God. Those who co-operated with the Reich Church committees therefore could not be of the Confessing Church. 'Whoever knowingly separates himself from the Confessing Church in Germany, separates himself from salvation', he wrote. (30) He could hardly have been more precise.

This precision, however, was not altogether one which ecumenical church leaders, whom Bonhoeffer tried assiduously to win over, found easy to accept. A paper written by Bonhoeffer in August 1935 on 'The Confessing Church and the Ecumenical Movement', (31) with this in mind, set out the theological and practical arguments (by now only too familiar) for the recognition of the Confessing Church, not merely as a true church but as the only Evangelical Church in Germany entitled to recognition in the ecumenical movement. The practical effect of this is evidenced by the correspondence which Bonhoeffer had with leaders of other churches at this time. Foremost among these were Bishop Bell of Chichester and Canon Leonard Hodgson, secretary of the Faith and Order movement. (32) In reply to Bonhoeffer's attempt to persuade Hodgson that the Confessing Church should replace the official Reich Church in ecumenical discussions, Hodgson was far from encouraging. Instead he pointed out that the ecumenical movement was intended to provide a platform and meeting-place for all churches professing Jesus Christ as God and Saviour. To this the Reich Church subscribed and was therefore entitled to be represented. Bonhoeffer's assertion (Hodgson continues) that the German State Church has in fact dissociated itself from the church of Christ, leaving only the Confessing Church to maintain the faith of Martin Luther, could not be sustained. It is difficult to see how the secretary of Faith and Order could have replied otherwise, in spite of Bonhoeffer's plea that the Confessing Church was fighting the battle for Christianity on a world front, unfortunately the principle of equal representation (which Hodgson offered) was unacceptable to Bonhoeffer and in 1939 he ceased to attend any more meetings.

The stage is now set for an examination of Bonhoeffer's concept of the church in *Ethics* itself, the earliest draft sections of which date from 1939. Since (as we have seen) *Ethics* consists of a collection of essays, written at various times between this date and 1943 (the year of Bonhoeffer's arrest), and also includes in Part 2 writings probably not intended to be part of the book, but of the same period, it is not possible to trace with certainty the precise way in which Bonhoeffer's ideas of the church changed over this period. Suffice it to say that, broadly speaking, there does seem to be traceable in *Ethics* views of the church, early on, which resemble those found in the chapter 'The Visible Community' in Bonhoeffer's *The Cost of Discipleship*, as well as those later on which are close to the spirit of the prison correspondence. It would appear, then, that the development in *Ethics* is one which moves from an exclusive Confessing Church concept, in which the church stands over against the world, towards a more inclusive one in which the boundaries of the church are very much less conspicuous.

It will be convenient for our purpose to summarize the main features of this development in *Ethics* under three heads. The first centres on the relation between the church and christology in *Ethics*; the second on the relation between the church and the world; the third concerns the church's responsibility for speaking concretely to the world. We begin with the relation between the church and christology. It has already been shown that in *The Cost of Discipleship* christology received heightened emphasis because of the need to encourage personal commitment and discipline within the membership of the Confessing Church. As a result christology begins to assume equal prominence in Bonhoeffer's mind with ecclesiology. Interest in the concept of the church, which until the middle 1930s had almost exclusively engaged Bonhoeffer's academic attention, is now expanded to include interest in the person of Christ so that, generally speaking, it may be said that in *Ethics* ecclesiology and christology exist as partners side by side.

This further stage in the development of Bonhoeffer's idea of the church could well be said to be characterised by a blurring of its boundaries due to its identification with a Christ who is now viewed as co-extensive with reality. It is conveniently illustrated by Bonhoeffer's use of the concept of 'conformation'. This means, (we remind ourselves), that the Christian is to allow Jesus Christ, as the incarnate, crucified and risen One, to be formed in him by submitting himself to be conformed to Christ's likeness. (33) This process, however, must begin with the church, where the form of Jesus first takes place. Bonhoeffer explains:

> '"Formation" consequently means in the first place Jesus's taking form in His Church. What takes form here is the form of Jesus Christ Himself.... The body is the form. So the Church is not a religious community of worshippers of Christ but is Christ himself who has taken form among men.... What takes place in her takes place as an example and substitute for all men.. ... The Church is nothing but a section of humanity in which Christ has really taken form.' (34)

It is still true, therefore, that 'Christ exists as community', but because of Bonhoeffer's new christological interests, especially in the Incarnation, the church is coming to be seen not in an exclusive sense (although it is doubtful whether Bonhoeffer ever wholly saw it as such) but, more important now, as the means of achieving the essential ontological unity which exists between humanity and God.

One important consequence of this new concentration upon the church as the place where christian formation begins is the insistence by Bonhoeffer of the need for the church, as a corporate identity, to confess to a fallen world its guilt for failing to proclaim Christ effectively, and for all the other moral failures which followed from it. Written probably in the aftermath of Hitler's victories in 1940 this confession was a particularly bold move, but it reflects Bonhoeffer's growing dissatisfaction with the ineffective witness of the Confessing Church during this period, and his conviction that genuine individual confession was only possible within the context of the church's own acknowledgement of guilt. So he writes:

> 'The place where this recognition of guilt becomes real is the

Church.... It is in here that Jesus realizes His form in the midst
of the world. That is why the Church alone can be the place of
personal and collective rebirth and renewal. (35)

In the same way the justification and renewal of the church becomes the
means whereby the justification and renewal of the western world is eventually
brought about. But whereas the church and its members are justified directly
by their becoming partakers of the form of Christ, the 'western world, as a
historical and political form, can be "justified and renewed" only indirectly,
through the faith of the Church.' (36)

It has to be admitted at this point that while Bonhoeffer's view of the
church, with its basic 'givenness' and essential 'notae' of Word, sacraments
and congregation, remains consistent with his earlier thinking in *Sanctorum
Communio*, and with Martin Luther's understanding of the church as the
place where the Word of God is preached and the sacraments are received,
an important change has in fact taken place within *Ethics*. Luther's view of
the church as the body in which God meets with men on the basis of a
personal encounter with Christ has now receded into the background. In its
stead an ontological dimension has been introduced in which the Body of
Christ is seen to embrace more than just the empirical church; it occupies a
position in relation to the reality of the world in a way which Luther certainly
did not conceive.

This leads on to a consideration of the second main feature of Bonhoeffer's
treatment of the church in Ethics. (Here it is important to remember that the
progress of Bonhoeffer's thinking in *Ethics* - as has already been noted - is
away from the Confessional Church concept towards a more worldly view. It
is this latter concept which is perhaps more typical of the Ethics and which
assumes prominence here.) This second main feature concerns the relationship
of the church to the world.

The subject of church-world relations attracts much attention in Ethics,
for obvious reasons, since Bonhoeffer's work with the Resistance necessitated
living a 'double-life' and being involved in both the church and the world at
one and the same time. Understandably in his treatment of it Bonhoeffer
diverges from his teacher, Martin Luther, while endeavouring to imply that
there is little or no disagreement between them. For example, in his account
of the break-up of the medieval unity of the *corpus christianum*, in the
sections 'Inheritance and Decay' and 'Thinking in terms of Two Spheres',
(37) Bonhoeffer (as we already know) suggests that the separation between
the church and the western world was not something which Luther by his
teaching intended. His doctrine of church-state relations, designed to prevent
the confusion or separation of the powers of the two authorities, was (according
to Bonhoeffer) 'misinterpreted as implying the emancipation and sanctification

of the world and of the natural.' (38) The practical consequence of this was
the rigid separation of sacred and secular spheres of activity from which the
West, and the Lutheran Church in particular, had suffered ever since. The
Ethics concept of the church sets out to remedy this by stressing a new
distinguishing mark - the church's responsibility to the world. This can be
undertaken only if, in the first place, the congregation is willing to recognise
this as its primary responsibility, thus:

> 'The congregation of Jesus Christ is the place at which Christ is
> believed and obeyed as the salvation of the whole world. This
> means that from the outset the congregation, according to its
> essential character, bears responsibility for the world which God
> lived in Christ. If the congregation fails to fulfil this responsibility
> it ceases to be the congregation of Christ.' (39)

In the second place, according to Bonhoeffer, the church's responsibility
for the world is exercised when the congregation *is* itself that responsibility,
that is, when it assumes the form of Christ:

> 'The Church is the man in Christ, incarnate, sentenced and
> awakened to new life. In the first instance, therefore, she has
> essentially nothing whatever to do with the so-called religious
> functions of men, but with the whole man in his existence in the
> world with all its implications. What matters in the Church is
> not religion but the form of Christ, and its taking form amidst a
> band of men.' (40)

The problems created, therefore, by a church standing apart from the
world, particularly when set in the kind of hostile relationship which obtained
between the Confessing Church and the German State Church, are no longer
to be solved (according to Bonhoeffer in *Ethics*) by having recourse to the
ghetto, or by bracing itself to meet the problems head-on. The church is co-
extensive with the world, and because of this is advantageously placed to
bring about the salvation of the world. It is this removal of the boundaries
between the church and the world in *Ethics* which provides Bonhoeffer with
the basic idea he needs to deal with the new problems he sees emerging in
church-world relations.

Even so there are theological problems. Reluctantly Bonhoeffer is forced
to admit that there are passages in the New Testament which accord with the
conception of the church having its own space in the world. This is, he
writes, 'a space which is delimited by her public worship, her organizations
and her parish life.... It would be very dangerous to overlook this, to deny

the visible nature of the Church, and to reduce her to the status of a purely spiritual force.' (41) There then follows an important qualification:

> 'it would be entirely wrong to interpret this space in a purely empirical sense.... the church of God is the place, in other words, the space in the world, at which the reign of Jesus Christ over the whole world is evidenced and proclaimed.... The space of the Church is not there in order to try to deprive the world of a piece of its own territory, but precisely in order to prove to the world that it is still the world, the world which is loved by God and reconciled with Him.... She asks for no more space than she needs for the purpose of serving the world.... The only way in which the Church can defend her own territory is by fighting not for it but for the salvation of the world.' (42)

This vital statement makes it clear that something of the tension of which Luther himself was aware existed between the idea of a folk-church and a 'hidden church' has now been transferred to Bonhoeffer's concept of a church which, at one and the same time, occupies space in the world, and yet is co-extensive with the world. Also the statement makes it evident that although the church is still regarded as the locus of revelation it is so only in a very special way. Revelation is not confined to spatial categories; these have broken down and others have to be found in order to describe its nature and significance. Among these, Bonhoeffer's use of the categories of the 'ultimate' and 'penultimate' is perhaps the most noteworthy. They do not however, in our consideration of the church, concern us at this stage.

More relevant to note is the extent to which Bonhoeffer's church-world teaching in *Ethics* has begun to undermine one of the fundamental Lutheran positions with regard to the place of the church in the world. The sharp division between the two (even if Luther himself had not intended it - as Bonhoeffer believed) was for most Lutherans an article of faith. It was implicit in Karl Barth's own teaching about revelation - indeed there are indications that Bonhoeffer may have partly blamed Barth for what he saw as the Confessing Church's preoccupation with its own security (43) - and Bonhoeffer's weakening of the boundaries between the church and the world could not therefore have pleased either his Lutheran or Reformed colleagues. The complete removal of the boundaries, when it eventually happened in *Letters and Papers*, was to strike them as something of an outrage.

The third principal feature of Bonhoeffer's concept of the church in *Ethics* concerns its responsibility for speaking a concrete word to the world. Much of what Bonhoeffer has to say about this is to be found in the important chapter 'Christ, Reality and Good'. (44) In *The Cost of Discipleship*, which may be said to sum up the second stage in Bonhoeffer's thinking about the church, to be a disciple of Christ means making a break with the world. In *Ethics* the oneness of the church and the world in Jesus Christ, by posing (as we have seen) the problem of separateness, raises the question 'how one is to conceive this distinction between Church and world without relapsing into these spatial terms.' (45) The difference is important if the church is to be seen to have any responsibility at all for preaching to the world. The paradox is that only by affirming its involvement in the world and its need to engage continually with it can the church truly be said to be the church and so be able to speak the word of salvation to it. Bonhoeffer's own view is expressed in the following sentences.

> 'The church is divided from the world solely by the fact that she affirms in faith the reality of God's acceptance of man, a reality which is the property of the whole world. By allowing this reality to take effect within herself, she testifies that it is effectual for the whole world. (46)

How is all this to be translated into the concrete word? Bonhoeffer's answer is to be found in his concept of the 'mandate'. The basic idea of a mandate stems from Luther who not only insisted that the Word of God should be heard, but also attached the greatest possible importance to the concepts of 'office' (*Amt*) and 'estate' (*Stand*), as divine creations through which God's commandments are organized and channelled. Bonhoeffer's preference for the use of divine mandates in *Ethics* arose from a wish to distance himself from the German Christians' misuse of Luther's concepts, and to emphasize 'the concrete divine commission which has its foundation in the revelation of Christ and which is evidenced by Scripture.' (47) Thus he defines a mandate as:

> 'the legitimation and warrant for the execution of a definite divine commandment, the conferment of divine authority on any earthly agent. The term "mandate" must also be taken to imply .the claiming, the seizure and the formation of a definitely earthly domain by the divine commandment.' (48)

Bonhoeffer lists four such mandates in *Ethics* as found in scripture: labour, marriage, government and the church. (49) Later these are listed as the church, marriage and the family, culture and government. (50)

Later still, in the prison letters, Bonhoeffer wondered about the place of 'culture' and its precise relationship to labour. (51) All four (Bonhoeffer believes) are imposed by God as tasks on all men to prevent any retreat from a 'secular' into a 'spiritual' sphere, and for the purpose of learning and practising the christian life. Their divine character comes from their relationship to Christ, for in themselves they are not divine, any more than the world itself is divine without a relationship to Christ. This is true even of the church which in this respect is no different as a mandate from the other three. So (Bonhoeffer argues) labour, for the sake of Jesus Christ, is the exercise of a divine responsibility laid upon man in which he responds to a concrete commandment given by God. Marriage, likewise, for the sake of Jesus Christ, is the human response to God's commandment to 'be fruitful and multiply'; and government, for the sake of Jesus Christ, is God's way of preserving and maintaining an orderly world through the agency of human beings. (52)

Thus the governing authority is entitled to obedience - for Jesus Christ's sake. If however a concrete form of labour, marriage, government or church persistently withholds this obedience the divine mandate lapses in this particular case. Yet the very fact of being a mandate ensures that these concrete forms retain a certain 'relative justification'. It requires however more than a single offence for each to acquire complete autonomy and for God to bring about its destruction. What is necessary is for each to return to its position of subordination and responsibility by adjusting its concrete form to its origin, continuance and goal in Jesus Christ. (53)

This leads Bonhoeffer into his explanation of the way in which the divine mandate of the church (although in other respects similar) differs from the other three. Since this bears directly on our purpose in considering the concrete word of the church to the world, Bonhoeffer's own words should be quoted here:

> 'The mandate is the task of enabling the reality of Jesus Christ to become real in the preaching and organization of the Church and the Christian life. It is concerned, therefore, with the external salvation of the whole world. The mandate of the Church extends to all mankind, and it does so within all other mandates.... The divine mandates in the world... are directed toward the whole man, as he stands in reality before God.' (54)

The prime duty of the church as a mandate, it seems, is to present and proclaim concretely to the world the reality of Jesus Christ. Upon this depends, according to Bonhoeffer, not only its own authority as a mandate but the authority of the other mandates as well. There is nothing here regarding the church's responsibility which, in principle, conflicts with what Bonhoeffer had always taught about the church. Similar teaching, for example, is to be found in his 1932 paper 'What is the Church?'; but from the standpoint of the church being 'a bit of the world, a lost, godless world, under the curse, a complacent, evil world' (55) Bonhoeffer's view of the world has been modified by the time *Ethics* has been reached. His view of the central purpose of the church, however, remains unchanged. The preaching of the Word and administration of the sacraments within the fellowship of the faithful continue to be its main function - following Luther - so that in this respect Bonhoeffer remained a loyal Lutheran, as he did in his own devotional practices and discipline.

Under the heading 'The Commandment of God in the Church' (56) Bonhoeffer shows a similar regard for the traditional channels of concrete commandment within the church (although this time in the church at large), through which the word of the revelation of God in Jesus Christ is made known. These, he declares, are preaching and confession (or ecclesiastical discipline). The Protestant Church is taken to task for concentrating too much on preaching without the necessary concern for personal discipline which must accompany it in its hearers (one is reminded here of the 'cheap grace' which is criticised in *The Cost of Discipleship*), while the Catholic Church is censured for the legalistic casuistry which is allowed to overshadow the preaching office. Both churches accordingly cease to possess a concrete ethic and need to remedy their deficiencies - the Protestants to return to personal discipline (which includes confession), the Catholics to the task of restoring preaching to its proper place.

In this important section, which unfortunately is incomplete, Bonhoeffer makes clear the ambivalent position in which the church stands as a result of his new view of the world and of reality. The attempt to locate the church fairly and squarely in the world as one of the four divine mandates, while at the same time endeavouring to reserve for it a special place as the 'home' of divine revelation does seem somewhat contrived. It is perhaps no more contrived, however, than some of Luther's own views, such as the simultaneity of law and grace, sinner and justified, and the visible and 'hidden' church.

It is thus clear that Bonhoeffer's *Ethics* may be regarded as marking the beginning of a third phase in Bonhoeffer's thinking about the church. In his early academic works, while holding firmly to Luther's ideas about the church's structure and purpose, he in effect broke new ground with his concept of 'Christ existing as community'. The middle period saw Bonhoeffer preparing the church for action in the struggle with the Nazis by defining its boundaries in terms of confessional commitment thus sharpening the church-world distinction. Bonhoeffer's third stage sees the emergence of the Christ-figure into a position in Ethics which might be described as 'co-sharer' with the church, and which is seen to be gradually moving into a position of ascendancy by the time we reach the prison correspondence. So it comes about that in *Letters and Papers* the presence of the crucified and risen

Christ is virtually indistinguishable from the everyday world.

While allowance must be made for the unsystematic character of the *Ethics* itself, and for the random nature of the references in *Letters and Papers*, a good case can clearly be made out for the conclusion that the logical development of Bonhoeffer's thinking about the church in *Ethics* is its near-disappearance in terms of traditional structures and form. (57) This case, however, would need to be argued very closely and in greater detail, bearing in mind what Bonhoeffer has to say about the radical church in 'Thoughts on a Baptism' and 'Outline for a Book' in *Letters and Papers*, as well as from his own private devotions (based on Lutheran practices) and references to an 'arcane discipline'. The general trend in *Ethics* nevertheless is plain - the movement of the church is outwards into the world. The *Ethics* account is not of a static, but of a dynamic, existential church, which finds its *raison d'être* in terms of a relationship with the world. In the nature of things its openness and vulnerability to changes and pressures in the world render it a 'servant church', whose main function is to exist for others.

How such a church, in Bonhoeffer's mind, should react to problems in the world may be seen in a separate essay in Part 1 of the *Ethics* entitled, 'On the Possibility of the Word of the Church to the World'. (58) It is believed to date from the Tegel imprisonment period. Discussing the degree to which the church is able to offer a solution to the world's problems, Bonhoeffer in fact rejects the suggestion that solutions on a human basis are part of the church's responsibility. Instead, he asserts that the 'Church's word to the world can be no other than God's word to the world. This word is Jesus Christ and salvation in his name.... (The) proper relation of the Church to the world cannot be deduced from natural law or from universal human rights, but only from the gospel of Jesus Christ.' (59) Even so, as the essay proceeds, Bonhoeffer seems not entirely to rule out the possibility of the church having a limited role to play in respect of worldly problems. Although he believes that the world is now sufficiently mature to grapple with its own problems, the church should not shy away from them altogether. Indeed it has within its responsibility a twofold function; first that of the 'office' - a divine function, which is to declare under the Word of God which economic attitudes or structures (for example) obviously obstruct belief in Jesus Christ; and second, that of the *'diakonia'* - an earthly task - by which christian specialists give of their expertise and so contribute to the creation of a new society. By stressing the church's duty to serve society not simply by ministering the Word and sacrament, but through the secular activities of its committed members Bonhoeffer claims a continuity with Luther. (60) This section however sits rather uneasily with Bonhoeffer's insistence that the church's main task is to summon people to faith and obedience to the revelation in Jesus Christ.

The continuity too with Martin Luther is only superficial; theologically, Bonhoeffer and Luther at this point are poles apart, starting, as they do, from different premises. Luther began by separating the 'two realms', church and the world, while at the same time recognising they had common interests. Bonhoeffer in *Ethics* teaches the ontological unity of the two, while seeking to explain in what way they are different. This oneness of the church and the world leads him to deny that there are any specifically 'christian' solutions to the world's problems; all come under the rule and judgement of God in the one salvific process of Christ- formation. What is needed is not solutions but redemption. In any case, need they all be solved?, he asks; their unsolved state may be of more importance to God than their solution - 'it may serve to call attention to the fall of man and to the divine redemption.' (61)

One final comment on Bonhoeffer's concept of the church in *Ethics* needs to be made. It relates to the emphasis which Bonhoeffer found himself increasingly placing on the church's identification with suffering humanity. In the early chapter in *Ethics*, under the heading of 'The Church and the World', (62), he takes up the cause of the not inconsiderable number of men of goodwill who, as a result of Nazi oppression, were in sympathy with much of what the Confessing Church was trying to do. These upholders of 'justice, truth, humanity and freedom', he maintained, who formerly spurned the church, were now seeking refuge and shelter with the Christ who himself was rejected and had nowhere to lay his head. Of them it could be truly said, 'He that is not against us is for us.' So it comes about that all who hold these values dear and seek the protection of Jesus Christ become subject to his claim. Because of this the church of Christ learns of the wide extent of her responsibility.

This may be said to be the point in *Ethics* at which Bonhoeffer begins to move away (theologically-speaking) from an insistence on strict boundaries for the Confessing Church to a greater interest in the secular world outside, where equally real men and women existed whose godlessness was often 'full of promise' compared with the 'pious godless' frequently found inside. Bonhoeffer himself believed that what impelled such persecuted people to seek the protection of Jesus Christ 'was not metaphysical speculation... it was the concrete suffering of injustice, of the organized lie, of hostility to mankind and of violence'.(63)

This would seem to indicate that by this stage Bonhoeffer's concept of the church is being shaped not so much by theological as by practical considerations; also that the dominion of Christ is a more helpful category to employ when dealing with the needs of suffering humanity than the dominion of the church. So the doctrine of the Incarnation comes into its own in *Ethics*, as Bonhoeffer describes the ontological reality of the form of Christ into which all men are to be drawn. So too the church is seen not so much as a bridge-head from which to evangelize the world, but as a representative section of humanity in which humanity can see itself as what it already is, in addition to what it might eventually become.

With Bonhoeffer's increasing involvement in suffering, both personal and national, the passion and crucifixion element in the 'form of Christ' begins more and more to dominate his mind. In *Letters and Papers* there are references to faith as meaning sharing in the sufferings of God in the world, (64) or watching with Christ in Gethsemane. (65) Furthermore in his poem 'Christians and Pagans', written at the end of his life, (66) Bonhoeffer ranks believers and unbelievers alike as equals before God in a fellowship of suffering, and therefore equally capable of receiving his forgiveness. Questionable though this extremely moving poem may be in terms of strict atonement-theology, it represents but one aspect of Bonhoeffer's hold on the revelation of God in Jesus Christ. God is also to be found, he insisted, at the centre of life 'and not only when death comes; in health and vigour, and not only in suffering; in our activities, and not only in sin.' (67) Swimming in dangerous waters as he undoubtedly was in his later years, because of his earnest desire for the church to exist for others, Bonhoeffer, it would seem, never entirely lost his belief in the conformation of Christ with *total* reality, nor of the church as the place where that reality is seen to take effect.

FOOTNOTES

(1)   *Cit.*, Bethge, EB., p.42.
(2)   See *LPP.*, 23:1:44, 21:2:44, pp.194, 216, 218.
(3)   *EB.*, p.42. For Bonhoeffer's reactions to Catholicism during his stay
       in the Benedictine monastery at Ettal 1940-1, see *NRS.*, pp.68ff. (*GS*11,
       pp.377ff.)
(4)   See pp.99ff. Note E. Feil's comment: 'Again and again (Bonhoeffer)
       had reason to take a stand against liberal theology'. *The Theology of
       Dietrich Bonhoeffer*, p.103.
(5)   *SC.*, p.197. See also the important 1938 lecture to younger theologians
       of Pomerania 'Our Way according to the Testimony of Scripture',
       TWF., p.178 (*GS*11, p.327).
(6)   See *SC.*, p.152.
(7)   *Ibid.*, pp.186f.
(8)   p.20.
(9)   See *LPP.*, 31:10:43, p.123.
(10) See *E.*, p.256.
(11) For a description of the position of the German Evangelical Church at
       this time, see E. Robertson, *The Shame and the Sacrifice*, pp.88ff.
(12) *NRS.*, pp.221-9, (GS11, pp.44-52).
(13) *Ibid.*, p.226 (p.49). However the same paper contains favourable
       references by Luther to the Jews.
(14) *Ibid.*, p.229, (p.53).
(15) See *ibid.*, pp.230ff. (pp.126ff.). For example, Barth was suspicious of
       the 'middle-line' approach of The Bethel Confession on the Jewish
       question which Bonhoeffer was helping to draft. (*NRS.*, pp.223, 240ff.
       *GS*11. pp.115-7, 130).
(16) See *NRS.*, pp.231f. (*GS*11, pp.127ff.).
(17) *GS*111, pp.270-85.
(18) E.g. at the Ecumenical Youth Conference April 1932 and the Youth
       Peace Conference in Czechoslovakia July 1932. See *NRS.*, pp.173-82,
       157-73, (*GS*1, pp.121-32, 140-58). For an authoritative treatment of
       the tensions present in Luther's teaching about the 'Two Kingdoms',
       see G. Ebeling, *Luther: An Introduction to his Thought*, Chapters 11
       and 12.
(19) *NRS.*, pp.153-4, (*GS*111, p.286). With regard to this passage, Burtness
       draws attention to the shift in Bonhoeffer's view of the church from
       having its own space (*CD.*, 1937) to not having its own space (*E.*,
       1940-3). Continuity (Burtness suggests) is provided by Bonhoeffer's
       insistence that the church is simultaneously under both sin and grace.
       Shaping the Future p.116, n.28.

(20) *NRS.*, pp.138f. (*GS*1, pp.116f.).
(21) See above, fn.18.
(22) *Ibid.*
(23) *Ibid.*, pp.162-3. (*GS*1. pp.145-6).
(24) At Fanö, state control of churches was condemned. See *GS*1, p.211.
(25) *CD.*, published 1937 was dedicated to Martin Niemöller then in prison. For similar views, see Bonhoeffer's paper on 'The Power of the Keys and Church Discipline' (1937), *TWF.*, pp.149-60, *GS*111, pp.369-81).
(26) In 'The Challenge of Dietrich Bonhoeffer's Life and Theology', *World Come of Age*, pp.58ff.
(27) *Cit., ibid.*, p.61.
(28) 'Zur Frage nach der Kirchengemeinschaft', printed in *GS*11, pp.217-41. See also paper on 'The Visible Church' (1936), *TWF.*, pp.42-51, (*GS*111, pp.325-34).
(29) Similar sentiments are to be found in Bonhoeffer's addresses and correspondence following the closure of Finkenwalde. See *TWF.*, pp.164-202 (*GS*11, pp.297-306, 320-45, 531ff.).
(30) 'Wer sich Wissentlich von der Bekennenden Kirche in Deutschland trennt, trennt sich vom Heil'. *Op.cit.*, p.238.
(31) *NRS.*, pp.362-44, (*GS*1, pp.240-61).
(32) See *GS*1, pp.230-9 and *WF.*, pp.206-10 (*GS*1, pp.282-6).
(33) See *E.*, pp.81f.
(34) *Ibid.*, p.83.
(35) *Ibid.*, p.111.
(36) *Ibid.*, p.117.
(37) pp.88-109, 196-207.
(38) *Ibid.*, p.96. See also p.103.
(39) *Ibid.*, p.322.
(40) *Ibid.*, pp.83-4.
(41) *Ibid.*, p.201.
(42) *Ibid.*, p.202.
(43) See *LPP.*, 8:6:44, pp.328f.
(44) pp. 188-213.
(45) *Ibid.*, p. 207.
(46) *Ibid.*, p.206.
(47) *Ibid.*, p.287.
(48) *Ibid.*
(49) See *ibid.*, p.207.
(50) *Ibid.*, p.286.
(51) *LPP.*, 23:1:44, pp.192f.
(52) See *ibid.*, pp.207ff.

(53) See *ibid.*, p.208.
(54) *Ibid.*, p.211.
(55) *NRS.*, p.153, (*GS*111, p.286).
(56) E., pp.292-302.
(57) For another view of church-state relations, see Bonhoeffer's draft paper
        and proclamation (1942) to follow the end of the Church Struggle
        after a political coup. *GS*11, pp.433-40.
(58) pp.354-62.
(59) *E.*, p.357.
(60) *Ibid.*, pp.361f.
(61) *Ibid.*, pp.355-6.
(62) pp.55-63.
(63) *Ibid.*, p.58.
(64) Letter, 18:7:44, p.361.
(65) Letter, 21:7:44, p.370.
(66) *LPP.*, pp.348-9.
(67) Letter, 29:5:44, p.312.

CHAPTER 4

BONHOEFFER AND JESUS CHRIST

'More than anyone Paul knew exactly what Christ is, and showed through his deeds what that man should be like who has been named after him. So clearly did he imitate Christ that he showed his Lord formed in himself. His imitation was so exact, the form of his soul was so transformed to conform to his model that the man who lived and spoke seemed to be no longer Paul, but Christ himself lived in him, as that good man says himself, knowing his own blessings: "Since you desire proof that Christ is speaking in me," and elsewhere: "It is no longer I who live, but Christ who lives in me."'

-St Gregory of Nyssa, (1).

Few would doubt that in this passage Gregory was right about St. Paul. It is a classic statement of Paul's understanding of the Gospel as centred on the experience of faith in Jesus Christ which, in contrast to Judaistic legalism, is alone capable of bringing about salvation. Mystical union and identification with Christ means for Paul a complete transformation - a washing and sanctification by incorporation into Christ's body in the power of the Holy Spirit. (2)

Reformation theology concentrated heavily on the work of Christ - for to know Christ was to know his saving benefits; christology tended to follow soteriology in the estimation of the Reformers who accordingly discouraged speculation about the person of Christ. This was also the view commonly held by 19th century German liberal theologians who regarded christological speculation as an unnecessary exercise which weakened the truth of the original gospel.

For Dietrich Bonhoeffer it was otherwise - christology came first. His course of lectures on christology, delivered in 1933, attracted audiences of up to two-hundred and marked the high point of his academic career. On his own admission no other series of lectures gave him so much trouble to prepare, (3) for in them he was crystallizing his thoughts about the basic theme on which his developing views about the church, reality and ethics were founded. The lectures make it clear that 'christology is not soteriology' and that the work does not interpret the person but the person the work.

Bonhoeffer's approach to the mystery of Christ's person, in these lectures, accordingly, is not one which, *prima facie*, would have commended itself to many of his Lutheran or Reformed colleagues. Moreover they were not based on speculative or exegetical enquiry focusing on the question How? This was the usual way preferred by the traditional dogmaticians and New Testament scholars, namely - How are the two natures related in the God-man? Instead, from the beginning Bonhoeffer ruled out the possibility of this approach. Neither dogmatic argument nor exegetical examination, pursuing the question How?, in his view, could arrive at the conclusion that Jesus is God. There had to be another route.

The route followed by Bonhoeffer in his christology lectures was opened up by two different questions, What is Jesus Christ? and Where is he to be found? These were questions which were to haunt Bonhoeffer throughout his life and which in 1944 lay behind the nagging query, 'who Christ really is for us today ?' (4) The answers given in 1933 make up the first part of his set of christology lectures. They turn upon the acceptance in faith of the *Christus praesens*. The Incarnate Lord has given, and continues to give, himself to mankind and to the world and is present to those with eyes to see. To the rest he is present incognito. 'The incognito of the incarnation makes it... impossible to recognize the person from his works'. In order to gain access to Jesus Christ one must 'attempt to be in the place where the person reveals himself in his own being, without any compulsion.... Only through the work of free self-revelation is the person of Christ, and thus his work, disclosed. (5)

Thus, according to Bonhoeffer, christology is primarily concerned with the being of Jesus Christ rather than with his action, although his action is necessarily involved from the beginning since the *Christus praesens* is the *Christus pro me*. For this reason existential interpretation is the key to the knowledge of Jesus Christ rather than theological or metaphysical speculation. Bonhoeffer himself had no doubt that the 'present Christ' was the proper starting-point of his enquiry. In his search for a concrete revelation the 'givenness' of Christ was a *sine qua non*, about which there should be no prior argument or discussion. In the seminary at Finkenwalde, as Eberhard Bethge tells us, the end wall of the chapel (a converted gymnasium) carried the word 'HAPAX' in shining gold letters to remind the worshippers of the 'once-for-all' nature of the divine redemptive event (cf., Hebrews 9,26-8). (6) It was also intended to bring to mind the declaration of the Barmen Synod of 1934 which based its authority as a Confessing Church upon the First Article of the 1933 constitution of the German Evangelical Church, namely:

'The impregnable foundation of the German Evangelical Church
is the Gospel of Jesus Christ, as it is revealed in Holy Scripture
and came again to the light in the creeds of the Reformation.' (7)

This was repeated and re-affirmed in the opening paragraph of the Barmen Declaration and provided the justification for unequivocal resistance to the destructive errors and teachings of the National Socialist State Church.

To this commitment to Jesus Christ as central to God's revelation to man, not simply as form but as content, Bonhoeffer remained consistently faithful. Indeed many influential commentators, such as Heinrich Ott, Jürgen Moltmann and John A. Phillips, have found in Bonhoeffer's christology the connecting-link between his many varied and often disjointed writings. (8)

The importance of christological thinking for Bonhoeffer is also shown in the two reports on the state of American religion and theology presented to his church authorities following visits to the United States in 1930 and 1939. (9) While detecting some signs of change in American church life by 1939, Bonhoeffer makes the point that, in his view, there was still too much concentration there upon ethics and the social gospel. Jesus Christ was not at the centre of American Christianity and, with the exception of the Fundamentalist churches, neglect of christology remained characteristic of the whole American church scene.

To return to the questions posed by Bonhoeffer in his christological lectures, Bonhoeffer replied to the first, What is Jesus Christ?, with a threefold answer to which he remained true in all his writings from the *Sanctorum Communio* of 1927 to the final prison correspondence. The answer given explicitly or implicitly in all these is the same - Jesus Christ is Word, sacrament and community. (10) In each case also he consider each must be interpreted dynamically not statically, existentially not metaphysically. The important fact is that Jesus Christ is present in Word, sacrament and community in his own person as a gift of God, and this involves us in a responsibility. Where there is concrete revelation there must needs be a response. (11)

Bonhoeffer is squarely within the Reformed tradition when he speaks of the Word as that which is preached and presented within the church. (12) But following his own understanding of 'Christ existing as the community' he also sees Christ as the Word spoken by the community. The individual member and the Body are one and the same, as is the Word whether directed within or outside the church. So that imperfect and human though that word may appear to be, it is still the Word of God to be heeded and acted upon as God's meeting point with man.

Similarly with regard to the sacrament, (13) Jesus Christ, the Mediator, acts spatially and temporally *pro me* and is existentially present wherever the sacraments are duly administered. Moreover the 'self-emptying' involved in taking form in the Word applies equally to the presence of the God-man in 'the penetration of fallen creation' (14) at the particular points represented by the sacraments. This is not a matter of intellectual comprehension - the result of struggling with the answer to the question How? (this was the mistake made by the medieval scholastics and the later Lutheran theologians) it is the only possible answer of the true Christian believer to the vital question, What is Jesus Christ?

The presence of Christ in the community (15) matches his presence both in Word and sacrament, according to Bonhoeffer; that is to say, in the same way that he is present as the Word and in the Word, as the sacrament and in the sacrament, he is also present as the church and in the church. 'His presence in Word and sacrament is related to his presence in the community as reality is to form (*wie Realität zur Gestalt*)'.(16) The important thing here is clearly the notion of the visible location of the whole person of Jesus Christ, both humiliated and exalted, in a community. As with previous elaborations on this theme, in *Communio Sanctorum* and *Act and Being*, the emphasis is upon Christ as the church itself, not separated from its members as its head (a dubious inference Bonhoeffer believed derived from the deutero-Pauline letter to the Ephesians), but fully identified with the historical, visible community itself. 'The community is the body of Christ, it does not *represent* the body of Christ.' (17) So it is to be regarded not simply as the recipient of the Word of revelation but is the concrete revelation of the Word itself.

The second of the two questions asked by Bonhoeffer in the first part of his christology course was, Where is Jesus Christ? This too is an existential question which is related to the real presence of Jesus Christ as Word, sacrament and community and to where the impact of that presence is to be found. Again Bonhoeffer returns a threefold answer - the real presence of Jesus Christ is to be found at the centre of human existence, at the centre of history and at the centre of nature. Students of Bonhoeffer's exposition of Genesis 1-3, given in Berlin University a few months previously, and later published under the title *Creation and Fall*, (18) will recognize in these answers some of the principal themes singled out for treatment in that course. The approach was theological rather than exegetical and owed much to Karl Barth's christocentric interpretation of scripture. Its main concern was to draw attention to the need to encounter the revealed God in Christ at the centre of things rather than on the periphery. It was a theme to be pursued more fully by Bonhoeffer in his *Ethics* and prison letters. (19)

Dominating the three answers again is the *pro me* element. Jesus Christ as the revelation of God is the Mediator (*Mittler*) who is both the centre (*Mitte*) and at the centre of reality *pro me*. Bonhoeffer insists that this centrality is not psychological in character but 'ontological - theological,' related not to our personality but 'to our being a person before God.' (20) It is not demonstrable. So when Bonhoeffer speaks of Jesus Christ being at the centre of human existence he is not referring to his being at the centre of our thoughts and feelings but is making an unconfirmable statement about reality. 'Christ is our centre even when he stands on the periphery of our consciousness'. He is 'being-there for men'. The law of human existence is such that man stands under judgement for his inability and unwillingness to keep it. Jesus is the one who alone has fulfilled it, but precisely at the same time that man is condemned for failing to fulfil the law's demands, Jesus as the centre is able to offer the possibilities of a new beginning. He both judges and justifies. (21)

As the centre in 'being-there for history' Jesus is to be seen as the fulfilment of the universal expectation of a messiah - or, in secular terms, as the meaning and purpose behind all history. Since the fate of God's messiah was to be humiliated and crucified, Jesus is able to offer simultaneously both the fulfilment and destruction of all human hopes and expectations. The heart of historical reality comprises both. The church is the outward form of Jesus Christ's real presence visible to man during the period extending between his resurrection and his return, so he is at the 'centre of a history which is made by the state.' As such he mediates between the state and God and is the hidden centre of the state as well as of all history. So for those who believe, it is possible to accept Luther's teaching about the 'two kingdoms', acknowledging that 'the state is the rule of God "with his left hand"'. Jesus Christ, the hidden centre of history, is therefore present in a double form as church and state, sustaining and redeeming the life of both whether recognized or not. (22)

With regard to Jesus Christ 'being-there for nature', Bonhoeffer admits that in the past Protestants have given little consideration to the place of Christ as mediator between God and creation. Nature, Bonhoeffer declares, no longer serves the purposes of God and creation as was originally intended when it first came into being. Under the curse of Adam it is in bondage and exists, like mankind and history, in a state of meaninglessness. Jesus Christ, the centre, is able to liberate and make it free to fulfil the Creator's purpose. Liberation is proclaimed in the preaching of the Word and anticipated in the transformation of the sacramental elements which, when duly administered, from being part of the old creation become constituents of the new. In this way too Jesus Christ is revealed to the eye of faith as being at one and the same time 'the end of the old world and the beginning of the new world of God.' (23)

It will now be apparent that the distinctive feature of Bonhoeffer's christology - and there is no reason to believe that he ever changed it - is the 'givenness' of Jesus Christ as the concrete embodiment of God's revelation to man, a revelation which embraces the whole of reality. Although strongly existential this approach is far from being Bultmannian. The stress is on the *hic et nunc* - the presence here and now - rather than on an existential response which then makes the living Christ a reality. The basis is ontological - not primarily existential - and is therefore closer to Hegel than to Bultmann. (24)

On the other hand, Bonhoeffer inherited from his Berlin tutor Seeberg a suspicion of metaphysics as such. This had the effect of leaving him unimpressed by the ontological controversies of the early church which had resulted in the formulation of the Trinitarian and christological dogmas. These controversies, Bonhoeffer believed, had been sparked off by an obsession with the question How? and were the product of speculation, rather than of commitment to the living Christ present here and now.

Even so, the Chalcedonian Definition (Bonhoeffer was convinced) served a useful purpose, for it laid down limits for theological thought and speculation beyond which it was not safe to go. It kept the mystery a mystery. By its use of such concepts as 'substance' and 'nature' Chalcedon demonstrated their inappropriateness; further development of the Definition was impossible along these lines; if required, such development would need to be inspired by another kind of approach. Only for this reason was Bonhoeffer prepared to concede that the 'Chalcedonian Definition is an objective, but living statement which bursts through all thought-forms.' (25) The person so defined (Bonhoeffer had declared earlier) is fundamentally different from Socrates or Goethe who also may be encountered as historical persons. The difference is that they are dead, and may be avoided, whereas Jesus Christ is alive. Upon our encounter with Christ hangs life or death, salvation or damnation. It is not so with Socrates and Goethe. So then the negative formulas of Chalcedon have their place, as does critical theology, in defining heresy; but for positive content we must rely upon the concreteness of the Incarnate One, Jesus Christ humiliated and exalted, who is the concern, not of reason but of faith.

If we return to our central theme of Bonhoeffer's *Ethics*, we find commentators vary only slightly as to the precise place of the *Ethics* within it. Thus there is a general acceptance of a three-stage course of development in which Bonhoeffer is seen to identify Christ, first with the church (1927-33), next with christian discipleship (1933-39), and in the final period (1939-45) with the world. These stages roughly coincide with the phases of Bonhoeffer's life when he was an academic, a Confessing Church leader, and lastly a member of the Resistance. Scholars also vary in the degree of emphasis which they place upon christology as the dominating motif in Bonhoeffer's thinking. Heinrich Ott and Jürgen Moltmann, for example, both stress the christocentric nature of Bonhoeffer's thought, as does John Godsey, while André Dumas finds the key in Bonhoeffer as 'Theologian of Reality'. In an important study of Bonhoeffer's concept of Christ and of reality, John A. Phillips in *The Form of Christ in the World* traces a radical shift from the ecclesiological Christ of the university dissertations and

Confessing Church period to the 'incognito Christ' of the secular world, which characterises the prison letters. (26)

Nevertheless, however one views the different stages in the progression of Bonhoeffer's thinking, and whatever interpretation one places upon them, it is scarcely open to question that the christocentric theme is a main thread running through them. Viewed in this light, *Ethics* must be seen as a connecting link between the *Christus praesens* of the church of *Cost of Discipleship* and *Life Together*, preceding it, and the *Christus praesens* of the world-come-of-age in *Letters and Papers*, which immediately followed it. Thus it is possible to detect a change in the presentation of Christ in *Ethics*, which contains traces of a synoptic-type, 'Sermon-on-the Mount' Jesus, in the opening chapters, and a pantokrator, Colossians-type Jesus in the chapters which follow. It is this latter presentation which makes possible the formulation of 'worldly Christianity' in the later parts of *Ethics* and *Letters and Papers*.

Behind all this, and indeed behind all Bonhoeffer's christology at whatever stage in his development, can be traced an indebtedness to Martin Luther. As Eberhard Bethge has pointed out, (27) in spite of Bonhoeffer's criticism of individual points of Lutheranism his christology was firmly based on Luther's. Bonhoeffer's criticisms were particularly noticeable during the Church Struggle when he felt it necessary to identify himself theologically more closely with his Reformed brethren, especially with Karl Barth, and when obedience in discipleship was absolutely vital. The effects of this seems to some Lutherans to minimize the importance of faith and to subvert what they normally understood as the strict relation between law and gospel.

However, when it came to christology and Luther's basic conviction that 'the finite could contain the infinite' (*finitum capax infiniti*) there was no capitulation to the conviction of his Reformed colleagues that 'the finite could not contain the infinite' (*finitum non capax infiniti*). (28) Luther was to be preferred to Barth. This in fact was the position taken up by Bonhoeffer from the beginning when, for example, in his inaugural university lecture of 1930, he anticipated some of the leading thoughts of his christological lectures three years later and declared that 'the rejection of the doctrine of *finitum incapax infiniti* follows from the emphasis on the transcendental nature of revelation.' (29)

It was in the same lecture, incidentally, that Bonhoeffer drew attention to his tutor Karl Holl's 'remarkably scant estimation of Luther's christology' (30) - a significant comment in view of the considerable debt which Bonhoeffer himself owed to Holl for arousing his interest in Luther studies. The importance of this interest is evidenced time and time again in the course of Bonhoeffer's treatment of christology as, for example, in his ready acceptance of the traditional Lutheran doctrines of Christ's ubiquity (much enhanced by the identification of Christ with reality in *Ethics*), the *communicatio idiomatum*, and *Christus pro nobis*, among others. (31)

The major debt however owed by Bonhoeffer to Luther was undoubtedly the latter's passion for concrete revelation which finds its noblest expression in his 'condescension-christology' - Jesus Christ is the humiliated one who empties himself *pro* me. In this, as in Philippians 2, the humiliation is, paradoxically, his exaltation and it is this which enables Christ to identify himself with our fallen humanity. Thus the glory, according to both Luther and Bonhoeffer, consists not in the fact of the Incarnation (God becoming man) but in Christ's subjection to our earthly conditions of sin and death. So (quoting from Christology):

> 'The scandal of Jesus is not his Incarnation - that is indeed the
> revelation! - but rather his humiliation.... Jesus Christ is Man as
> the Humiliated and Exalted.' (32)

Our meeting with Christ is therefore always a meeting with the humiliated God-man.

As we have already seen, within the overall framework of Luther's kenotic-theology it is possible to trace a development in *Ethics* itself of Bonhoeffer's conception of Christ from that of lordship over the church and its individual members to that of lordship (in an ontological sense) over the whole world. Acceptance of this view, however, turns upon agreement with the ordering and dating of the diverse and scattered papers, making up *Ethics*, which Eberhard Bethge has attempted in the 1963 German edition. This arrangement (he believes) 'makes Bonhoeffer's inner development from the *Cost of Discipleship* to the threshold of *Letters and Papers from Prison* somewhat clearer'. The anticipated publication of a new German critical edition of the *Ethics* (*Ethics*, Volume 6 of Bonhoeffer's *Werke*) is likely to suggest (with Bethge's approval) a slightly different arrangement, for example, the inversion of the order of Chapters 2 and 3. However, this should not seriously affect Bethge's account of the development of Bonhoeffer's thinking during this period. (33)

On this basis - to illustrate Bonhoeffer's inner development - it is possible to quote examples from both the earlier and later parts of *Ethics*. Thus, the 'costly discipleship' note is evidenced at the beginning in the insistence that dominical precepts are to be obeyed literally, and in the fact that scriptural injunctions abound - not least from the Epistle of James (Luther's 'epistle of straw'). (34) So specifically:

> 'The sermon on the mount is there for the purpose of being done
> (Matt.7,24ff.). Only in doing can there be submission to the will

of God.' (35)

or again:

'The hearer of the word who is not at the same time the doer of
the word thus inevitably falls victim to self-deception (Jam.1,22)'.
(36)

By contrast, in the final phase of *Ethics* we are told that 'in ethics, as in
dogmatics, we cannot simply reproduce the terminology of the Bible', (37)
and - more important in considering Bonhoeffer's doctrinal development -
we read:

'The cross of atonement is the setting free for life before God in
the midst of the godless world; it is the setting free for life in
genuine worldliness.'

Significantly Bonhoeffer adds - 'a life in genuine worldliness is possible
only through the proclamation of Christ crucified'. (38)

Bethge's arrangement of the separate sections of *Ethics* into some form of
chronological sequence in the 1963 edition, is based upon four different
starting-points, or approaches, which he endeavours to date more or less
precisely. (39) It will be useful in considering Bonhoeffer's christological
development during the *Ethics* period to examine these four approaches
more closely. The first approach, which Bethge himself entitles 'Cost of
Discipleship', while retaining (as we have seen) something of the christological
exclusiveness of the earlier book, picks up the ontological features found in
Bonhoeffer's university dissertations and moves into the inclusiveness of
Christ's dominion over the world. The special interpretative treatment of
Genesis 1-3 in *Creation and Fall* is also brought into play to set the stage
for the distinctive *Ethics'* theme of the unity of God and Christ in the world.
Disunity with God and man (Bonhoeffer suggests), and the knowledge of
good and evil, are products of the Fall, which can only be overcome by
accepting the exclusive claim of Jesus Christ over our lives. This at the same
time brings us into union with the inclusive being and dominion of Jesus
Christ over the world. Hence:

'The more exclusively we acknowledge and confess Christ as
our Lord, the more fully the wide range of His dominion will be
disclosed to us.' (40)

The second approach, described as 'Conformation', (41) deals with the need to conform to the Incarnate One who, crucified, risen and ascended, has taken form in the world. The point made here is that submission to being conformed to the likeness of the total Christ is in fact to submit to reality and to become real men as God intended us to be.

> 'Jesus is not *a* man. He is *man*. Whatever happens to Him happens to all men, and therefore it happens also to us. The name Jesus contains within itself the whole of humanity and the whole of God.' (42)

In this section there is also a break with the ecclesiological connection in order to relate the concrete revelation of Christ more specifically and intimately with the world and human reality. So now in Bonhoeffer's thinking 'the Church is nothing but a section of humanity in which Christ has really taken form.' (43)

Under the heading 'Justification', Bethge's title for the third approach, Bonhoeffer's christology moves on a further stage. Starting from the 'event' of justification by faith he sees that which goes before justification, namely the 'penultimate' way of life, as a form of encounter with Christ which continues to retain its own individual autonomy. For Bonhoeffer the 'penultimate' is a term for the particular way in which Christ engages the world as a preparation for his ultimate coming in judgement and mercy. Its relationship to the 'ultimate' is described as follows:

> 'The ultimate has become real in the cross, as the judgement upon all that is penultimate, yet also as mercy towards that penultimate which bows before the judgement of the ultimate.' (44)

So the possibility now opens up of an encounter with the Lord of Life which is not directly dependent upon the church as such. This carries with it, however, the risk of dissolving the 'form of Christ' in a formless cosmic reality unless other spatial and concrete locations can be found. The four divine mandates of labour, marriage, government and the church provide Bonhoeffer instead with a solution whereby Christ may assume concrete form in the world. But the concept of mandates became the subject of serious doubts later and it was not really pursued after *Ethics*. (43) Such evidence as we have suggests that Bonhoeffer was less than happy with it and this will occupy our attention later.

The fourth approach, described by Bethge as 'Incarnation', moves towards a full acceptance of the identification of Jesus Christ with total reality:

'It is from the real man, whose name is Jesus Christ, that all factual reality derives its ultimate foundation and its ultimate annulment, its justification and its ultimate contradiction, its ultimate affirmation and its ultimate negation.' (46)

Because of the ontological coherence of God's reality and that of the world, brought about by the Incarnation, the one reality of Jesus Christ makes it possible for man to be conformed to his likeness by everyday involvement in ordinary life. From this undoubtedly stems Bonhoeffer's notion of a 'genuine worldliness' which comes to dominate his later thinking. The contrast with the christology of *Cost of Discipleship* could hardly be greater.

Nevertheless the problem of the spatial and concrete location of Jesus Christ as the 'structure' of reality continues to vex Bonhoeffer. In this section, too, he dwells on the subject of the divine mandates but supplements it with another concept - that of 'deputyship' (*Stellvertretung*), (47) the origins of which are to be found in his earlier interest in sociality and the 'collective person'. (48) Although the basic meaning is that of a representative who engages in vicarious activity, fulfilling responsibilities on behalf of others, Bonhoeffer's use of 'deputyship' extends its meaning to include 'the complete surrender of one's own life to the other man.' (49) Jesus Christ is consequently *the* deputy, responsible for reality itself before God as well as for action on behalf of humanity with whom he is also identified. So our guilt is his guilt, our repentance is his repentance; just as his death is our death and his resurrection also ours. In like manner we ourselves are called upon to act as deputies for our fellow-men. This is what it means to live responsibly and to manifest concretely the form of Jesus Christ within ourselves. 'Only the selfless man lives responsibly, and this means that only the selfless man *lives*', (50) declares Bonhoeffer; it is also - as becomes clear in the succeeding section - what he means by 'correspondence with reality' (*Wirklichkeitsgemässsheit*). (51)

The foregoing survey of the principal characteristics of Bonhoeffer's christology and their development up to and including the *Ethics* finds here a natural conclusion. Scholars differ as whether the subsequent prison writings represent a logical continuation of this christology or not. For example, Hanfried Müller points to a radical discontinuity between Bonhoeffer's position in the *Ethics*, where a nostalgia for a christian theological heritage can be traced, and *Letters and Papers*, where he thinks Bonhoeffer's christology amounts to little short of humanism. (52) Similarly Heinrich Ott believes that while it is the triumphalism of an ontological christology which predominates in the *Ethics*, this is superseded by a *theologia crucis* approach in *Letters and Papers*; (53) others are convinced that Bonhoeffer's course of theological development remains even and undisturbed. (54)

It is not however our purpose here to pursue this particular theme. It is sufficient instead to remind ourselves that Bonhoeffer's progress overall in *Ethics* was in the direction of a deeper and more complex christology as it came to grapple ever more intensely with the problems of an adult world. (55)

There remain two questions, arising out of Bonhoeffer's approach to the person and work of Christ, to be considered. The first concerns the concept of the *imitatio Christi*. It is well known that Bonhoeffer frequently turned to the classic work of St Thomas à Kempis, of that name, for his devotional reading, and indeed retained a copy up to his death. In prison during Advent 1943 he was reading it in the Latin version (which he preferred to the German) and its gentle directness and charm could scarcely have failed to influence him. (56) The 'imitation-theology' of Martin Luther with its emphasis upon humiliation and 'becoming Christ for another' must also have left its mark upon him.

However, in the one work of Bonhoeffer which would seem to be most closely concerned with the call to follow and imitate Christ, namely, The *Cost of Discipleship*, the final chapter 'The Image of Christ' confronts us with a 'conformation-theology' reminiscent of *Ethics*, rather than an 'imitation theology', as the following passage indicates:

> 'To be conformed to the image of Christ is not an ideal to be striven after. It is not as though we had to imitate him as well as we could. We cannot transform ourselves into his image; it is rather the form of Christ which seeks to be formed in us.' (57)

This is not quite the same point however which Bonhoeffer makes earlier in the book when expounding Matthew 5-7, where in accordance with what he believes to be Luther's approach he calls for strict obedience to the literal commands of Jesus - 'when Christ calls a man he bids him come and die.' (58)

Again, it is only with difficulty, if at all, that one detects any signs of direct commitment to the imitation of Christ pattern in Bonhoeffer's earlier works, *Sanctorum Communio* and *Act and Being*, in spite of references in both books to the need to be 'in Christ'. Moreover the context is invariably that of Christ's solidarity with the church rather than that of the individual's personal following of Jesus.

The *Letters and Papers from Prison* reveal another apparent change in Bonhoeffer's attitude to '*imitatio*'. This is in fact remarked upon by Karl Barth in a letter to Superintendent P. W. Herrenbrück in 1952, after reading the prison letters,

'what (Bonhoeffer) says about sharing in the suffering of God,
and so on, seems to me to be clearly a variation of the idea of
imitatio which he rightly stressed.... Was it Bonhoeffer's view
that the whole of theology must be put on this basis? It is
possible that in his cell he did at times think this'. (59)

Barth was without a doubt correct in sensing a change of attitude in this
respect at this late stage in Bonhoeffer's life. It is detectable too in the
paper, 'After Ten Years', written at the end of 1942 for the benefit of
Bonhoeffer's fellow conspirators. (60) In this he identifies christian action
with sharing in 'Christ's large-heartedness' and in his love for others,
indicating that 'we are certainly not Christ', but as Christians we are called
to enter into the sufferings of those for whom Christ died. (61) The 'imitation'
theme also becomes explicit in the prison letter of 18 July 1944 where
Bonhoeffer refers to the many ways in which the New Testament speaks of
participation in the messianic sufferings of God in Jesus Christ. These include
the call to discipleship, fellowship with sinners and acceptance of children
in Jesus' name. They all have in common the offering of an opportunity to
share in the sufferings of God in Christ through faith. (62)

In sum, it would seem that, as long as Bonhoeffer's christology remained
tied to an ecclesiology which concentrated upon locating Jesus Christ within
the confines of the church in a visible and concrete way, he had little concern
for teaching the need for a traditional *imitatio Christi*. Once, however, the
Church Struggle had begun, the need for a more definite and visible form of
christian discipleship became apparent; this Bonhoeffer identified with
membership of the newly- formed Confessing Church. Disappointment with
this church and his more active involvement in world affairs from 1939,
seems to have contributed to a change (reflected in *Ethics*) in which
discipleship is associated with 'being conformed with Christ', who in turn is
thought of as identified with total reality. The pattern of the Christian's
involvement in the humiliation and exaltation of his Lord nevertheless remains
constant throughout. As freedom from the restrictions of the church (traceable
in *Ethics*) becomes complete, the continuing need for a 'spatial' and 'concrete'
revelation of Jesus Christ leads Bonhoeffer to turn wholly to the secularised
world in which Christ is to be recognized mainly through the sufferings of
others. As Karl Barth pointed out, participation in the being of Jesus, whose
only concern is for others, is in fact a form of *imitatio Christi*, which
Bonhoeffer's own sufferings in prison certainly helped to shape and influence.

The other question which requires some consideration follows from the
way in which Bonhoeffer deals with the work, rather than with the person, of
Christ in the *Ethics*. At the outset it must be said that, because of his
overwhelming concern for the concrete revelation of a divine Christ, he

never ceased to draw attention to the 'once-for-all' event in which God was reconciling the world unto himself. Furthermore, throughout Bonhoeffer's life, belief in salvation is never assumed except on the basis of a faith-commitment to Jesus Christ in which the believer is required to die and rise again with Christ. (63) At the beginning the stress is on membership of the church as a sacramental and mystical body and as the true repository of the Word of God. During the 'middle' period the emphasis is jointly on both Confessing Church membership and individual discipleship. In the final 'worldly' period the stress is on an individual sharing of the sufferings of Christ, based on a 'theology of the cross'. Even here the need for a church, however conceived and structured, is not completely ignored. (64)

As for *Ethics* itself, it must be conceded that the idea of redemption in the full biblical sense of a conversion of man to God is given little or no prominence. In his chapter 'On the Possibility of the Word of the Church to the World' (65) Bonhoeffer refers to the Word of God as 'not a solution of problems, Jesus brings the redemption of man, and yet for the very reason He does really bring the solution of all human problems as well... but from quite a difference plane.' (66) This is a rare reference to redemption as such in *Ethics* and illustrates Bonhoeffer's apparent reluctance to speak of soteriology in traditional terms. Jaroslav Pelikan in a symposium on Bonhoeffer's thought, *The Place of Bonhoeffer*, published in 1963, asks whether Bonhoeffer in his christological thinking does sufficient justice 'to the full range of biblical language and imagery about Jesus Christ'. (67) While Pelikan has principally in mind the 1933 lectures on christology, the question is equally applicable to references to the saving work of Christ in *Ethics*, where the relevant New Testament texts quoted are fewer in number than those referring to Christ's person and teaching. Along with this there is a less than liberal sprinkling in *Ethics* of references to the need for individual confession of guilt and conviction of sin. This might be regarded as surprising in a Reformation theologian.

Instead, much of *Ethics* deals with Christ's redemptive activity in terms of 'knowledge' and 'realization'. There is an early instance of this when Bonhoeffer is discussing the 'knowledge of the Pharisees':

> 'Whoever knows God in his revelation in Jesus Christ, whoever knows the crucified and risen God, he knows all things that are in heaven, on earth and beneath the earth. He knows God as the ending of all disunion, all judgement and all condemnation.... (The) knowledge of the Pharisees is disruptive, but the new knowledge is redemptive and propitiatory'. (68)

This trend away from specific references to sin and guilt as concerns to be dealt with in the traditional way by the justifying grace of God through Christ continues in *Letters and Papers*. The theological truth remains but Bonhoeffer's preoccupation now is with the lordship of Christ exercised in powerlessness and service through the cross, and with the need for Christians to demonstrate this in their own lives.

Thus it would appear that, while Bonhoeffer throughout the course of his life undoubtedly remained loyal to the Reformation insight of justification through faith in Jesus Christ alone, the fact of the Incarnation, because of its implications for reality as a whole, came more and more to occupy the foreground of his thinking. The structuring of that reality (it must be remembered) did indeed take the 'form' of Jesus Christ crucified, risen and glorified, so that 'at-one-ment' is woven into the very fabric of Bonhoeffer's attitude to life.

Nevertheless it can hardly be denied that, as the dialectical theologian of earlier days came under the influence of what can only be described as an Hegelian view of reality, the use of traditional language and imagery of salvation was dropped. Redemption in terms of liberating men from an earthly to a heavenly reality no longer seemed to Bonhoeffer to make sense in a non- religious world which had 'come-of-age'. So Jesus is described in *Ethics*, not as a saviour or redeemer, but as God's deputy who acts through divine mandates and structures all reality, thereby restoring to man his proper 'form' - the image of God - which God purposed at Creation. (69)

Early on in this chapter mention was made of the way in which Bonhoeffer distinguished between christology and soteriology in order to assert the priority of christology and his own belief that 'the person interprets the work'. While the distinction is a common one in systematic theology, it will have become evident by now that it is not one which Bonhoeffer maintains consistently throughout his writings. Although there is certainly evidence of a more traditional approach to the doctrine of justification by faith during the Confessing Church period, especially in his book *The Cost of Discipleship*, generally speaking for Bonhoeffer Jesus Christ's being and action were inseparable; *Christus praesens* is always the *Christus pro me*. The importance of the *Ethics* for this purpose therefore is that in it the Incarnation is at one and the same time the Atonement. Bonhoeffer sees the Incarnation as the starting-point for redemption and the Cross the place where mankind and reality take on Christ's pattern of humiliation and glory. (70)

However, any suggestion that in the course of his life Bonhoeffer jettisoned the doctrine of justification by faith, the *articulus stantis et cadentis ecclesiae* in which he had been brought up, cannot be sustained. The evidence is that he held firmly to it throughout while at the same time seeking to give it meaning and significance for his own day and age. To the end Bonhoeffer remained a devoted disciple of Martin Luther no less than of Jesus Christ and, like Martin Luther, nothing could shake his fundamental conviction that when he pointed to the infant Jesus he pointed to God.

FOOTNOTES

(1)   'On Christian Perfection' (P.G.46, 254-5) in *From the Fathers to the Churches*, ed. Brother Kenneth CGA., Collins, 1983, p.450.

(2)   Cf., 'Justification is the new creation of the new man and sanctification his preservation until the day of Jesus Christ.' *CD.*, p.250.

(3)   See Bethge's forward to *GS*111, p.9: 'ihm keine Vorlesung so viel Not bereitet hatte wie diese.' The German text of *Christology* is in *GS*111, pp.162-242.

(4)   See *LPP.*, 30:4:44, p.279, also Bethge, *DB.*, p.784.

(5)   *C.* p.39. (*GS*111, pp.177-8).

(6)   *WB.*, p.348, cf., *E.*, p.120.

(7)   In E. H. Robertson, *Christians Against Hitler*, p.48

(8)   See Ott, *Reality and Faith*, Moltmann, *Two Studies in the Theology of Bonhoeffer*, Phillips, *The Form of Christ in the World*; also J. W. Woelfel, *Bonhoeffer's Theology Classical and Revolutionary*, pp.280f.

(9)   *NRS.*, pp.86-118 (*GS*1, pp.323-54). See also *E.*, pp.104-5 for a further view of the relationship between American democracy and Christianity.

(10)   'Gemeinde' is variously translated by Bonhoeffer students as 'church', 'congregation', 'community' - none of which is entirely adequate. We have usually followed E. H. Robertson and J. Bowden in their preference for 'community', in most cases see (e.g.) *C.*, p.13, cf., J. Pelikan 'Bonhoeffer's *Christologie* of 1933' in *The place of Bonhoeffer*, p.149.

(11)   In the original there is a play on words here: 'Aus Anrede wird Antwort und Verantwortung,' *GS*111, p.185. See *C.*, p.51.

(12)   *C.*, pp.49-53.

(13)   See *ibid.*, pp.53-9.

(14)   *Ibid.*, p.59.

(15)   See *ibid.*, pp.59-61.

(16)   *Ibid.*, p.59. We translate 'Gestalt' here as 'form' rather than 'figure' (E. H. Robertson) or 'structure' (A. Dumas) cf., (*GS*111, p.193).

(17)   *Ibid.*, p.60.

(18)   In German as *Schöpfung und Fall*, Munich 1937. E.T., 1939. Later published as *Creation and Temptation*, London, 1966.

(19)   For christology as the centre of the *universitas litterarum*, see *C.*, p.28. *LPP.*, pp.273-333.

(20)   *C.*, p.62 (*GS*111, p.195 - 'nicht psychologischer, sondern ontologisch - theologischer Art.')

(21)   *Ibid.*, pp.62f.

(22)   *Ibid.*, pp.63f., cf., application of Luther's 'two realms' doctrine as only a 'polemical unity' in *E* pp.196-9. For an extended comment on

Bonhoeffer's treatment of Luther's concept of 'two realms', see T. R. Peters, *Die Präsenz des Politischen in der Theologie Dietrich Bonhoeffers*, pp.96-103.

(23) *C.*, p.67.

(24) For an authoritative account of ontology as the basis of Bonhoeffer's thinking see Ott, *Reality and Faith*. Also Dumas for a thoughtful comment on Ott's book, and on Bonhoeffer's ontological thinking in *C.* in particular, *Dietrich Bonhoeffer: Theologian of Reality*. pp.269ff. and pp.30ff.

(25) *C.*, p.92, cf., p.35.

(26) See especially pp.73-75: also *LPP.*, pp.185,245. J. W. Woelfel summarizes several interpretations in *Bonhoeffer's Theology*, Chapter 10.

(27) In *DB.*, p.476.

(28) For a concise summary of Reformed and Lutheran differences in christology see W. Nicholls, *The Pelican Guide to Modern Theology*, Vol. 1, 1969, p.198.

(29) Cited by Bethge in DB., p.135, cf., *NRS.*, p.64, (GS111, p.79).

(30) In NRS., p.61, (*GS*111, p.76).

(31) See *C.*, pp.92ff.

(32) Phillips' sharper translation in *The Form of Christ in the World*, p.272, fn.21 is to be preferred to that of Robertson, *C.*, pp.46-7, (*GS*111, p.181). Peters draws particular attention to Bonhoeffer's indebtedness to Luther's *Deszendenz - Christologie in Die Präsenz des Politischen*, p.113.

(33) See 1963 preface to *E*, p.iii, and De Gruchy, *Dietrich Bonhoeffer: Witness to Jesus Christ*, Collins, 1988, pp.221f., also Bibliography and p.261 below.

(34) See *E.*, Index of Biblical References, p.380.

(35) *E.*, p.43.

(36) *Ibid.*, p.45.

(37) *Ibid.*, p.223. cf., pp.84-5.

(38) *Ibid.*, p.297.

(39) For Bethge's 1963 arrangement see *ibid.*, pp.i-iv. For revised arrangement (cf., p.121 aove and below pp. 147f., 261, 308.) see Clifford Green, *Bonhoeffer's Ethics: A Research Brief*, an unpublished paper presented to a conference of the International Bonhoeffer Society, Oxford, March 1980.

(40) *Ibid.*, p.58, cf., *NRS.*, p.161, (*GS*1, pp.143-4).

(41) It is an intriguing question how far Bonhoeffer's insistence on 'conformation' was intended to supplant the Nazi concern for 'formation'. See Robertson, *NRS.*, p.15.

(42) *E.*, p.72.
(43) *Ibid.*, p.82.
(44) *Ibid.*, p.132.
(45) See *LPP.*, 23:1:44, pp.192f.
(46) *E.*, p.228.
(47) 'The bearer of the mandate acts as a deputy in the place of Him who assigns him his commission.' *Ibid.*, p.287. See also pp.289,299ff. For a modern treatment of Bonhoeffer's idea of deputyship, based on Richard Neibuhr's book *The Responsible Self.* See E. H. Robertson, *Bonhoeffer's Heritage*, pp.45-49.
(48) E.g., in *SC.* and *AB.*
(49) *E.*, p.225.
(50) *Ibid.*
(51) *Ibid.*, pp.227ff. See also *Ethik*, pp.241ff.
(52) In *Von der Kirche zur Welt*, pp.357ff., cited by Ott, *Reality and Faith*, p.106, fn.,3. See also Müller, 'Concerning the Reception and Interpretation of Dietrich Bonhoeffer's in *World Come of Age*, pp.182-214.
(53) See *Reality and Faith.*
(54) For an authoritative summary of Bonhoeffer's approach in *E*, see Bethge, *DB.*, p.625.
(55) See Marty, *The Place of Bonhoeffer*, p.20. 'Bonhoeffer's christological concern is born in a sociological setting and moves to an ethical one.' cf., Peters' reference to the current debate on 'a sociologically informed theology *(eine gesellschaftsbezogene Theologie)* in *Die Präsenz des Politischen*, p.16 fn.,26.
(56) See *LP.*, Advent iv, 22:12:43, pp.170-175. These and similar references to his devotional practices in prison *(ibid.*, pp.387,391), surely dispose of the charges of 'humanism' sometimes brought against Bonhoeffer.
(57) p.272.
(58) *Ibid.*, p.79.
(59) Cited in *World Come of Age*, p.91.
(60) See *LPP.*, p.1-17.
(61) *Ibid.*, p.14.
(62) *Ibid.*, p.362.
(63) For further evidence of Bonhoeffer's views about the person and work of Christ, see his Finkenwalde circular letters, 1939-40, in *TP.*, pp.28ff, (*GS*111, pp.388ff.).
(64) See especially 'Outline for a Book', *LPP.*, pp.382f.
(65) *E.*, pp.354-62.
(66) *Ibid.*, p.355.
(67) p.162.

(68) *E.*, p.34.
(69) See also Bonhoeffer's rejection of the idea of Christianity 'as a religion of redemption' in letter 27:6:44, *LPP.*, p.336. But cf., his description of Jesus as one who 'brings the redemption of men'. *E.*, p.355.
(70) *E.*, p.116.

CHAPTER 5

BONHOEFFER AND THE NATURAL

'Ich beginne jetzt mit dem Teil über das "Natürliche Leben"; Du hast recht, es ist gefährliche Materie, aber gerade darum so reizvoll.'

This remark in a letter from Dietrich Bonhoeffer to his friend Eberhard Bethge (1) provides us with unusually precise information about the date and setting of Bonhoeffer's important section in *Ethics* on 'The Natural'. (2) The letter is dated 10 December 1940, and was written from the Benedictine abbey at Ettal in Bavaria where Bonhoeffer was staying as a guest of the Roman Catholic community during the winter of 1940-1941. Bonhoeffer's excitement at beginning this part of *Ethics* stems from his conviction that his own church had sadly neglected the concept of the natural - indeed (to quote his opening words) it had 'fallen into discredit in Protestant ethics' - and the time had now come for its rehabilitation. However, Bonhoeffer himself had shown little or no interest in the natural, as such, up to this point. In a letter to his brother-in-law, Rüdiger Schleicher, four years earlier, in reply to an enquiry about how to live a christian life in the real world, Bonhoeffer had responded in a typically protestant way - 'The Bible alone is the answer to all our questions' (*Die Bibel allein die Antwort auf unser Fragen ist*), (3) provided one asks repeatedly and humbly. But by 1940 his thinking about reality, and especially about the world had changed profoundly. From then on the problem of the relation of the reality of God to the reality of the world was to occupy his mind incessantly; it was to prove singularly fruitful, especially for his understanding of the natural.

Nevertheless the seeds of a later interest in the natural were being sown at an earlier date. For example, in Bonhoeffer's university dissertations, *Sanctorum Communio* and *Act and Being*, where the emphasis is upon Christ's presence in the church, as the place where God meets with man, the obligation of Christians to look outward to the world is not entirely overlooked. In the case of *Act and Being* the recognition of God's dominion over creation is specific. Thus:

'God is still the Lord even of this world, and, looking to the hope offered by the resurrection of the historical (*geschichtlich*) Christ and my life with him, to which is promised a new Heaven and earth, faith must believe that in spite of its falling away the world is God's creation.' (4)

It is interesting, as a matter of fact, that throughout the whole of his university period, when Bonhoeffer was most heavily influenced by Karl Barth's revelation theology - so much so that even Barth himself accused him of 'killing everything with grace' (5) - Bonhoeffer was occupying himself increasingly with the problem of worldly reality. The reason for this undoubtedly sprang from his pastoral and evangelistic concern, aroused by his parochial ministries in Barcelona and Berlin, and from his active involvement in ecumenical affairs.

Bonhoeffer was searching at this time for a concrete ethical word to give to his expectant congregation, and this led him in Barcelona in 1929, for example, to declare: 'Ethics is a matter of earth and of blood, but also of him who made both; the trouble arises from this duality.... The earth remains our mother, just as God remains our Father'. It was in the same address that Bonhoeffer quoted Nietzsche's favourite myth about the giant Antaeus, whose strength remained constant as long as his feet rested firmly on the ground. (6)

A similar insistence on the importance of earthly reality and of the need for the church to be involved in the world is to be found in a succession of addresses dated three years later, 'Dein Reich komme!', 'What is the Church?' and 'A Theological Basis for the World Alliance'. It was in the paper, 'What is the Church?' that Bonhoeffer refers most explicitly to the ambivalent position of the church, which 'is a bit of the world, a lost godless world, under the curse', but which is also 'the presence of God in the world... called by God to God.' (7) By the winter of 1932-33 Bonhoeffer's growing interest in God's creation had moved him to expound Genesis 1-3 in what was to be one of his final sets of lectures. Commenting on Genesis I verses 25-26 - God saw the original creation as good, and then created man in his own image and likeness - Bonhoeffer makes it clear that 'the work is good only because the Creator alone is good'; there can be no intrinsic goodness in creation itself. In the fallen world man no longer rules, but is ruled by the world. Only through the Incarnation does it become possible for man to exercise his true dominion over the earth in a proper relationship with God and his fellow man, 'for God, our brother, and the earth belong together.' Furthermore (Bonhoeffer continues) God's image and likeness in man consists in man being-free-for God, and also for his brother. This is a relationship bestowed upon man by God through the Word - and more fittingly described in terms of an *analogia relationis* than an *analogia entis*. (8) This is an original point being made by Bonhoeffer which needs to be borne in mind in all his subsequent thinking about the natural.

With the advent of the Church Struggle, however, Bonhoeffer's attention was taken up more with equipping the church to face the world than with working out the theological implications of the reality of the world. In each of the two publications representative of this period, namely, *Life Together* and *The Cost of Discipleship*, Bonhoeffer's chief concern is with exploring the kind of christian life required to withstand the mounting secular pressures from outside. The principal purpose of this is still church witness, but the need to battle for the existence of the Confessing Church left him with little time to investigate the natural. Understandably there are eschatological overtones evoked by the onset of persecution to be found in these writings, particularly in *The Cost of Discipleship*. 'The world is growing too small for the Christian community', declares Bonhoeffer, 'and all it looks for is the Lord's return. It still walks in the flesh, but with eyes upturned to heaven, whence he for whom they wait will come again.' (9) In spite of the undoubted prominence of the witness motif in Bonhoeffer's mind, the overall impression is of a ghetto-mentality rather than of openness to the world. The church-world distinction is sharpened and the disciple's glance is directed upwards rather than outwards.

An interesting comment by James Burtness draws attention to the way in which Bonhoeffer in *The Cost of Discipleship* uses the words 'visible' and 'hidden' as contrasts, in the place of visible' and 'invisible', when speaking of the church and discipleship. (10) These categories (Burtness believes) correspond to Luther's use of *Deus revelatus* and *Deus absconditus* to describe the revealed and hidden God. In his view, Bonhoeffer employs them to support the Chalcedonian concept of the church as a visible reality, which does not equate reality with invisibility but with the presence of the 'hidden' Christ in his Body, recognizable to the eye of faith. So there are not two realities, the visible and the invisible, but one unity- in-duality, both visible and hidden simultaneously. (11) The point is well made since here we see Bonhoeffer introducing the theme of 'one reality' (already to some extent anticipated in *Creation and Fall*) which later came to dominate the *Ethics*. The scene is thus set for a transition from the 'ghetto-type' church of the Church Struggle period to the more this-worldly church of the *Ethics* and the prison correspondence.

It is generally agreed that about 1939-1940 a radical change in Bonhoeffer's thinking took place, particularly with regard to his attitude towards the world. T. R. Peters in *Die Präsenz des Politischen in der Theologie Dietrich Bonhoeffers* presents a case for associating Bonhoeffer's positive attitude to the world with the rise of National Socialism in the early 1930s - and its obsession with world domination. This dating is rejected by Ernst Feil in both the original and revised editions of *The Theology of Dietrich Bonhoeffer* where the 1939 date is preferred. J. A. Phillips in his account of Bonhoeffer's christology, *The Form of Christ in the World*, supports this view of a major change in Bonhoeffer's theological outlook as taking place at the outbreak of war. (12) That a change is discernible is not open to doubt, but it is a moot point whether the movement was not more a matter of acceleration than of transformation, since (as we have seen), Bonhoeffer's interest in the world and creation, which now begins to loom large, can be detected in some of the earliest writings of his university days.

In his book Phillips also mentions a number of factors, dating roughly from the publication of *The Cost of Discipleship* in 1937, which helped to steer Bonhoeffer's mind away from church-exclusiveness to the more open church-worldliness of his later period. (13) These may be summarized as follows; firstly Bonhoeffer's distancing of himself from the Confessing Church, due largely to government restrictions on his church activities, and to the Confessing Church's over-preoccupation (as he saw it) with its own security. Next, his resolve to find another sphere of activity, among a new set of associates, leading to involvement in the anti-Nazi *Abwehr* conspiracy; this brought him into touch with 'men-of-the-world' who were outside the strict limits of ecclesiastical politics. Third, Bonhoeffer's theological and general reading (the former including Rudolf Bultmann's 1941 'demythologizing' essay 'New Testament and Theology', which he warmly welcomed), (14) which consisted largely of nineteenth-century histories and biographies, with (significantly) some scientific works, such as C. F. von Weizsäcker's *Geschichte der Natur*. These all indicate (according to Phillips) an 'open-window' attitude towards the world. Lastly Phillips refers to Bonhoeffer's new interest in the problems of post-war reconstruction, which presented Bonhoeffer with realistic and practical questions to bite on rather than questions of a purely theological kind. As an example, Phillips quotes Bonhoeffer's response, along with W. A. Visser't Hooft, to William Paton's paper 'The Church and the New Order' (1941) which sought to plan for the new society which would be needed in Europe after the war and, more specifically, for the role of the churches within it. (15)

Such, undoubtedly, were the major external influences which from 1939 onwards brought Bonhoeffer face to face with the wider reality of the world itself. His response to it, once the opportunity for thought and reflection opened up, was characteristically theological - how to relate the reality of God to the reality of the world. The problem (as we have shown) had been with him since the thirties, but the world situation had now changed radically, and so had Bonhoeffer. His view of the church, too, was in process of change since he could no longer wholeheartedly believe in it as the sole locus of salvation. Nevertheless, its prime responsibility, and that of individual Christians, remained the same - God's commandment must be preached both inside and outside the church, and be recognized and heard by fallen humanity.

The new insights which Bonhoeffer worked upon for this purpose in *Ethics* need only be briefly mentioned, since we have already referred to them; (16) they are very familiar and lie behind the whole of the thinking in *Ethics*: they are - the unitary concept of reality, the christocentric nature of reality, and 'conformation' with Christ as ethical reality. In our examination of the way in which Bonhoeffer treated the natural in *Ethics* these foundation thoughts will be assumed, and not developed further except where necessary in the interests of clarification.

Bonhoeffer's section on 'The Natural' falls within the chapter 'The Last Things and the Things before the Last', which, together with the chapter, 'Christ, Reality and Good', marks (according to Bethge) the third of Bonhoeffer's starting-points in the writing of *Ethics*. With some hesitation he attributes its writing to the summer of 1941. (17). It is one of the few pieces of sustained writing in Ethics; and even then it is incomplete. Already Bonhoeffer had written the chapters, 'The Love of God and the Decay of the Word' and 'The Church and the Word', which concentrated attention on the God-world relationship, as well as having completed the important chapter, 'Ethics as Formation', which focuses on Jesus Christ's taking form in the church and the world. It is possible to detect in these earlier pages a movement away from what may be described as a *'Cost of Discipleship'* understanding of Christ's Lordship over the church, towards a concept of Christ's taking form in the world, with the church being regarded as 'nothing but a section of humanity in which Christ has really taken form'. The movement is not uniform but the general direction is clear; external pressures were building up to compel Bonhoeffer to turn his attentions to the problems created by the need for Christians to live in the twentieth century world.

Bonhoeffer did not however come to this part of *Ethics*, devoted to a consideration of the natural, without being theologically well prepared. Apart from those already mentioned - dissatisfaction with a dualistic view of reality, emphasis upon christology rather than ecclesiology, and christian-living as a sharing with Christ in total reality - there were at least two other important theological influences at work. The first derives from Bonhoeffer's commitment to the Lutheran doctrine of justification by grace and faith alone. This, he was convinced, stands at the centre of christian life and gives it its ultimate meaning. The need, however, for Bonhoeffer to distance himself from the protestant tendency to downgrade the natural, on the one hand, and, on the other hand, from the catholic tendency to exalt it, led him to attempt a reformulation of the doctrine of justification in terms of the concepts of the 'ultimate' and the 'penultimate'. By speaking of justification as an event (or the last word) in both a qualitative and a temporal sense, he hoped to exclude the possibility of making an idol of the natural (now thought of as the penultimate). The former error, according to Bonhoeffer, results in

'compromise', which 'springs from hatred of the ultimate', and is exemplified
by Dostoievsky's Grand Inquisitor; the latter error produced 'radicalism',
which 'arises from hatred of creation', and is exemplified by Ibsen's dramatic
character Brand.

In a striking passage in *Ethics*, where these points are made, Bonhoeffer
contrasts the two positions:

> 'Radicalism hates time, and compromise hates eternity. Radicalism
> hates patience, and compromise hates decision. Radicalism hates
> wisdom, and compromise hates simplicity. Radicalism hates
> moderation and measure, and compromise hates the immeasurable.
> Radicalism hates the real, and compromise hates the world'.
> (19)

Only in the justifying event of Jesus Christ are the two dimensions brought
together. 'In Him alone lies the solution for the problem of the relation
between the ultimate and the penultimate'. (20) This relation between the
ultimate and the penultimate lies at the heart of what Bonhoeffer has to say
about the natural, and it is vital to accept, as he himself insists, that the
penultimate exists for the sake of the ultimate, and not the other way round;
the penultimate has a *raison d'être* only because of Christ, for it has no
intrinsic value of its own. The advantages of this reformulation of the doctrine
of justification for Bonhoeffer are twofold; it enables him to take both the
natural and the supernatural seriously, and it enables him to preserve a
balance between the 19th century liberal view of revelation, which he believed
reduced it to the level of the natural, and the Barthian view, which he saw as
elevating revelation beyond the reach of the natural.

The other theological influence which had a bearing upon Bonhoeffer's
'rediscovery of the natural' was that of Friedrich Nietzsche. According to
Bethge, Bonhoeffer quite early on 'read all of Nietzsche very carefully, and
Nietzsche's tremendous plea for the earth and for loyalty to its creatures
never left his mind.' (21) This interest persisted and we are told that
Bonhoeffer continued to read Nietzsche's books even in prison. (22) As we
have already seen, (23) Bonhoeffer's Barcelona address of 1929 made use of
the Antaeus myth to illustrate the need to remain firmly in contact with the
ground (it also recurs in the draft of his play written in Tegel in 1944), as
well as to put forward a strong plea in favour of ethical freedom. This was
the point at which he questioned the need for absolutes in christian ethics
(even asking whether Christianity and ethics are necessarily connected),
holding out the prospect (as Nietzsche did) of a morality which was 'beyond
good and evil. (24)

Again, while Bonhoeffer's home background and social tastes had accustomed him to the 'good life', there seems little doubt that his wholehearted acceptance of them as a Lutheran pastor, without any sense of guilt or inconsistency, owes much to Nietzsche's belief in naturalistic values, and affirmation of life as it is. Alike they were both in agreement about the importance of worldly reality, and fought against a false 'Platonized Christianity,' which reduced the Gospel to the status of an unworldly set of ideals. However, as André Dumas trenchantly argues, 'Bonhoeffer disagrees with Nietzsche about the nature of that reality. For Nietzsche it is the courage of frozen solitude, while for Bonhoeffer it is the acceptance of the givenness of co-humanity'; it is for Nietzsche 'the superman protesting against the deception of ideas, whereas Bonhoeffer maintained that it is Christ with man in the midst of the world.' (25)

It will be convenient for our purpose - in order to explore Bonhoeffer's concept of the natural in *Ethics* in more detail - to consider it in three parts; first, acceptance of the secular, next the natural as christological, and third, christian life as worldliness. Under the first head, acceptance of the secular, it is important to make clear that, looked at as a theological concept secularity was a relatively new interest for Bonhoeffer. He was of course familiar with the idea of the secular (Lat. *saeculum* meaning 'age') in its contemporary sense of 'non-religious' as contrasted with 'religious', but the process of 'secularization' (i.e., 'becoming secular') was one which he seldom referred to in his early writings. A possible explanation for this may be found in the *Sanctorum Communio* where he declares his belief that 'the meaning of history cannot be progressive development, but that "every age is in direct relationship with God" (Ranke)', (26) that is to say, the early Bonhoeffer viewed history vertically rather than horizontally.

Such however was Bonhoeffer's later concern with the phenomenon of godlessness that by the time he had started on *Ethics* he found it necessary to take up the challenge of secularization, and to attempt to trace its origins and progress on two separate occasions in the book. The first occasion occurs in the section, 'Inheritance and Decay', (27) where he states his belief that the Reformation destroyed the unity of Christendom and, in so doing, left the way open for the emergence of a different kind of unity - that of godlessness. Accordingly the secular is something to be deplored and to be regarded as almost equivalent to atheism. However, in the second of these two historical surveys, 'Thinking in Terms of Two Spheres', (28) 'secularism', understood as the product of the secularization process, is viewed much more tolerantly. The unifying of the sacred and secular in one reality through Christ, Bonhoeffer asserts, makes it possible to affirm 'a better secularity;' the coming of Jesus Christ makes all the difference; as a result:

'The world, the natural, the profane and reason are now all taken up into God from the outset. They do not exist "in themselves" and "on their own account". They have their reality nowhere save in the reality of God, in Christ. It is now essential to the real concept of the secular that it shall always be seen in the movement of being accepted and becoming accepted by God in Christ .... (that) which is Christian (is) to be found only in that which is of the world, the "supernatural" only in the natural, the holy only in the profane, and the revelational only in the rational. (29)

It is significant that Bonhoeffer seems to have retained a lasting dislike for the word 'secularization' (it is used only three times in the *Ethics*), probably because of its negative overtones, while the word 'secular', with its later positive link with Christ, continues to be employed. By the time *Letters and Papers* is reached it has become descriptive of the reality of the world-come-of age in which the presence of the suffering God is to be found and experienced.

In the light of all this it becomes possible to understand Bonhoeffer's concern to revive an interest in the concept of the natural. At the outset (as we have indicated) he admits that the concept had fallen into disrepute in protestant ethics, and had been abandoned entirely to the Catholics. (30) Furthermore, for Protestants, the natural was associated with sinfulness because of its identification with creation since the Fall, being nothing without grace. On the other hand, for Catholics, the natural tended to be separated from the supernatural and become autonomous, thus suggesting it had rights of its own. If therefore we are to look for the origins of Bonhoeffer's new understanding of the natural, we must look neither to wholly protestant nor to wholly catholic sources, but elsewhere.

The true source from which Bonhoeffer's interest in the natural springs is in his approach to total reality as centred in Christ. In this section in *Ethics* on 'The Natural' Bonhoeffer insists that the concept of the natural (derived from *nasci, natura*) is not the same as the concept of the 'creaturely' (derived from *creare, creatura*) 'in that it implies an element of independence and self-development.' (31) As a result of the Fall the 'creature' becomes 'nature', and its original direct dependence on God gives way to the relative freedom of natural life. This is not absolute freedom for God and one's neighbour, which is the ideal, but 'a relative openness and relative closedness for Christ'. (32) The recovery of the concept of the natural can therefore only be brought about on the basis of the gospel. So Bonhoeffer defines the natural as 'the form of life preserved by God for the fallen world and directed towards justification, redemption and renewal through Christ.' Alternatively (using his new terminology) by means of the Incarnation 'natural life becomes the penultimate which is directed towards the ultimate'. (33) Form and content in the natural thus defined are then distinguished - formally the natural can be known only in relation to Jesus Christ, while its contents remain open to recognition by reason.

Bonhoeffer accordingly has the best of both protestant and catholic worlds; on the one hand, his protestant inheritance ensures a continuing belief in the radical corruption of nature by the Fall, so that both the natural and the unnatural are equally condemned; on the other, his catholic leanings predispose him in favour of the natural, which because of the advent of Christ, is separated from the unnatural by its openness to him. This readiness to concede a relative validity to the natural in spite of its total involvement in the Fall is illustrated by Bonhoeffer's treatment of reason, which, while less restricted in its fallen state than many Protestants would accept, cannot be given the degree of intrinsic validity which Catholics confer upon it. Reason, he asserts, is totally 'embedded in the natural' and so is affected by the Fall. It does not retain a 'certain essential integrity' as Catholics would argue, nor is it unaffected and sovereign, as Enlightenment thinkers would contend. It is fallen and can become natural or unnatural according to the way in which it relates to the coming of Christ; so that,

> 'reason does not now cease to be reason, but it is now fallen reason, perceiving only the datum of the fallen world, and perceiving it only in the aspect of its contents.' (34)

Under our second head, that of the christocentric character of Bonhoeffer's understanding of the natural, it is first necessary to remind ourselves of the heart of the matter as he himself sees it, namely, that:

> Natural life must not be understood simply as a preliminary to life with Christ. It is only from Christ Himself that it receives its validation. Christ Himself entered into the natural life....Only through the incarnation of Christ do we have the right to call others to the natural life and to live the natural life ourselves.' (35)

In view of the point already made about Friedrich Nietzsche's influence upon him, it is worth spending a moment looking a little closer at Bonhoeffer's concept of 'natural life'. Bonhoeffer is quite adamant in his rejection of Nietzsche's commitment to life as an absolute, or end in itself. In his section 'Natural Life', Bonhoeffer describes this as 'vitalism', which can be found in both individual and social life. Vitalism is self-destructive and finds its end in nihilism. With the spectacle of the Nazi idolatry of life in its crudest and most unrestrained forms before him, Bonhoeffer had no option but to warn that the absolutization of life in itself 'is a void, a plunge into the abyss.... It does not rest until it has involved everything in this movement of destruction.' (36) Similarly, Bonhoeffer continues, it is possible to 'absolutize' life by making it the means to an end, as well as an end in itself. This occurs, for example, where the individual or community are understood only in terms of their usefulness in a larger organization, or for a superior idea. Bonhoeffer describes this as a 'mechanization of life' - it has equally baleful consequences for both individuals and society; life is sacrificed in the process, and when mechanization has killed off all life, mechanization itself must collapse. From this fate only the coming of Jesus Christ can save it:

> 'Natural life stands between the extremes of vitalism and mechanization.... In relation to Jesus Christ the status of life as an end in itself is understood as creaturehood, and its status as a means to an end is understood as participation in the kingdom of God'. (37)

So in this context, as one awaits Christ's coming, involvement in natural life carries with it certain definite rights and duties. The rights come first as part of the givenness of natural life, and the duties follow after. 'God gives before He demands' and the duties 'derive from the rights themselves, as tasks are implied by gifts' (*wie die Aufgaben aus den Gaben*). They are implicit in the rights. (38)

One of the inferences which Bonhoeffer draws from his previous consideration of the ultimate-penultimate relationship just before his section on 'The Natural', and which is also relevant to the foregoing description of natural life, is his statement that 'whatever humanity and goodness is found in this fallen world must be on the side of Jesus Christ.' (39) Such a concern for the recognition of the proper place of humanity and goodness in the divine scheme of things, even in a fallen creation, anticipates of course Bonhoeffer's later emphasis upon a God who is to be met at the centre of life, and not only in situations of weakness. While humanity, goodness and such-like virtues must not be thought of as having value in themselves, nonetheless they must be claimed for Christ, just as the father's love in the New Testament parable was lavished on the elder son who stayed at home, as well as on the prodigal.

In the remainder of the chapter on 'The Last Things and the Things before the Last' it was clearly Bonhoeffer's intention to deal with rights and duties in a number of specific areas in natural life, as now interpreted. Although some are considered (under the title of 'The Right to Bodily Life'), (40) such as marriage, suicide, reproduction and nascent life, further sections under 'The Natural Life of the Mind' and 'The Natural Right to Work and Property' (and possibly others) were not written.

How therefore Bonhoeffer would have dealt with these practical ethical issues is not known. Instead what we have is an approach to them on the basis of the position which he had already adopted and outlined, namely, that the natural means being open to Jesus Christ and to the will and purpose of God, and the unnatural means the opposite. Thus, for example, in the case of marriage its natural character is emphasized, together with the natural right of full bodily union based on mutual love, as distinct from the right of reproduction. Rights springing from nature, however, must be exercised rationally, and 'the relation between nature and reason in particular instances is a matter which can be decided and answered for only as the individual case arises.' (41) Bonhoeffer frankly admits that reason and nature reach an accord in relatively few contemporary marriages, but that this has to be accepted. Just at the point at which he is prepared to say that the christian faith is able to harmonize reason and nature, he breaks off the discussion, with a promise to take it up later. Tantalizingly therefore we are left with little or no indication of the way in which Bonhoeffer would have dealt with this problem in detail. The same is broadly true of the other specific areas he discusses in this section. Were we in possession of this important information, it would have provided us with much needed content with which to assess the validity, or otherwise, of Bonhoeffer's christocentric approach to the natural. As it is, however, we are left with the impression that what matters in ethical situations is the context and the method of dealing with them. Given these the practical outcome could well be allowed to differ from problem to problem and from person to person - and this, in spite of a remark by Bonhoeffer in a letter to Eberhard Bethge about the same time, 'I find Catholic ethics in many ways most instructive, and more practical than ours.' (42)

There remains still to be dealt with under this head the question of the part played by natural law in Bonhoeffer's exposition of the natural. It has to be admitted at the outset that, whatever he had in mind to deal with later in this part of *Ethics*, there is very little indication that the subject of natural law loomed very large in his thoughts. It has to be borne in mind of course that Bonhoeffer came from a tradition which for the most part had broken with belief in natural law, and also that the notion of a body of 'fixed principles' located in the nature of things, and recognizable by reason, was anathema to him. The probable reasons, however, for not giving it very much consideration spring from the central position he accords to Jesus Christ in his view of reality, which renders invalid any concept of natural rights which fails to take Christ into account; also (as has been shown), for Bonhoeffer the place of reason after the Fall is strictly limited to the examination of the contents which are part of the givenness of the fallen world. In Bonhoefler's own words - 'Reason... is the conscious perception of the natural as it, in fact, presents itself.... (It is) the form of consciousness of the preserved life.' (43) As a result, reason is only adequate to grasp truths appertaining to unredeemed nature, not to comprehend eternal truths laid up in the constitution of nature itself.

The closest in fact Bonhoeffer gets to anything like a statement on natural law is in his short section on the *Suum cuique* of Roman law, (44) which formulates the natural rights of each individual man in relation to the right of others. Here he seems to allow for the existence of innate rights within men, which nevertheless may come into conflict with the natural rights of others. (45) Due account must also be paid to the reality of the fallen world, according to Bonhoeffer, of which it is the responsibility of reason to be aware. In short:

> 'The principle of *suum cuique* is the highest possible attainment
> of a reason which is in accord with reality and which, within the
> natural life, discerns the right which is given to the individual by
> God (of whom reason knows nothing). (46)

The conclusion of this particular matter then would seem to be that, against the background of the two realities, the divine and the human, the sacred and the secular, which have been brought together in Christ, Bonhoeffer firmly accepts the natural order as fallen, and as having involved reason along with it. Nevertheless, because of its openness to Jesus Christ, the natural acquires the status of a penultimate in which rights and duties, as well as ethical problems, are to be seen in the light of the ultimate. The centrality of the gracious justifying action of Christ is therefore paramount, and the notion of a direct access to any kind of 'natural law', by way of reason, for the solution of ethical problems in consequently out of the question.

The subject under the third main head - christian life as worldliness - follows quite logically. Bonhoeffer in dealing with the natural declares it to be 'the true means of preserved life.... It is in the last analysis life itself that tends towards the natural and keeps turning against the unnatural and bringing about its downfall'. Life itself (Bonhoeffer affirms) is on the side of the natural, and rooted in it is an 'entirely immanent optimism'; it acts as a physician when either physical or mental health is threatened, and enables us to take an optimistic attitude to human history. The conclusion follows that man has a natural right to bodily joys, since the body is made for preservation not sacrifice.

Bonhoeffer rejects the idealistic view that the body is only a means to an end. Instead he asserts that it is an end in itself, buttressing this hedonistic suggestion with appropriate quotations from Ecclesiastes. (47) Later in the *Ethics*, in the section 'The Warrant for Ethical Discourse', (48) the same theme is pursued, this time in the larger context of the making of ethical decisions. Ecclesiastes is again cited to make the point that in all human existence there is a time and a season for every activity. Thus, in Bonhoeffer's opinion, 'the "ethical" as a theme is tied to a definite time and a definite place.' (49) Moralists make the mistake of thinking that every moment of life must be seen *sub specie aeternitatis* and involve a deliberate choice between good and evil. While there are occasions when the 'ethical phenomenon' may supervene, and the need for a conscious decision on a matter of good or evil becomes apparent; generally speaking, life should be taken in its stride without undue moralising in order to 'prevent a pathological overburdening' by the ethical. More intriguingly still, Bonhoeffer believes that straightforward ethical issues, such as helping someone in distress, pose no real ethical problem. It 'goes without saying' what one should do; on the other hand,

> 'it is quite a different matter when we have to deal with the small everyday troubles such as the "common cold" and the "perversity of inanimate objects", that is to say, with all the thousand and one ways in which great and high-principled undertakings may be "frustrated" by trivial and insignificant untoward outward happenings.' (50)

Bonhoeffer's most useful answer to the problem of maintaining a correct balance between over-moralising and under-moralising, with regard to the happenings of everyday life, is given in the section 'The Structure of Responsible Life', (51) which it is not necessary to enter into in detail. Briefly, he suggests, responsible life is structured in the sense that correspondence with reality becomes possible primarily through conformation with Christ. Responsible human living is a matter of reconciling the order, which comes from man being bound to God, with the freedom which comes from human life itself. God's ordering of his creation is apparent in a number of ways, such as through divine mandates, vocation, deputyship and conscience, and within the context of Christ-formation it thus becomes practicable to combine freedom with obligation. Action of this kind, moreover, allows the world to be the world, because it is the same world which Christ loved, judged and restored, and by corresponding with reality man sees things as Christ sees them. Man's responsibility for dealing with good and evil is limited, in the sense that human beings do not deal with good and evil as they are in themselves. This Christ has done, and continues to do; man is thereby set free to enable 'the world ever anew to disclose its essential character to him.' (52)

Already we are fast approaching the point at which 'worldliness' (*Weltlichkeit*), one of the major themes of *Letters and Papers*, is beginning to take shape in Bonhoeffer's mind. Sharing in the world and entering fully into everyday living is now in *Ethics* the test of 'being in Christ', and hence the way to being good. Ethical behaviour also means helping other people to throw themselves into the processes of life, 'not out of the motive of "shall" and "should", but from the full abundance of vital motives... and from free acceptance and will.' (53)

It is clear, whatever is read into Bonhoeffer's later references to 'worldliness' in the prison writings, that the Christ-figure is the connecting link which holds together the changing attitudes to the world that we find in *Ethics*. In the earlier part, in a way reminiscent of *The Cost of Discipleship*, the church is almost triumphalist in its attitude to the world. By the end of the *Ethics* we have reached a stage in which responsible christian living is virtually identical with total immersion in worldly affairs. Yet the centrality of Jesus Christ stays constant throughout; his cross of atonement 'is the setting free for life before God in the midst of the godless world... (and) for life in genuine worldliness.' (54)

For a rounded assessment, however, of Bonhoeffer's thinking about the natural in *Ethics* it is necessary to look beyond its pages to the correspondence which occupied so much of his time and attention in the few years that remained to him. Students of *Letters and Papers*, as is well-known, are divided on the extent and significance of the differences which are undoubtedly to be found in moving from one set of writings to the other. Hanfried Müller, for example, in his book, *Von der Kirche zur Welt*, (55) believes that a truly radical shift in Bonhoeffer's approach to the secular appears in his letter of 30 April 1944, (56) with the introduction of the idea of 'religionless Christianity'. According to Müller, in *Ethics* the secular is treated 'clerically', within the historical context of Christendom's past. In *Letters and Papers* the church is left behind, and secularity enters into its own, becoming an end in itself; so the way is opened for a purely human interpretation of ethics, which Müller sees as nonetheless christian. Other commentators, like John D Godsey, (57) see the changes more in terms of 'theological fragmentation', which one should be wary of organizing into a coherent whole, and which consequently leaves many questions unanswered. Many follow Eberhard Bethge in tracing a basic continuity in the development of Bonhoeffer's thought from its beginnings in the *Sanctorum Communio* to its culmination in *Letters and Papers*. (58)

One fixed point, however, in the progress of Bonhoeffer's thinking after the *Ethics*, is to be found in some outline notes for a book which Bonhoeffer sent to Bethge in August 1944, in which he evidently intended to set out his new theological ideas. (59) From this we can glean something of the direction in which his mind was moving at this time. It will make for simplification if this is approached under the three headings of, the secular, christology and worldliness which we have already been considering. First, with regard to the secular and secularization, it becomes apparent from Bonhoeffer's 'Outline for a Book' that his interest in the secular as such (in spite of a separate note referring to it in the proposed 'Chapter 2') has been replaced by a new concept - that of the 'world- come-of-age' (*die mündiger Welt*). The process of secularization, which from his letter of 8 June 1944 (60) Bonhoeffer dates from the thirteenth century, had resulted not so much in godlessness, in the negative sense (as in the early pages of *Ethics*), as in maturity. Man is now of age and well able to live without depending on God for solutions to all his problems. Religionlessness is therefore to be welcomed not deplored, and the great biblical concepts of creation, fall, atonement and such-like should be re-interpreted in this light. Where this leaves the church, when one is bidden to live *esti Deus non daretur*, is not dealt with in the letter of June 8th; it is however taken up in the 'Outline' notes where Bonhoeffer exhorts the church, and individual Christians, to 'exist for others', as did their Lord. This 'being there for others' he describes as the experience of transcendence. (61) Thus the historical movement away from God, so hesitantly treated in *Ethics*, is wholly accepted as adulthood by Bonhoeffer at the end of his life. Sadly the full implications of all this remain for us a mystery.

When we come to consider our second heading, Bonhoeffer's christological approach to the natural, it becomes clear that, in spite of increasing radicalism, Bonhoeffer does not discard his concept of the centrality of Christ when he comes to *Letters and Papers*. Although, as we have seen, he welcomed Bultmann's demythologising procedures in New Testament study - and continued to do so in the cause of intellectual integrity and honesty - he refused to accept a reduced Christianity, which in effect disposed of the divine Christ. In his 'Outline for a book' Bonhoeffer's notes for 'Chapter 2' are vital in this respect. The question, who Christ really is for us today, continues to haunt him and is implicit in his insistence on the fact that an encounter with Jesus is the same as an encounter with God. The notes speak of 'participation in this being of Jesus (incarnation, cross and resurrection)' as essential to the encounter, which consists of 'being there for others'; abstract belief in God can never be a substitute for a genuine experience of God. (62) An important comment by Eberhard Bethge in his book, *Bonhoeffer: Exile and Martyr*, on this point deserves to be quoted in full. He writes:

'The experience of God certainly takes place in meeting Christ, the Incarnate, Crucified and Risen One, who is there for others. At this point Bonhoeffer answered Feuerbach's question about the truth and reality of theology. Feuerbach's dissolution of theology into anthropology had unmasked theology as an expression of the promise to fulfil men's this-worldly desires in a world beyond, and to relieve their needs. Bonhoeffer took this up but changed it around. He accepted Feuerbach's criticisms of religion; but for him the Christian experience of God through the biblical Christ says exactly the opposite: man does not delegate himself to an almighty God, but God in weakness delegates himself to man. For Bonhoeffer, the substance of faith is not man existing for a despotic God, but the experience that a total transformation of human existence is given in the fact that Jesus is there for others. Feuerbach endeavoured, by making "the candidates of the hereafter into students of this world", to change them into atheists; but Bonhoeffer, with the same phrase, wanted to make them into Christians.' (63)

If Bethge is correct in his interpretation, it is decisive for the view that, even in the *Letters and Papers* phase, Bonhoeffer's christocentric theology continues to embrace the natural. It makes all the difference too as to whether we regard his later statement as, in effect, emptying all human life and activity of any christian content whatsoever, or whether he was correct in believing that they could be re- established on an entirely 'secular', though still 'christian' foundation. Again, Bonhoeffer's premature death prevents us from ever knowing.

Under the third heading, namely christian living as worldliness, we need to bear in mind the importance which Bonhoeffer throughout attached to the fact of sheer living. Both his background and personal inclinations, together with his concern for the concrete, predisposed him to engage fully in the business of living, and identify this with what he considered to be God's purpose for himself and for the world. In one of the few published letters to his fiancée, Maria von Wedemeyer, written from prison in 1943, (64) Bonhoeffer refers to the need for faith; not the kind of faith which shuns the world, but which is in love with the world and willing to accept whatever amount of suffering it has in store for them. 'Our marriage', he continues, shall be a yes to God's earth; it shall strengthen our courage to act and accomplish something on the earth. I fear that Christians who stand with only one leg upon earth also stand with only one leg in heaven.' (65)

Theologically speaking, Bonhoeffer's commitment to 'earthly living' is derived from Old Testament roots. The religion of the Old Testament was for him almost entirely a thing of this world, encouraging total involvement in the here-and-now; and the great redemption stories on which the Hebrew religion is based, are historical redemptions 'i.e. on *this* side of death. ' (66) For the same reason he was attached to the Jeremiah text (45:5) - mentioned five times in *Letters and Papers* - (67) which speaks of the reality of God amid the chaos of historical events; he was also curiously attracted by W. F. Otto's book, *The Gods of Greece*, with its account of worldly-minded gods who were made in the likeness of men. (68) Bonhoeffer especially approved of the inclusion of the sensual *Song of Songs* in the Old Testament canon, arguing in a letter to Bethge that the association of Christianity with the restraint of passion was not justified by this Old Testament example. Instead the book is a good illustration of the way in which an undisturbed acceptance of the reality of God can provide a kind of *cantus firmus* to the polyphony of life. So long as the *cantus firmus* is kept going, life can be lived to the full and the counterpoint developed to its limits. (69)

Bonhoeffer however was no 'naturalist' in the romantic sense of wanting to live close to nature. For his first point in 'Chapter l' of his 'Outline for a Book', he proposed to deal with the fact that, in modern society, organization has replaced nature as a man's immediate environment. The only indication we are given as to how he intended to treat this particular problem is his note to the effect that 'in the last resort it all turns on man.' (70) The inference is that man is under an obligation to be completely honest with himself, if example is to prevail over precept, and so be effective. (71) By this time Bonhoeffer was living in the aftermath of the failure of the July bomb plot, when Hitler narrowly escaped assassination, and his mind was turning more and more away from thoughts of resistance to those of submission. Christian example is to be seen in terms of acceptance of all kinds of experiences, especially suffering, and worldliness as 'living unreservedly in life's duties, problems, successes and failures, experiences and perplexities.' This comes to mean nothing less than taking the sufferings of God in the world seriously - and indeed participating in them. (72)

So christian-living in the world, by the end of Bonhoeffer's life, finds its true freedom (one of the major themes of *Ethics*) in the complete surrender of human life to God - through the successive stages of discipline, action, suffering and death, as his poem 'Stations on the Road to Freedom' expresses it. (73) Paradoxically, at the last - as this moving poem suggests - living and worldly dying, for Bonhoeffer, became one and the same.

FOOTNOTES

(1)   *GS*11, p.389 (*TP.*, p.83).
(2)   See pp. 143-87.
(3)   *GS*111, p.26.
(4)   *AB.*, p.172.
(5)   Bonhoeffer in a letter to Erwin Sutz, *NRS.*, p.121 (*GS*1, p.20).
(6)   See *NRS.*, pp.46-47 (*GS*111, pp.56-8).
(7)   *Ibid.*, pp.153-4 (p.286).
(8)   *CF.*, pp.36ff.
(9)   *CD.*, p.243.
(10) In *Shaping the Future*, pp.4lf. (cf., *Cost of Discipleship*, pp.141f.)
      This and the following Chapter 6 owe much to the lively analytical
      thinking of Burtness in his book.
(11) *Ibid.*, p.42.
(12) See Peters, p.39, fn.70 and p.116. Feil, p.83. Phillips, p.129.
(13) See *The Form of Christ in the World*, pp.128ff.
(14) In an unpublished letter to a friend, 25:3:42, reproduced in the original
      and in translation in Appendix 1, *The Form of Christ in the World*,
      pp.249f.
(15) Original and E.T. in *GS*1, pp.355-71, 479-88. See also Bethge, *DB.*,
      pp.643ff.
(16) See above Chapter 2.
(17) *E.*, p.ii. Clifford Green links it with either Chapter 3 or 6 - probably
      the latter. See above, p.90, fn.39.
(18) *Ibid.*, p.83.
(19) *Ibid.*, p.130.
(20) *Ibid.*
(21) In 'Bonhoeffer's Life and Theology', *World Come of Age*, p.27. For a
      critical study of Bonhoeffer's use of Nietzsche see Peters *Die Präsenz
      des Politischen*, pp.133-144.
(22) Dumas, *Dietrich Bonhoeffer: Theologian of Reality*, p.285, fn.7.
(23) Above, p.142.
(24) *NRS.*, pp.44,41 (GS111, pp.53,50). See Nietzsche's book *Beyond
      Good and Evil.*
(25) *Op. cit.*, pp.161-2.
(26) p.198.
(27) See pp.88-109.
(28) *Ibid.*, pp.196-207.
(29) *Ibid.*, p.198.
(30) *Ibid.*, pp.143f, and above p.86.

(31) *Ibid.*, p.145.
(32) *Ibid.*
(33) *Ibid.*
(34) *Ibid.*, p.146.
(35) *Ibid.*, p.145. See also Feil, interpreting Bonhoeffer, 'The fact of God's incarnation alone is the basis of that task'; (viz., to serve this world) 'solely within it are we to seek the basis for a positive relation to the world and for our service' in *The Theology of Dietrich Bonhoeffer*, p.83.
(36) *Ibid.*, p.149.
(37) *Ibid.*, p.150.
(38) *Ethik.* p.161 (E., p.151).
(39) *E.*, p.142.
(40) *Ibid.*, pp.155ff.
(41) *Ibid.*, p.180.
(42) *TP.*, p.86 (GS11, p.394).
(43) *E.*, p.146.
(44) *Ibid.*, pp.151-5.
(45) H. Funamato rightly points out that Bonhoeffer's belief in the existence of a natural right of the individual springs from the will of God to create individuals and to endow them with eternal life. See 'Penultimate and Ultimate in Dietrich Bonhoeffer's Ethics' in *Being and Truth*, p.382.
(46) *E.*, p.154.
(47) *Ibid.*, pp.147ff.
(48) *Ibid.*, pp.263-76.
(49) *Ibid.*, p.264.
(50) *Ibid.*
(51) *Ibid.*, pp.224-54.
(52) *Ibid.*, p.233.
(53) *Ibid.*, p.269.
(54) *Ibid.*, p.297.
(55) See the condensed version 'Concerning the Reception and Interpretation of Dietrich Bonhoeffer' (translated from *Die Mündige Welt* IV, pp.52-79) in *World Come of Age*, pp.182-214.
(56) *LPP.*, pp.278-81.
(57) In *The Theology of Dietrich Bonhoeffer*, 1960, pp.195ff.
(58) See *DB.*, especially pp.609-26 and pp.757-95.
(59) *LPP.*, pp.380-3. See also Bethge, *DB.*, pp.764-7 and *Dietrich Bonhoeffer, Exile and Martyr*, 1975, pp.138ff.
(60) *LPP.*, pp.324-9.
(61) *Ibid.*, pp.382f.

(62) *Ibid.*, p.381.
(63) p.148.
(64) In *LPP.*, pp.414f.
(65) *Ibid.*, p.415.
(66) See *LPP.*, 27:6:44, p.336.
(67) See pp.105,219,297,370,379.
(68) *Ibid.*, p.365.
(69) *Ibid.*, 20:5:44, p.303.
(70) *Ibid.*, p.380.
(71) See *ibid.*, p.382.
(72) *Ibid.*, 21:7:44, p.370.
(73) *Ibid.*, pp.370-1.

CHAPTER 6

BONHOEFFER AND THE COMMANDMENT

'Rarely perhaps has any generation shown so little interest as ours does in any kind of theoretical or systematic ethics. The academic question of a system of ethics seems to be of all questions the most superfluous. The reason for this is not to be sought in any supposed ethical indifference on the part of our period. On the contrary it arises from the fact that our period, more than any earlier period in the history of the west, is oppressed by a superabounding reality of concrete historical problems.' (1)

Bonhoeffer's words of more than half a century ago have a contemporary ring about them. Intriguingly enough, they were written against the background of Adolf Hitler's succession of military victories in 1940 when ethical systems, as such, were likely to attract more respect than they do today. The National Socialist view of ethics was seen by patriots like Bonhoeffer as a view which substituted evil for good, darkness for light, and slavery for freedom. In practice it was a negative system - nihilism - which separated man from God, from his fellows, from things and from himself. (2) Worse still, the Nazi tyranny not only ensured its widespread acceptance, but also induced a state of moral insensibility and paralysis in the nation as a whole. The immediate practical effect on Bonhoeffer was to destroy any lingering doubts he might have had about the 'unchristian' nature of engaging in conspiratorial activities against the state, and led him to offer his services to the *Abwehr*, as a double-agent committed to the overthrow, and if need be, the assassination of Hitler. The importance of 'action' for Bonhoeffer as an essential ingredient in ethical decisions will become apparent as we proceed. Another related ingredient, of which we need to remind ourselves, is the remarkable consistency which obtained between Bonhoeffer's life and his ethical thinking. The two were closely related and interacted, the one influencing the other. His *Ethics* therefore cannot be conceived of as an objective or systematic study of ethics for its own sake; the fruits of Bonhoeffer's own life and experience are pervasive throughout.

From an early stage in his academic life Bonhoeffer was preoccupied with the problem of authority. The product of a middle-class background, in which authority was taken for granted, he came to recognize the need, once his theological education had begun, for a firm foundation in divine authority to provide the necessary warrant for public and private morality. His first academic publications, *Sanctorum Communio* and *Act and Being*, concentrated on the problem of authority within the church, and soon after, as his mind turned towards ordination, it was the responsibility of speaking an authoritative word to his congregation which occupied his attention. His anxieties on this score are in fact reflected in his first sermons, preached in Barcelona, where Bonhoeffer served as an assistant pastor to a German-speaking congregation from 1928-9. Comments on his experience as a preacher abound in letters to his parents and to a fellow-student, Helmut Rossler, during this period. In one letter to Rossler (significant in the light of his later thinking) Bonhoeffer distinguishes sharply between 'real' people (*Wirkliche Menschen*), whom he met with outside the church, and church members themselves (*die christlich Welt*), whom he addressed in his sermons and who were more likely to be under wrath than grace, from his point of view. (3) The perennial problem of how to bring both into an encounter with God was here evidently facing Bonhoeffer for the first time.

The following years 1929-32 were consequently years in which the ethical theme began to dominate Bonhoeffer's thoughts. Reinhold Seeberg, his perceptive tutor, possibly anticipating this, had attempted to influence Bonhoeffer's choice of an habilitation thesis in 1928 by suggesting (among other subjects) something in the field of ethics or morality, but Bonhoeffer settled for *Act and Being*. (4) However the practical pressures were such that, even before it was completed, his mind had begun to work on fundamental questions regarding the nature of christian ethics, as well as on their application to contemporary problems. The results of his thinking can be seen in a series of theological addresses given about this time.

Three of the most important addresses may be selected to illustrate three of the leading thoughts which were to direct Bonhoeffer's ethical thinking for the rest of his life. The first of these basic thoughts occurs in the Barcelona address of 1928 'What is a Christian Ethic?' Among a number of other important points in the address, Bonhoeffer declares that ethical decisions cannot derive from a set of abstract or timeless principles, not even from the principle of love; absolute moral laws make for legalism and casuistry, when applied to actual situations, and have the effect of restraining freedom. To quote Bonhoeffer's own words:

> '(If) there was a generally valid moral law, then there would be a way from man to God.... So, to some extent, I would have control over my relationship to God.... And, most important of all, in that case I would once again become a slave to my principles. I would sacrifice man's most precious gift, *freedom*.'
> (5)

The outright rejection of Kantian transcendentalism, as well as traditional moral teaching, is here only too apparent. Instead, Bonhoeffer refers approvingly to Nietzsche's Superman who 'creates new tables' i.e., his own standards of good and evil for himself. The Christian too, Bonhoeffer insists, should be free to interpret ethics as something which lies beyond good and evil and which comes into being 'only on the completion of the act, not in the letter of the law.' (6)

The second leading idea emerging at this early stage governs the thinking of a lecture, 'The Theology of Crisis', (7) which Bonhoeffer was invited to give to American theological students in Union Theological Seminary, New York in 1931 - the idea is commitment to a belief in the historical revelation of God's purposive will in Jesus Christ as fundamental to all ethical discourse. So Bonhoeffer explains:

> 'The revelation of God in Christ is not a revelation of a new morality, of new ethical values, a revelation of a new imperative, but a revelation of a new indicative. It is not a new "you ought" but "you are". In other words the revelation of God is executed not in the realm of ideas, but in the realm of reality.' (8)

The main purpose of the lecture was to introduce to his 'liberal' American colleagues the new dialectical theology of Karl Barth. Its principal thrust was both philosophical and theological, but its importance for our purpose lies in its insistence that the authoritative source of man's moral behaviour lies not in his reason, conscience, nor sense of justice, but in God's coming. For Bonhoeffer, as for Barth, God speaks 'not in ideas, but in historical facts; not in imperatives, but in indicatives; not in generality, but in once-ness.'

The third of Bonhoeffer's leading ideas from this period is that of concreteness. The address given to the 1932 Youth Peace Conference in Czechoslovakia entitled 'A Theological Basis for the World Alliance', has already been mentioned in this connection. (10) It concentrated on the need for the churches within the Alliance to speak concretely to the world on the subject of peace. This was no new idea for Bonhoeffer, but its application to the ecumenical scene at a time when the international situation was beginning to take on a threatening look gave it a new sense of urgency and relevance.

Bonhoeffer in the address asks the question, 'How can the Gospel and how can the commandment of the church be preached with authority, i.e., in quite concrete form?' The answer he gives is: 'The Gospel becomes concrete in the hearers, the commandment becomes concrete in those who preach it.... A commandment must be definite, otherwise it is not a commandment.' (11)

For this reason, Bonhoeffer goes on to say, the preacher must take into account the contemporary situation when articulating the commandment so that the commandment is relevant and applicable to those to whom it is addressed. The only possible source of such a commandment is the divine revelation in Jesus Christ - no biblical law, none of the traditional Lutheran 'orders of creation', no amount of reasoning by man can enable the church to preach to man's needs. Only the Word of God is the word of authority, and 'only as a concrete saying is it the Word of God to me.... God's commandment now requires something quite definite from us. And the church should proclaim this to the community. (12)

These three leading ideas provide us with the basic assumptions which were to influence much of what Bonhoeffer was to write and say about ethical behaviour later on. They have been singled out because they highlight the difficulties facing Bonhoeffer as he attempted to work out a new approach to christian ethics. On the one hand he could no longer accept the authority of the customary christian norms and standards (*as* norms and standards); on the other, he sought an ethic of command and obedience which could result in concrete modes of behaviour. His attempted solution was to see ethics as very much a matter which concerned both the world and God, and in which man was required to share by taking both into account. Authoritative speech and behaviour, therefore, was only possible when revelation was experienced as something concrete and definite - all else lacked divine worldliness. The necessity for combining the revelatory event with the concrete act is well expressed by Bonhoeffer in the Barcelona lecture referred to earlier:

'Ethics is a matter of earth and blood, but also of him who made both; the trouble arises from this duality. There can be ethics only in the framework of history, in the concrete situation, at the moment of being addressed.... Thus there cannot be ethics in a vacuum, as a principle; there cannot be good and evil as general ideas, but only as qualities of will making a decision.' (13)

This is the point at which some clarification of Bonhoeffer's use of the word 'ethics' and the word 'commandment' may be helpful. In his *Ethics* Bonhoeffer devotes much of Chapter VII (particularly the sections 'The Warrant for Ethical Discourse' and 'The Commandment of God') (14) to this task. In these sections he contrasts the 'ethical', which defines the formal and negative boundaries of the discussion, with the 'commandment', which is the speech of God to man, or the concrete claim which God makes on man. The object of a christian ethic therefore is something which lies beyond itself, namely, the divine will seeking expression. Thus the commandment includes the ethical, but not vice-versa. Similarly the biblical law (e.g., found in the Decalogue and the Sermon on the Mount) is comprised within the commandment (or command). So Bonhoeffer concludes - while the ethical stakes out a space within which man may encounter God, who is the fullness of life, the commandment enables him to participate in that very life itself through its concrete nature and demands. The ethical and the commandment, accordingly, operate on different planes, as it were, but it is the commandment alone which gives life and has the authority to command obedience, to save or to condemn. (15)

We have seen that Bonhoeffer's academic interests from 1929-32 were very much concentrated on the search for authority, particularly with a view to enabling the church to preach a concrete command. The onset of the Church Struggle with the Nazis in 1933 led him to concern himself more with justifying the need for a Confessing Church (*Bekennende Kirche*), and with emphasizing the importance of obedience to the Word of God within the church itself. *The Cost of Discipleship*, with its stress on the price to be paid for true discipleship, together with other writings based upon Bonhoeffer's experience in the Finkenwalde community, were products of this period. As a result the strictly ethical theme was not seriously pursued. Nevertheless the problem of concretion in preaching - provoked by the needs of his Finkenwalde ordinands - as well as his ecumenical concern for the church to speak authoritatively to the world - continued to occupy Bonhoeffer's attention and assumed greater prominence with the passage of time.

As he reflected upon what he considered to be an overriding obligation on the part of the church, as the *Christus praesens*, to proclaim an appropriate word to the world, Bonhoeffer was faced with the obvious questions - how could the church, or the preacher representing the church, be certain of his message. The answer was of course that certainty was not possible. Bonhoeffer took this point - his favourite text at this time was 2 Chronicles 20:12, 'We know not what to do, but our eyes are upon thee' (*Wir wissen nicht, was wir tun sollen, sondern unsere Augen sehen nach dir*). (16) In his World Alliance speech of 1932 Bonhoeffer had quoted the first half of the text and followed it immediately with the equally plaintive text from Psalm 119, 'O hide not thy commandments from me.' (verse 19). The verse was also mentioned in a letter to Karl Barth explaining his somewhat abrupt departure for a London pastorate in 1933, (17) as well as in a report to the *Yorkshire Post* on the Gland conference in Switzerland by the Bishop of Ripon, where Bonhoeffer had (in the bishop's words) used it as a kind of refrain. (18)

Uncertainty, however, according to Bonhoeffer, should be no impediment to the preaching of a concrete word. As he was to emphasize repeatedly in *Ethics*, the preaching of the commandment is grounded in the forgiveness of sins, and even if the preacher's word turns out eventually to be wrong there is always forgiveness. The important thing is prayerful thought and preparation before committing one's self to the concrete, revealed will of God. As a last resort, one could always have recourse to 'qualified silence' (*qualifiziertes Schweigen*), as a positive and not simply negative act, if the word cannot be spoken in full confidence and faith. (19)

Much of what the church had to say to the world at this time stemmed from the need to define the limits which should exist in the church-state relationship. The new Confessing Church, fortified by its public commitment to the lordship of Christ in the Barmen Declaration of 1934, sought to declare its position in relation not only to the German Reich Church but to other European churches as well. Bonhoeffer took a prominent part in all this. At the Fanö Life and Work Conference in the same year, and in a set of notes prepared for the 1937 Oxford Conference (which he did not attend), on 'Church, Community and State', Bonhoeffer stressed the obligation of the churches to speak peace to the nations (20) (the Fano address opened with a reference to Psalm 85,8, 'I will hear what God the Lord will speak: for he will speak peace unto his people, and to his saints.') (21) This was a call not for pacifism but for a positive, creative peace-making operation between the nations, which Bonhoeffer firmly believed to be God's concrete commandment to the nations of the world at that time.

As a further contribution to the church-state relationship, Bonhoeffer, - in his two papers, 'What is the Church?' (1932) (22) and 'The Visible Church in the New Testament' (1936) (23) insists that the church's function is not to 'christianize' the state but to declare its limitations, and to proclaim a concrete commandment from within the setting of these limitations. This is coupled in the second paper with a stern reminder of the church's responsibility to be obedient itself to the Word of God, since the church is constituted by practising what it preaches under the guidance of the Holy Spirit. (24)

Throughout all this, Bonhoeffer (as did his mentor Karl Barth) kept in mind the fact that God's commandments were the products of his gracious promises, which in their turn received their fulfilment in Jesus Christ. The commandment of God is therefore at all times a gracious commandment and for that reason always a joy to keep. So Bonhoeffer explains:

> 'It is a grace to know God's commandments. They free us from self-made plans and conflicts. They make our steps sure and our way joyful. God's commandments are given us to be obeyed, and his "commandments are not grievous" (1 John 5:3) for those who have found salvation in Jesus Christ. Jesus himself was under the law and fulfilled it in complete obedience to the Father, God's will is his joy, his meat and drink. So in us he thanks God for the grace of the law and gives us the joy he has in fulfilling

it.' (25)

The above quotation is taken from Bonhoeffer's exposition of the Psalms given in Finkenwalde between 1935-1937. Like his earlier exposition of Genesis 1-3 it is treated christocentrically, so that God's commands, in the Old Testament as well as the New Testament, are interpreted within the context of God's gracious act in Christ. All God's commands, whether to Adam and Eve in Genesis or through the Decalogue in Exodus, are linked to his redemptive work, which is inseparable from his self-giving in Jesus. As a result Bonhoeffer was prepared to say that the imperative becomes the indicative and does not follow from it; indeed the indicative *is* the imperative. (26)

Bonhoeffer's decision to take up again the serious study of ethics in 1939 is clearly connected with his commitment to political resistance and to his growing involvement with the *Abwehr*. Forbidden to preach or to publish any writings, he found himself drawn into a life of deviousness and deceit which, in later years, led him to confess with his fellow conspirators that learning how to equivocate and pretend had made them secretive and suspicious of their fellow men. (27) This appalling experience, without a doubt, lies behind the astonishing assertion with which he began his *Ethics* in 1939, 'The knowledge of good and evil seems to be the aim of all ethical reflection. The first task of Christian ethics is to invalidate this knowledge.' (28)

As we consider Bonhoeffer's treatment of the divine commandment in *Ethics* in detail, it will be helpful to use as our guide the three leading ideas of his early period mentioned in the early pages of this chapter. No weakening of Bonhoeffer's hold on these basic ideas is discernible in the years which follow - if anything, his belief in the relevance of the real world (on the one hand) and in the reality of the divine revelation (on the other) were immeasurably strengthened by his involvement in the Church Struggle and political affairs.

It will be recalled that the first of Bonhoeffer's early ideas was the radical one of rejecting all norms and principles as unhelpful for the purpose of ethical discourse; there is no such book of rules and standards available to the ethicist. In Bonhoeffer's own words:

'An ethic cannot be a book in which there is set out how everything in the world actually ought to be but unfortunately is not, and an ethicist cannot be a man who always knows better than others what is to be done and how it is to be done.' (29)

In *Ethics* this idea is related to total reality and to man's participation in it. The justification for this turns upon Bonhoeffer's attitude to what he describes as 'two-sphere' thinking - a legacy (he believes) from the Middle Ages - which cannot now be sustained. As we already know, central to his view of reality is the Incarnation which must be taken seriously as both an historical and ontological fact. Ethics therefore has to do with recognizing and sharing in God's presence, through Christ, in the world. The world is no longer the reality of God's original creation, but alienated through sin and from its Creator. The birth, death and rising again of Jesus Christ both reconciled and continues to reconcile the world to its origin, but, until the consummation of all things, good and evil are seen to be co-existing within the fabric of the one reality, which is no longer divided, spiritual from material, but brought together in Christ.

As Bonhoeffer frequently suggests in *Ethics*, there can be no true knowledge now of good and evil since its essence consists in its basic relationship to God. The unredeemed man is a 'god against God' and knows good and evil only from this standpoint, not as God knows it himself. Consequently, according to Bonhoeffer, all ethical discourse must start from the brute fact of man's disunion with God and with everything else, including himself. The Incarnation therefore becomes the key to Bonhoeffer's approach to ethics, the starting point of which is the church, the Body of Christ. The church is a part of humanity in which the form of Christ is being realized and also both the instrument and affirmation of the new reality which is coming into being in the world. (30)

Bonhoeffer is quick to point out the weaknesses of the 'two-sphere' ethical mentality which separates the spiritual from the material, the sacred from the profane. In philosophical terms he sees it as resulting either in a system of idealistic ethics, generating moral absolutism or casuistry, or in a scheme of positivistic ethics productive of crude situationalism and power politics. An important passage in *Ethics* makes this clear:

> 'There is a way of basing ethics upon reality which differs entirely from the Christian way. This is the positive and empirical approach, which aims at the entire elimination from ethics of the concepts of norms and standards.... This conception is undoubtedly superior to the idealist conception in that it is "closer to reality". God does not consist here in an impossible "realization" of what is unreal, the realization of ethical ideas. It is reality itself that teaches what is good.... The Christian ethic speaks... of the reality of God as the ultimate reality without and within everything that is.' (31)

The importance of this quotation for our purpose is that it points to the two vital concepts upon which Bonhoeffer's rejection of ethical norms and standards, whether they issue from a positivist or an idealist view, is based. The first concept is his unitary view of reality which brings together God and the world; the second concept links reality not only with God but with what is good. This reality (Bonhoeffer continues) is not just an idea, for christians believe it as a fact (*Tatsache*) that in Jesus Christ the reality of God entered into the reality of this world. (*In Jesus Christus is die Wirkliches Gottes in die Wirklichkeit dieser Welt eingegangen*). (32) This statement represents the linchpin on which Bonhoeffer's teaching about ethical and moral attitudes depends. It is for this reason that he regards the commandment of God as more important than ethical discussion or ideas, and why for him the commandment includes the ethical, and not the other way round.

A further implication of Bonhoeffer's unitary view of reality has to do with its sacramental character. We already know that Bonhoeffer in his World Alliance address was led to describe reality as 'the sacrament of command'. By this he was seeking to suggest that just as grace is communicated through the material reality of water, or bread and wine, so equally judgement and forgiveness are conveyed sacramentally by the preaching of God's command. Thus Bonhoeffer writes 'What the sacrament is for the preaching of the Gospel, the knowledge of firm reality is for the preaching of the command. Reality is the sacrament of command.' (*Was für die Verkündigung des Evangeliums das Sakrament ist, das ist für die Verkündigung des Gebotes die Kenntnis der konkreten Wirklichkeit. Die Wirklichkeit ist das Sakrament des Gebotes*). (33)

Curiously enough this sacramental language, which so readily fits in with Bonhoeffer's total view of reality in *Ethics*, does not appear in this form in *Ethics*. Instead he relies on other concepts, such as the divine mandates, to express the intimate connection between spiritual reality and that of the world. In broad terms, however, Bonhoeffer is able to deduce from his viewpoint in *Ethics* that ethical behaviour is action in accordance with reality, or 'responsible living', (34) which in turn is action which is in conformity with Christ. So again, the ethical task is not to be seen as the attempt to live according to certain timeless principles, but as taking on the form of Jesus Christ. He is life itself, restoring to man his true manhood as he stands before God. He also allows the world to be the world, so that in ethical enquiry we are no longer asking what is good in itself, nor treating it as an absolute. 'Good is not a quality of life. It is "life" itself. To be good is to "live".' (35)

Already students of *Letters and Papers from Prison* will be able to detect more than a hint of Bonhoeffer's later thinking about 'worldliness' and living life to the full in these references from *Ethics*. The discussion has taken us from Bonhoeffer's rejection of any form of ethical activity, which involves abstraction from life, to action which is concerned with looking deeply into life - indeed to engaging with life itself. It is only a short step from here to the startling prison statements, 'God is in the facts themselves' (36) and 'God meeting us no longer as "Thou", but also disguised in the "It".' (37) For our present purpose, however, it is necessary simply to note the possibility of a link.

Bonhoeffer's second leading idea, to which reference has been made, and which from the beginning determined the shape of his ethical and moral thinking can be formulated in terms of his dependence upon the Barthian concept of revelation. For Karl Barth the gracious God is a commanding God, so that ethical questions emerge as a part of dogmatics - many chapter headings, for example, in Barth's *Ethics* and *Church Dogmatics* include the word 'command'. Bonhoeffer took up this notion early on with so much enthusiasm that at their first meeting in 1931 Barth accused Bonhoeffer of 'making grace into a principle and killing everything else with it.' Barth preferred at this point to believe that there were smaller lamps, in addition to the one 'great light in the night', to which man might look for guidance, but Bonhoeffer rejected any suggestion of 'relative ethical criteria' as undermining the absolute authority of the divine revelation. (38)

The later Bonhoeffer moderated his position as his interest in the unity of reality grew, and as he began to allow more and more room for the 'natural'. The development in Ethics of his 'penultimate' - 'ultimate' distinction to meet this shift, led Bonhoeffer to believe that Barth was laying far too much stress on the ultimate, at the expense of the penultimate. So in *Ethics* Bonhoeffer believes it possible that remaining deliberately in the penultimate may be the means of pointing 'all the more genuinely to the ultimate, which God will speak in His own time (though indeed even then through a human mouth)' (39). The change in emphasis is clear - Bonhoeffer by this time is no longer willing to look for 'ultimate' solutions to ethical problems in the way he believed Karl Barth was still prepared to do.

Nevertheless, Bonhoeffer continued to remain faithful to Barth's basic approach to revelation as the declaration of God's gracious will and commandment in Jesus Christ.

The difference emerging between the two in *Ethics* is in the context of reality in which the will of God is seen to operate; in Barth the 'two sphere' framework is presupposed, whereas in Bonhoeffer it has been discarded; but for both, knowledge of the will of God is an indispensable part of the ethical endeavour. So Bonhoeffer makes his own position clear in Ethics:

> '(Instead) of asking how one can be good and do good, one must ask what is the will of God. But the will of God is nothing other than the becoming real of the reality of Christ with us and in our

world.... After Christ has appeared, ethics can have but one purpose... participation in the reality of the fulfilled will of God.... (which) is possible only in virtue of the fact that I myself am already included in the fulfilment of the will of God in Christ, which means that I am reconciled with God.' (40)

The form in which the will of God, as thus described, meets with man is that of the divine commandment, or command. Bonhoeffer's understanding of the word 'commandment' (*Gebot*) is very much influenced by its biblical background. It is close to the Hebrew '*Mitzvah*' which conveys the suggestion of a positive out-pouring of grace, a partnership with God in the world. It also takes on something of the meaning of *Torah* with its creative and reconciling functions (it is no accident that Psalm 119 was Bonhoeffer's favourite psalm). (41) All in all, therefore, the thrust in the meaning of the word 'commandment' for Bonhoeffer was existential, stressing the outgoing, positive movement of the will of God towards man, which could either save or destroy. In this interpretation Bonhoeffer broke with classic Lutheran theology which carefully distinguished between Law (*Gesetz*) and Gospel (*Evangelium*) as contrasting judgement with grace. Karl Barth's interpretation (with which Bonhoeffer began) had the effect of giving the Gospel priority while including the Law within it, seeing both as channels of grace through the Word of God. Bonhoeffer's view in *Ethics*, while not rejecting entirely the traditional distinction in theory, brought the two together in his definition of God's commandment as 'the total and concrete claim laid to man by the merciful and holy God in Jesus Christ.' (42)

The section in *Ethics*, 'The Commandment of God.' (43) from which this definition is taken, is unfortunately incomplete. It may well have been among the last sections Bonhoeffer was able to write before his arrest in 1943, but in spite of this there is much that is valuable in what remains. For example, there is his emphasis on the total and unconditional nature of God's commandment, which not only binds but sets free and which embraces the whole of life. An interesting anticipation of this 'wholeness' of approach is to be found in the lectures given by Bonhoeffer at Finkenwalde some years before, now available under the title, *Spiritual Care (Seelsorge)*. (44) Here Bonhoeffer regards spiritual care as including both preaching and *diakonia* i.e., the ministry to the outsider which seeks to bring him back into the arena of proclamation. Law and Gospel come into play in both activities of spiritual care, since the main purpose of both aspects of this care is to make clear the commandment of God concentrated in the sermon. Repentance, forgiveness and healing are all the work of grace and may be found in *diakonia* as well as preaching. (45)

A similar unified approach is to be seen in Bonhoeffer's treatment of the

Decalogue in relation to the commandment as a whole. The early Bonhoeffer tended to think in strictly traditional terms of the condemnatory function of the Ten Commandments, and traces of this remained even after his commitment to a non-prescriptive type of ethics. For example, in the *Ethics* section on 'The Confession of Guilt', (46) written in 1940, he speaks of the church breaking all ten commandments and so defecting from Christ. (47) However, his main line of thinking, as we have seen, is concerned with stressing the unity rather than the distinction between Law and Gospel. At times this leads him into explanations which could be described as more academic than practical. Thus in his account of the 'responsible' man, that is, the man who lives according to reality, Bonhoeffer states that such a man is not simply obedient to the Law, nor free from the Law, but lives midway between obligation and freedom, bearing the tension and offering himself and his actions to God. It is in this context that he quotes Martin Luther to the effect that 'in obedience man adheres to the decalogue and in freedom man creates new decalogues'. (48)

Although the *Ethics* includes a paper which deals rather technically with the meaning of the *primus usus legis* (the negative use of law in Lutheran theology), the climax of Bonhoeffer's thinking about the commandment and Decalogue comes with his conclusion that the Decalogue and the Sermon-on-the-Mount are not two different ethical ideals but 'one single call to concrete obedience towards the God and Father of Jesus Christ', (49) and that 'the whole law and the whole gospel of God belong equally to all men.' (50) The final logical step from this position in *Ethics* to that in *Letters and Papers* is the glossing over of any difference between the inner and outer disposition, and the recognition only of the '*anthrôpos teleios*', the whole man. (51)

By far the most interesting part of the *Ethics* section dealing with the commandment of God (in view of Bonhoeffer's later insights) is that which describes the commandment as giving 'permission to live'. By this he means, allowing a man to be a man before God. An important point to notice here is that 'permission' does not imply 'permissiveness'; it means permission to act responsibly. Man's fallen nature does not permit him to live in complete unity with the will of God', full acceptance of God's commandment does, and this brings with it freedom - not the absolute freedom to choose between right and wrong (*posse non peccare*), but the freedom which is found in obedience to the will of God (*non posse peccare*). So, in Bonhoeffer's own words, 'the commandment of God.... allows the flood of life to flow freely. It lets a man eat, drink, sleep, work, rest and play.... (It) allows him to live and act with certainty and with confidence in the guidance of the divine commandment.' (52) Not only does this broad commitment to what the divine will has in store for us day by day provide a sure defence against antinomianism and legalism, according to Bonhoeffer, but it prevents us standing endlessly at the crossroads agonizing over the right decision. The right decision is seen to come behind us and not always before us. (53)

Once more we are well on the way to the kind of approach which Bonhoeffer describes in his prison correspondence. His letter of July 21, 1944 to Eberhard Bethge, set within a discussion on saintliness and what is meant by faith, advocates an attitude of 'this-worldliness', by which he means, 'living unreservedly in life's duties, problems, successes and failures, experiences and perplexities. In so doing we throw ourselves completely into the arms of God'. (54) By this time Bonhoeffer was only too well aware that this experience would be primarily one of sharing in God's sufferings in the world, but the principle of responsible living in accordance with the will of God is still what he has in mind.

The third leading idea (we suggested) upon which Bonhoeffer based his ethical thinking from the outset was that of concreteness. Interestingly, an editorial footnote at the close of the unfinished section, 'The Commandment of God', indicates that Bonhoeffer had it in mind to conclude with a series of questions about the concreteness of the will of God. (55) It was clearly his intention to settle any doubts he might have raised in his readers' minds with regard to this particular aspect of the divine commandment. Accordingly, in his summary of points still to be made, he includes statements such as, 'the will of God is always concrete, or else it is not the will of *God*' and, 'the good will is from the outset a concrete deed; otherwise it is not Christian will.' (56)

Bonhoeffer was not innovating here, since (as has been shown) a concern for the concrete word had been with him almost from the beginning. For him it was inextricably bound up with the question of authority to which he turned for meaning in so much of his life and ministry.

Ever since he had tried to come to grips with the nature of revelation in *Act and Being* (1930), where he referred to God as being 'haveable' and 'graspable' within the Church through Jesus Christ, (57) the concrete nature of the Word of God had dominated Bonhoeffer's thinking. By the time we reach *Ethics*, concreteness is being linked with his unitary view of reality and its historical focus in the Word made flesh. Concreteness now becomes a matter of 'realising' the form of the crucified and resurrected Jesus Christ in our lives and in the world.

We now know that the principal means, in Bonhoeffer's view, whereby God's commandment, revealed in Jesus Christ, confronts man and the world is in the divine mandates, namely, the church, marriage and family, labour (or culture) and government. (58) These are concrete divine commissions which originate in the revelation of Christ. Their purpose (according to Bonhoeffer) is to confer divine authority upon those so commissioned, for example, ministers, parents, employers and rulers, who thereby act as deputies for Jesus Christ. The mandates, in addition, mark out a definite earthly domain which may be seen and identified as rightly belonging to the commandment, The effect is to dispose of the traditional Lutheran 'orders' or 'estates', which for Bonhoeffer approximated to autonomous, secularized centres of authority, and to replace them with designated areas of life which could act as focal points for the concrete commandment of God.

Although, according to Bonhoeffer, the mandates function separately as channels for the creative and redemptive activity of God in Christ, by performing in different ways the various tasks assigned to them by God, none can properly act alone. They are all interrelated and interact one with another, since they are all 'directed toward the whole man, as he stands in reality before God.' The unity of reality can only begin with man, and this unity becomes possible when man permits himself to be faced 'with the accomplished reality of the incarnation of God and of the reconciliation of the world' in Jesus Christ. The responsibility for bringing this about is the special task of the church which in other respects is on an equal footing with the other three mandates. The key passage for this deserves to be quoted in full:

> 'The divine mandate of the Church is different from these three. This mandate is the task of enabling the reality of Jesus Christ to become real in the preaching and organisation of the Church and the Christian life. It is concerned, therefore, with the external salvation of the whole world. The mandate of the Church extends to all mankind, and it does so within all the other mandates. (59)

It has to be admitted that we have all too little from Bonhoeffer about the precise relationship of the church, the body of those who hear God's word and keep it, to the other three mandates. The main section dealing with the mandates and their interrelationship is regrettably unfinished, (60) although we are given a useful discourse on preaching and ecclesiastical discipline as concrete demonstrations of the commandment of God, a subject aired by Bonhoeffer in other writings. The earlier point about the church's responsibility for proclaiming the commandment in a representative capacity on behalf of the world is again taken up, with a firm reminder that the dominion of Christ's commandment over all creation is not to be equated with any dominion of the church.

On this point, Bonhoeffer seems to admit the anomalous position which the church (as he describes it) occupies in relation to the other mandates. On the one hand, the church, through the Word of God which it proclaims, is part of humanity in which Christ has become real. On the other, it is the mandated means whereby Christ's lordship is made effective within itself and over the whole world. So the congregation (Bonhoeffer suggests) is both an instrument in God's hands for dealing with the world and, at the same time, its goal and centre, As a result of the church's preaching the commandment of Christ, creation is set free to fulfil the law of its own being. It has to be admitted that this explanation seems singularly unconvincing in view of Bonhoeffer's insistence that the other mandates are there precisely to enable the divine commandment to 'enter' the created order on an equal footing. Either the mandate of the church is decisive for making the commandment effective throughout the world, or it has an equal place in effectiveness with the other three. It may have been the unsatisfactory nature of this relationship which led Bonhoeffer in the later *Letters and Papers* virtually to drop the idea of mandates (it is mentioned only in one letter). (61) Instead, the theme of Christ's lordship over the world and mankind is heavily stressed, to the point of reducing the place and purpose of the church to something of an enigma.

The question of the concreteness of commandment in the mandates raises also the question of the concreteness of decision-making once the commandment is heard. In the early pages of *Ethics* this is considered under the form of 'proving God's will'. For the most part this concentrates on the effort to be made by the individual to discover, by careful consideration and reflection, what the will of God is to be when faced with a variety of situations in his everyday life. Simple intuition or a flash of inspiration are out of the question. For the revealed will of God to be properly understood and interpreted, the whole man, 'the heart, the understanding, observation and experience must all collaborate'. (62) Moreover there must be a recognition of the fact that we live within a nexus of historical experiences and responsibilities, as part of human existence, from which we cannot escape. Central to this should be our awareness that 'we stand already in the midst of Christ's taking form, in a section of history which He himself has chosen.' (63) This too must be taken into account.

To those who would argue that this, in effect, represents a capitulation to 'situationism' Bonhoeffer would no doubt point to the centrality of Jesus in his scheme of things. Not only does commitment to him in prayer and action ensure that we are always experiencing his mercy and judgement, but the emphasis upon the 'realising' of Christ's form within us guarantees the necessary 'backcloth' of continuity and content which the ethicist seeks. The concrete making real of reality itself (Bonhoeffer might well argue) is the surest safeguard against situationism.

Heinrich Ott in *Reality and Faith* makes this situational approach of Bonhoeffer the subject of an intriguing comparison with Karl Barth's approach. In Ott's view Barth's understanding of theology as a system rather than a method means that its proper symbol is that of a survey instead of a journey. The converse is true, he believes, of Bonhoeffer's theology where discovery of reality (and so of the divine commandment) happens step by step. Ott also sees in Bonhoeffer's existential interpretations which demonstrate the presence of Christ, not the 'atomizing of theological thought' but 'pattern cases' - 'existential interpretation deals with pattern cases and not with principles of an abstract and general nature.' (64)

Whatever we make of this interpretation, there is little doubt that Bonhoeffer came to see ethical enquiry very much as a pilgrimage, with decision-making thought of as 'stations' on the way. Not only is his celebrated poem *Stations on the Road to Freedom* evidence of this, but his fondness for the Old Testament - particularly during his imprisonment) was based largely upon its presentation of the people of God as pilgrims and sojourners upon the earth. The earth was more real to Israel than any expectation of a life to come, but it lived its life *sub specie aeternitatis* which gave it a quality which Bonhoeffer admired. Consequently the Old Testament fascinated him not only because of its enthusiasm for the good things of life but also because of its references to lying, killing, stealing, murdering - often to the glory of God. (65) Hence the appeal which the 'penultimate' had for Bonhoeffer, for (as he came to believe) it was only in the penultimate that men are vouchsafed intimations and expectations of the 'ultimate'.

It was in this spirit of concrete commitment to the world, as it is, that Bonhoeffer wrote his essay in Tegel on 'What is meant by "Telling the Truth"?' (66) Under interrogation, for example, he believed that deception, and even lying, could be more in correspondence with reality than adhering to the strict truth. Reality, if it includes Christ, is the sacrament of the ethical, and participation in it is the first consideration rather than striving for a principle not rooted in the earth. Always, too, there is forgiveness. The rightness or wrongness of a concrete ethical decision can never be known in advance, but the responsible man, who combines simplicity with wisdom, is acting in accordance with reality and so committing himself to Christ.

In attempting to summarize Bonhoeffer's treatment of the commandment of God, one must take into account his starting-point, namely the search for authority. This led to an early emphasis upon three foundation ideas - the rejection of timeless principles, acceptance of a historical revelation, and commitment to a concrete Word - upon which Bonhoeffer proceeded to base his view of an authoritative commandment from God. Given these foundations, Bonhoeffer in *Ethics* began to construct, within a framework of Christ-centred, all-embracing reality, a theory of responsible ethical behaviour as life lived in correspondence with that reality. This - responsible living - was the way in which a human being could fulfil the divine commandment, which is concretely manifested in the biblical old and new law and the four mandates.

As work on the *Ethics* progressed, Bonhoeffer seems to have become aware that he was in fact in the process of describing a new kind of man. If Eberhard Bethge's 1963 arrangement of the chronological sequence of the different sections is accepted, it would appear that Bonhoeffer's early accent upon Christ taking form in the world and in men gives way, in the later pages, to a greater emphasis upon men and the world conforming to reality. On this view, the concern of much of *Letters and Papers* with 'worldly' Christianity can be seen as consistent with the development of his thinking in *Ethics*.

What Bonhoeffer understands by the new kind of man, who alone, he regards as capable of coming to terms with the reality of living in the secularized world of the twentieth century, is to be found in his report 'After Ten Years', written for the benefit of his fellow conspirators at the end of 1942. In it is the recognition that the old securities have gone - there is 'no ground under our feet' - and that 'the great masquerade of evil has played havoc with all our ethical concepts'. The only hope for the future lies in the action of responsible men who are willing to commit their lives in response to the call of God: 'Only the man whose final standard is not his reason, his principles, his conscience, his freedom or his virtue, but who is ready to sacrifice all this when he is called to responsible action in faith and in exclusive allegiance to God' is capable of standing fast, and entitled to be called 'responsible'. (67)

As is well-known, the practical implications of this sort of living are less clearly delineated in Bonhoeffer's prison letters than we should like. Among the collection of often disconnected theological insights and reflections which make up *Letters and Papers*, perhaps the most persistent is Bonhoeffer's exhortation to Christians to participate in the sufferings of God in the world. This is in line with his thinking in 'After Ten Years' which, together with its concern for future generations, and a reconstructed Germany, is very much coloured by the suffering and turmoil of his own day.

Is Bonhoeffer's 'responsible living' then only an interim ethic, improvised and applicable only for his own day? There is no evidence that he thought of it as such. Conceivably Bonhoeffer would be prepared to argue that the principle of participation in worldly reality in order to obey the commandment of God would apply, whatever the conditions of the time, and that it is this which marks out the responsible man. However, the two tantalizing references in *Letters and Papers* to an *Arkandisziplin*, (68) along with scattered remarks about the need on occasions for reticence and silence, indicate a more than passing interest in the belief that Christians should be prepared to practise a 'secret discipline' as part of their way of life in a world-come-of-age. Whether the secret discipline is practised for its own sake (as did the early Christians), or is regarded as a means of 'holding the line' until the advent of more propitious times, the inference would appear to be that Bonhoeffer did not think it possible for commitment to worldly reality to be total or complete. But we cannot know now if Bonhoeffer at this stage contemplated alternative approaches to responsible living appropriate to other conditions.

In one respect, however, Bonhoeffer remained consistent in his concept of living responsibly as a man before God; it is in his insistence upon the uniqueness of persons who alone can make the necessary response of penitence and faith to the divine commandment and to one another. Responsible living, both in *Ethics* and *Letters and Papers*, is demonstrated in living responsibly with one's neighbour. This, according to Bonhoeffer, is possible 'only in the complete surrender of one's own life to the other man. Only the selfless man lives responsibly, and this means that only the selfless man *lives*.' (69)

FOOTNOTES

(1) *E.*, p.64.
(2) See *ibid.*, p.20.
(3) See *NRS.*, pp.37ff. (*GS*1, pp.51ff).
(4) See Bethge, *DB.*, p.88.
(5) *NRS.*, p.43 (GS111, p.52).
(6) *Ibid.*, pp.44f. (p.54f).
(7) *Ibid.*, Appendix 2, pp.361-72 (pp.110-26).
(8) *Ibid.*, p,362.
(9) *Ibid.*, p.363.
(10) See above, Chapter 3.
(11) *NRS.*, pp.162-3 (GS1, pp.145-6).
(12) *Ibid.*
(13) *NRS.*, p.46 (GS111, p.56).
(14) See pp.263-76, 277-85.
(15) See pp.284f.
(16) E.g., Exaudi Sunday Sermon, 1932. (*GS*1, p.133), cf., Bethge, DB., p.140.
(17) See *NRS.*, p.237 (GS11, p.133).
(18) See Bethge, *op. cit.*, p.188.
(19) See the World Alliance speech, NRS., pp.160, 164, (*GS*1, pp.143,147).
(20) *TWP.*, pp.147-9 (*GS*1, pp.276-8).
(21) *NRS.*, p.289 (*GS*1, pp.216 and 289).
(22) See *NRS.*, pp.153-7 (GS111, p.286-91).
(23) See *TWF.*, pp.42-51 (*GS*111, pp.325-34).
(24) *Ibid.*, p.48 (pp.330f.).
(25) *Psalms: The Prayer Book of the Bible*, 1982, pp.10-11.
(26) See *CF.*, p.20.
(27) See 'After Ten Years', *LPP.*, p.16.
(28) p.17.
(29) *E.*, p.269.
(30) *Ibid.*, pp.83ff. Summarized concisely by Feil: 'Ethics has to address human beings in the concrete, historical and social situation which is given in and through Jesus Christ.' *The Theology of Dietrich Bonhoeffer*, p.35.
(31) *Ibid.*, pp.193-4.
(32) *Ibid.*, p.194 (*Ethik*, p.207). Feil p.44.
(33) *NRS.*, p.164 (*GS*1, p.147). Feil p.36.
(34) See *E.*, pp.227ff.
(35) *Ibid.*, p.221.

(36) *LPP.*, 23:1:44, p.191.
(37) *Ibid.*, 21:2:44,p.217.
(38) See above, p.141. Burtness attributes a similar remark about 'killing everything with Grace' to Reinhold Niebuhr. See *Shaping the Future*, p.104.
(39) p.126.
(40) p.212.
(41) See *Spiritual Care*, pp.88, fn.44 and p. 83, fn.20.
(42) p.277.
(43) pp.277-85.
(44) Translated by Jay C. Rochelle, 1985, from *GS* V.
(45) pp.30ff.
(46) pp.110-16.
(47) p.l5, cf., *NRS.*, p.44 (*GS*111, p.53).
(48) p.253.
(49) p.359.
(50) p.358.
(51) See *LPP.*, 8:7:44, p.346.
(52) p.283. See also Burtness, *Shaping the Future*, pp.109-115 from which the substance of this paragraph is taken.
(53) pp.283f. cf., *NRS.*, p.45, 'there is ethics only on the completion of the act, not in the letter of the law.' (*GS*111, pp.54-5).
(54) *LPP.*, p.370.
(55) *E.*, p.285. Feil provides an excellent summary of the implications of Bonhoeffer's concept of God as 'the *Concretissimum*' in *The Theology of Dietrich Bonhoeffer*, pp.37-55.
(56) *Ibid.*
(57) pp.90f.
(58) For Bonhoeffer's extensive treatment of the mandates, see *E.*, pp.207-13, 286-302, 344-6.
(59) *Ibid.*, pp.211-2.
(60) pp.286-302.
(61) 23:1:44, pp.192-3.
(62) p.38.
(63) *Ibid.*, p.87.
(64) See pp.441ff.
(65) See especially *LPP.*, 21:1:44, 5:12:43, pp.181, 156f.
(66) *E.*, pp.363-71.
(67) *LPP.*, pp.3,4,5. See also E., pp.224-62. For sympathetic treatments of Bonhoeffer's concept of responsibility see H. Richard Niebuhr, *The Responsible Self*, 1963 and E. H. Robertson, *Bonhoeffer's Heritage*, pp.43-9.

(68) In 30:4:44, 5:5:44, pp.281, 286, cf., p.300.
(69) *E.*, p.225.

CHAPTER 7

ASSESSING BONHOEFFER'S 'ETHICS'

'On four occasions, I have taken part in explosive discussions about Bonhoeffer's thought. The first was provoked by the famous phrase about salvation being found only in the Confessing Church; here Bonhoeffer is accused of being an "enthusiast". The second took place around the problem of costly grace; this time he was taken for an obscure pietist. Then there was the clamour over "contacts with the enemy" during the war, and he was accused of high treason. And now the debate centres on non-religious interpretation of Christianity, and a well-meaning colleague conjectures at a pastors' conference that one should hope that at the very end of his life Bonhoeffer recovered his faith.'

This intriguing comment of Eberhard Bethge (1) must be seen against the background of what was mainly a series of German discussions on various aspects of Dietrich Bonhoeffer's life and work. Reactions to Bonhoeffer of course vary from individual to individual, but in fact they may also be said to vary according to one's national viewpoint. Thus German interest tends to concentrate on his theological ideas while for the most part ignoring, if not actually condemning, his political activism. Americans, assiduous students of continental theology, warm to him, attracted by his protestant seriousness and evident zest for life. The pragmatic English, as might be expected, genuinely admire Bonhoeffer's courageous witness but remain bewildered by his theology. (2)

That there is substance in the view that Bonhoeffer presents us with a picture of a highly complex and many-sided personality, arising from the kaleidoscopic character of his life, is surely not open to doubt. The key to it all is to be found in the consistency with which (it is generally agreed) he lived a life in accordance with his convictions, a life which like a Greek tragedy unfolded itself logically and inexorably towards an inevitable end.

The path pursued, however, was not in isolation, separate from the world of affairs and his fellow men. Bonhoeffer himself would have been the first to admit that he was a 'part of all that he had met'. Many experiences went to make up the man - a comfortable bourgeois background, extensive travel both at home and abroad, ecumenical contacts, involvement in church and national politics, and finally imprisonment in a Nazi gaol on a charge of conspiracy. All these experiences provided the material for the thinking that went into his *Ethics*. (3)

One important element in this broad set of experiences was that of an academic, fostered both at home and at university. In so far as Bonhoeffer endeavoured to live out his beliefs in a demonstrably concrete (a favourite word!) way, he would have declined the description of a 'pure academic'. Nevertheless his beliefs were powerful, the product not simply of his own fertile and original brain but of some of the most influential German theological and philosophical thinkers of his day. In Tübingen, where Bonhoeffer studied for a year, he was attracted both by Adolf Schlatter's interest in the relevance of the gospel to the normal and the good, (4) and by Karl Heim's concern for the unbeliever and the sceptic in an age of science. Although Bonhoeffer was later to criticize both in the light of his dialectical thinking, he was nevertheless indebted to Heim for introducing him to Schleiermacher and to Ritschl, for whose sound scholarship, along with that of Harnack, he always maintained a healthy respect. However, it was during his time at Berlin University that Bonhoeffer, as a student in the late 1920s, came into direct contact with some of the foremost liberal-minded scholars of his day - Adolf Deissmann, Ernst Sellin, Hans Lietzmann, Adolf Harnack, Ernst Troeltsch, Karl Holl and Reinhold Seeberg. According to Bethge, it was under Seeberg, 'the mediating spirit between idealism, orthodoxy, and modernism', that Bonhoeffer became a Hegelian specialist, with momentous results for his later understanding of the nature of the church and of reality. Bethge sums up the influences of these student years as follows:

> 'These were formative influences.... Troeltsch's interest in the sociological realities of Christianity, Holl's reawakening of the genuine Luther, Harnack's intellectual incorruptibility, and Seeberg's philosophical openness.' (5)

Although there are those like Hanfried Müller who maintain that, generally speaking, Bonhoeffer remained remarkably independent of his liberal training, Bonhoeffer himself later on in life recorded his indebtedness to nineteenth century liberal theology (6) and more particularly to Adolf Harnack personally. (7) Honesty in face of the facts was undoubtedly the principal gift which liberalism conferred upon him.

Equally helpful to us in this brief survey is a consideration of four major figures whose theological and philosophical ideas also helped to shape the thinking of Bonhoeffer in the writing of the *Ethics*; these are Hegel, Barth, Luther and Nietzsche. For our purpose it will be sufficient to concentrate upon one key area in each case in order to illustrate the way in which Bonhoeffer's thinking was affected by them. These areas are not to be sharply distinguished, one from another; instead, together they should be seen as indispensable ingredients in the *Ethics* as a whole.

We begin with G. W. F. Hegel, from whom Bonhoeffer borrowed the concept of a unified reality and of God's close identification with it, which is such a prominent feature in *Ethics*. As we have frequently noted, in the place of the traditional 'two-sphere' division of reality, which Bonhoeffer believed to be a legacy of the Renaissance and Reformation, he introduced the Hegelian notion of 'one sphere of the realisation of Christ, in which the reality of God and the reality of the world are united.' (8) Bonhoeffer's chief concern in *Ethics*, however, is with the 'ethical' and with how, interpreted as the commandment of God, it can be made concrete in human life and in the world. In his own words, 'the ethical cannot be detached from reality, and consequently continual progress in learning to appreciate reality is a necessary ingredient in ethical action.' (9) So that, contrary to the idealist view, which sees the good in the realizing of ethical ideals, reality itself teaches what is good, (10) and 'correspondence with reality' is seen as being of the essence of ethical behaviour. (11)

Bonhoeffer's preoccupation with a unified reality, therefore, is wholly ethical, whereas Hegel's concern is primarily philosophical, and of this Bonhoeffer was well aware. Among numerous annotations in Bonhoeffer's collection of books by Hegel there are to be found comments critical of Hegel's abstract approach, for example; 'The question of reality... world history... a total abstraction!' 'Each isolated concept (sin, etc.) is seen clearly in itself, but is understood in the total scheme only as a moment of becoming.' 'Not "thy will be done" but "*it* is done".' (12) With Hegel, in the last resort, it is reason which overcomes; in Bonhoeffer's case it is faith. Although there are those who see Bonhoeffer as substantially succumbing to the seductions of Hegel's 'incarnational ontology', i.e., the complete identification of the Incarnation and God with total reality, with no separation between God and the world, Bonhoeffer's continual insistence on the concrete commandment as a divine-human personal encounter keeps him from becoming a complete Hegelian.

The next influential figure behind the thinking in *Ethics* was Karl Barth. Critical as Bonhoeffer was from time to time of details in Barth's theological stance, he remained throughout committed to Barth's dialectical approach, particularly in the field of revelation. For both of them revelation disclosed the way of God to man through the Word, rendering 'religion' (man's way to God) at best suspect - at worst idolatrous. Soon after discovering Karl Barth's writings about 1925, Bonhoeffer came to grips with the problem of the relationship between 'act' and 'being'. His book of that name (as we know) was an attempt to deal with this against the background of Kantian transcendentalism and Heideggerian existentialism. Using Barth's theology of the Word, and Hegel's 'theology' of ontological presence, Bonhoeffer believed it to be possible to reconcile the two. For Bonhoeffer the supreme revelatory event of Jesus Christ gives rise to the reality of the being of the church, where Christ affirms and gives effect to reality, and his taking form is both proclaimed and accomplished. (13) The church accordingly, as the Body of Christ, becomes the point of departure for christian ethics since, 'the question of good becomes the question of the participation in the divine reality which is revealed in Christ. (14)

It is clear that this is one of the points at which Bonhoeffer parted company with Barth. Barth's conception of the church was more eschatological and less concrete than Bonhoeffer's, and his Calvinist background prevented him from allowing that the 'finite could contain the infinite'. Hence to the later Bonhoeffer Barth's positivistic approach to revelation (*Offenbarungspositivismus*) seemed altogether too much a matter of 'take it or leave it' (*Iss, Vogel, oder stirb*), (15) and as such no real answer to the misguided liberal belief in the goodness of man. Instead Bonhoeffer believed in a gracious God, who in the act of revelation makes himself available to man by establishing his presence ontologically both in the church and in the world.

A third important influence was Luther's. Without a doubt Bonhoeffer's commitment to a christological foundation for his ideas on reality and the revealed Word came largely from Luther, although of course he would not have denied the existence of a considerable Barthian element in his christology too. The Lutheran influence however for Bonhoeffer was decisive, coming as he did from a Lutheran circle and trained by such dedicated Lutheran teachers as Reingold Seeberg and Karl Holl. The influence of the Danish Lutheran theologian Søren Kierkegaard cannot be discounted either.

As the large number of references to Luther in *Ethics* demonstrate, Bonhoeffer's indebtedness to Luther is very great. We shall concern ourselves here simply with the way in which it relates to Bonhoeffer's thinking about Jesus Christ, the pivot of his ideas about reality and ethical behaviour. Starting from Luther's *Kondeszens* - Christology Bonhoeffer proceeds in the *Ethics* to combine the conception of a self-emptying, *pro me* Jesus Christ (evident in his earlier works) with a triumphalist, universal Christ, unifier of heaven and earth. As with Luther, the one who unifies also reconciles. So in one of the few direct references to the Atonement in *Ethics* Bonhoeffer declares:

> 'The world is not divided between Christ and the devil, but, whether it recognizes it or not, it is solely and entirely the work of Christ.... In the body of Jesus Christ God is united with humanity, the whole of humanity is accepted by God, and the

world is reconciled with God. In the body of Jesus Christ God took upon himself the sin of the whole world and bore it.' (16)

As we know, in his later thinking Bonhoeffer was to take this central concept of the presence of the crucified, risen Lord in creation and (according to some), by stressing the suffering rather than the victorious Christ, thereby incur a shift from a *theologia gloriae* to a *theologia crucis*. Karl Barth was certainly among those who thought that, by so doing, Bonhoeffer had contracted more than a touch of the 'Lutheran melancholy' prevalent in the North German Plain. (17)

The truly Lutheran element in Bonhoeffer's christology, however, as contrasted with Barth's, which Bonhoeffer himself pointed out in *Act and Being*, is the fact that God is not free *of* man in his eternal non-objectivity, but free *for* man in his *given* Word. (18) By insisting on the 'havable, graspable' nature of Christ the Word, Bonhoeffer remained faithful to Luther's concrete and realistic view of the condescension of Christ, however crudely Luther expressed it. Thus Bonhoeffer quotes Luther directly:

'It is the honour and glory of our God (*unseres Gottes Ehre*), however, that, giving himself for our sake in deepest condescension, he passes into the flesh, the bread, our hearts, mouths, entrails, and suffers also for our sake that he be dishonourably (*unehrlich*) handled, on the altar as on the Cross'. (19)

The fourth major figure influential in Bonhoeffer's ethical thinking was F. W. Nietzsche. Some indication of the attraction, which this radical critic of a morality grounded in reason, had for Bonhoeffer has already been noted in connection with the 1929 Barcelona address, 'What is a Christian Ethic?' In this address Bonhoeffer's adherence to Nietzschean 'principles' is unmistakable - rejection of the universal norms, attachment to the earth, reaching beyond good and evil, and moral élitism worthy of supermen. It is difficult for those coming to Bonhoeffer via his *Letters and Papers*, with their overt life-affirming Christianity, not to sense the kinship between the two writers; (20) both - though for different reasons - similar in their fragmentary and aphoristic approach; both fascinated by the vision of a race of 'free spirits'.

In the *Ethics* Nietzsche's influence is particularly noticeable in Bonhoeffer's refusal to accept idealism as a basis for ethical enquiry. The contrast between what 'should be' and 'is', for Bonhoeffer as for Nietzsche, is destructive of a genuine ethic. It 'arises (according to Bonhoeffer) 'from fear of the fullness of everyday life and from an awareness of incapacity for life'. Instead good is not a quality of life' 'it is "life" itself. To be good is to "live".' (21) In their joint search for a moral standard which could be found beyond the universal norms they turned to that which was concrete and definite, and discernible only in life itself, For Nietzsche this meant a revaluation of all accepted values; for Bonhoeffer it meant the commandment of God which lay behind the ethical, and which he defined as 'the total and concrete claim laid to man by the merciful and holy God in Jesus Christ.' (22)

In spite therefore of seeming resemblances between the two at this point, the difference is really fundamental. Nietzsche's injunction to treat life as an absolute or an end in itself is for Bonhoeffer pure vitalism, leading ultimately to nihilism. In its place he insisted that life must be understood as the reality given by God, which is embodied in Jesus Christ. (23) Once again the fundamentally christocentric nature of reality is the distinctive feature which Bonhoeffer brings to the consideration of ethics. Accordingly, in a world which is rooted and grounded in the reality of Christ, Bonhoeffer declares the necessity of coming to terms with all its contradictions - 'growing and dying, health and suffering, happiness and renunciation, achievement and humility, honour and self-abasement'. The parting shot, as far as Nietzsche is concerned, comes in the following sentence from the *Ethics*:

> 'The actions of the Christian do not spring from bitter acquiescence in the irreconcilable cleavage between vitality and self-denial, between "secular" and "Christian" or between "autonomous ethics" and the "ethic of Jesus", but they spring from joy in the accomplishment of the reconciliation of the world with God'. (24)

Bonhoeffer may have drawn inspiration from Nietzsche's view of morality as being of the 'earth earthy', but his concept of reality, and therefore of the world, was based not on the absence of God but on his presence there in Christ. While they appeared to have much in common in their iconoclastic attitude to conventional morality, the basic assumptions of the two could not have been more different.

With this consideration of four major figures - Hegel, Barth, Luther and Nietzsche - whose thinking undoubtedly contributed to the shaping of the *Ethics* - we turn to consider what distinctive Bonhoefferian feature, if any, governed his philosophical and theological approach to ethical questions in the book. Again, its essentially fragmented and kaleidoscopic character must be fully taken into account; in addition the point must be made that the *Ethics* is unrevised and incomplete. Moreover Karl Barth's question, arising from his reading of the prison correspondence, as to whether Bonhoeffer, 'an impulsive, visionary thinker', really had a systematic viewpoint, is also applicable to *Ethics*. (25)

One fact nevertheless about Bonhoeffer's method of approach in *Ethics* - however disjointed the presentation - was undoubtedly his practice of occupying the middle-ground between opposing positions. The method is dialectical - his conclusions sometimes paradoxical - but the tenor of Bonhoeffer's writings, taken as a whole, suggests that this is characteristic of the way he dealt with theological and ethical questions. Substance is lent to this view from a remark made by Bonhoeffer himself in 1944 with regard to understanding and interpreting 'religionless Christianity', namely, that a heavy responsibility would fall on those living in Germany, 'midway between East and West', to undertake this interpretation. (26) The midway position referred to here is geographical, but it may perhaps also be seen as typifying the way Bonhoeffer's mind worked. Certainly it is the case that commentators from time to time have understood Bonhoeffer as variously offering a middle way between Barthianism and liberalism, between Barth's objectivism and Bultmann's existentialism, between Catholicism and Protestantism, and even between Marxism and Christianity. (27) With his later radicalism very much in mind, a French writer in similar vein intriguingly describes Bonhoeffer as a 'piétiste tentant d'être irreligieux'. (28) There seems therefore to be something of a consensus among a number of writers, each from his own particular stand-point, that Bonhoeffer can be described as a creative thinker who acted as a catalyst in relation to a number of varying viewpoints and positions.

After this discussion of the personal, academic and, more specifically, theological influences which provide the background to Bonhoeffer's thinking in the *Ethics*, we now turn to examine three important areas of contrasting positions which Bonhoeffer in *Ethics* seems to bring together in a creative synthesis. The first to claim our attention is clearly fundamental, in the sense that it dominated his thinking from earliest times and underlies most of what he has to say in *Ethics*. The problem is stated in the opening pages of *Act and Being* - 'the whole of theology, in its theory of the knowledge of God, of man, of sin and grace, crucially depends on whether it elects to stress concepts of act or of being at the outset.' (29) From here Bonhoeffer goes on in *Act and Being* to set himself the task of attempting 'to unify the aims of true transcendentalism and true ontology within an "ecclesiastical thought".' (30) The solution he arrived at, as we know, was in terms of revelation within the church, but the 'act' versus 'being' problem was not thereby disposed of; it remained a hidden factor in most if not all of Bonhoeffer's theological thinking, not least in that of the *Ethics*.

The 'act-being' relationship is especially relevant to the question of reality which, as Gerhard Ebeling has pointed out, (31) raises questions about the concrete reality of the church as well as of the commandment and the world. Bonhoeffer's answer, as we have it in *Ethics*, is to bring the customary two 'spheres' or 'realms' of reality into a 'polemical unity', thereby seeking to avoid the alternatives of either spiritual seclusion or worldly indifference. The remedy, as we are aware, is a dynamic rather than a static view of reality - a unity-in-tension which (if it may be so expressed) has the best of both worlds. The unifying process is based on the Incarnation which, through the ontological Christ enables the reality of the world and the reality of God to come together as one. So:

> 'There are not two spheres, standing side by side, competing with each other and attacking each other's frontiers.... (the) whole . reality of the world is already drawn in into Christ and bound together in Him.... The unity of the reality of God and of the world, which has been accomplished in Christ, is repeated, or, more exactly, is realized, ever afresh in the life of man. (32)

Heinrich Ott, who (as we have seen) emphasizes the importance of such New Testament passages as Colossians 1,16ff., and others in the Deutero-Pauline Epistles, for Bonhoeffer's christological ontology, sees this as the key to Bonhoeffer's thinking about reality, as well as an attempt (albeit not completed) 'to satisfy the challenge of the existential question of faith, who Jesus Christ really is for us today,' (33) Ott also draws attention to the similarities in this respect between Bonhoeffer's approach and those of later writers such as Teilhard de Chardin, Paul Tillich and Karl Rahner. (34) Likewise André Dumas, who writes approvingly of Ott's presentation of Bonhoeffer's theology as getting 'closest to the heart of Bonhoeffer's theology of reality and of the credibility of Christian faith in the midst of reality', (35) believes that Bonhoeffer's openness to the existentialism of the actualists and the essential being of the ontologists prevents him from becoming trapped within false alternatives such as,

> 'fact versus interpretation, *extra nobis* versus *in nobis*, otherness versus openness, God-in-himself versus God-for-us, objectivity versus subjectivity, givenness versus relationship, "positivism of revelation" versus existential interpretation, cosmology versus anthropology, revelation outside the world versus the world outside revelation, orthodoxy without dialogue versus existentialism without an object, dogmatics versus hermeneutics, the duty of belief versus the possibility of belief'. (36)

The list is long and formidable, but it highlights what is at stake in

Bonhoeffer's attempt to reconcile 'act' with 'being'. Essentially Bonhoeffer's treatment of reality in *Ethics* should be seen as an endeavour to grapple with the same problem.

The second area of contrasts, or polarities, which illustrates Bonhoeffer's 'unity-in-tension' approach in *Ethics*, centres on his view of the natural and unnatural life. Here in reaction to two-sphere thinking, which tended to associate God with the supernatural and the world with the natural, Bonhoeffer instead contrasts the natural with the unnatural. The reason for this rests on the fact of the Fall. The change is designed to replace the customary connection which sinful nature has with the Fall, with the notion of creaturely dependence which, since the Fall, Bonhoeffer believes to be characteristic of nature - 'we speak of the natural rather than of the sinful so that we may include in it the creaturely', he writes. (37) In effect this means that the decisive event for mankind and for the world is no longer the Fall but the Incarnation. Bonhoeffer may not have intended that, but the conclusion seems inevitable, following from the natural-unnatural contrast which he draws and with which we are already familiar: (38) 'The natural is the form of life preserved by God for the fallen world and directed towards justification, redemption and renewal through Christ', or, in other words, which 'opens its doors to Christ'; the unnatural, on the other hand, 'is that which, after the Fall, closes its doors against the coming of Christ.' (39)

For this novel interpretation of an important distinction in christian soteriology Bonhoeffer has to hand (as we know) a new set of categories, namely, the concepts of the 'penultimate' and the 'ultimate'. The coming of Christ (once more crucial to Bonhoeffer's dialectical approach) as the ultimate, confirms the post-Fall natural life as the penultimate; so that the natural is the penultimate seen in proper relation to the ultimate, and the unnatural is the penultimate seen as unrelated to the ultimate. According to Bonhoeffer the penultimate cannot be considered as a state or condition in itself - its status is determined by the judgement passed upon it by the justifying action of Christ i.e., the ultimate. So that 'concretely, two things are called penultimate in relation to the justification of the sinner by grace, namely, being man (*Menschsein*) and being good.' (40)

The Japanese ethicist, Hiroki Funamoto, paying tribute to this as a new and unique approach, traces the origin of the ultimate-penultimate concept to Bonhoeffer's Lutheran heritage and to Catholic tradition, backed by his interest in the Old Testament. Pointing out that Protestantism tends to regard the ultimate as destructive of the penultimate, and that Catholicism is apt to forget that the ultimate does not simply follow on behind the penultimate, Funamoto sees in Bonhoeffer's approach an ethic which addresses itself to the centre rather than the edges of life. His words are worth quoting:

'Catholic theology usually deals with the penultimate (e.g., the natural and culture) in the light of the ultimate (the supernatural) which perfects it, while in Protestant theology righteousness by faith alone is too much emphasized and as a result the ultimate (grace) frequently repudiates the penultimate as insignificant or even sinful. Bonhoeffer, however, with an approach quite original in ethical theory, begins with the ultimate, which undergirds and safeguards the penultimate, just as the New Testament and the gospel of the crucifixion and resurrection send us back to the Old Testament and to life here on earth,' (41)

There is much more in Bonhoeffer's treatment of the last and penultimate things which illustrates his predilection for the dialectical technique, as, for example, his understanding of God's justifying word as final in two senses - the qualitative (it is beyond human capacity and reason) and the temporal (it is always preceded by something penultimate). However, a concluding example may perhaps be cited from the section in *Ethics* on 'Natural Life', which was touched upon in the earlier remarks about Nietzsche. Bonhoeffer, explaining that natural life is served and given form by the natural immanent within it, rejected the view that life could be regarded as a means to an end or as an end in itself; it stands between both extremes. However, since there is some truth in each of these positions - life as an absolute confers certain rights, and as a means imposes certain duties - Bonhoeffer suggests that natural life is able to provide a framework within which the gospel can operate. So, provided life's rights and duties are accepted in their proper order, since God gives before he demands, a harmonization of life's privileges and responsibilities becomes possible by this means. (42)

Another important area of polarities dealt with by Bonhoeffer can be described concisely by reminding ourselves of Bonhoeffer's own words from the section in Ethics, 'Christ, Reality and Good'. 'The problem of Christian ethics', he writes, 'is the realization among God's creatures of the revelational reality of God in Christ.... The place which in all other ethics is occupied by the antithesis of "should be" and "is", idea and accomplishment, notice and performance, is occupied in Christian ethics by the relation of reality (*Wirklichkeit*) and realization (*Wirklichwerden*), past and present, history and event (faith)'. (43) The area concerned may be described as that of the contrast between the ideal and the real, and involves the problem of the concrete commandment. In the sentence which follows the above quotation Bonhoeffer describes the problem as one of the relation between Jesus Christ and the Holy Spirit, as indeed it is; but it is one of the few references to the Holy Spirit to be found in the *Ethics*, where 'realization' takes the place usually occupied by 'salvation' in the christian scheme of things.

In this particular area, accordingly, Bonhoeffer seeks to avoid the usual conflicts and dilemmas, which bedevil the traditional ethical encounter between the ideal and the real, by replacing them with a commitment to the ontological Christ who both unifies and reconciles all reality. For just this reason (Bonhoeffer explains) human beings are no longer creatures subject to conflict; by living in the world he is not separated from Christ, and by being Christians they are not separated from the world. (44)

As Bonhoeffer indicated on a number of occasions in *Ethics*, (45) this approach supplies the concrete warrant which he believed to be essential to ethical discourse, if it was not to be conducted in a vacuum or in purely abstract terms. By this means too it can be associated with an authoritative office, and be seen as conforming to the pattern of a definite structure of society. Its merit is that it avoids having to be dependent upon either an empirical or metaphysical positivism, thought of in terms of reality as it is given, or as it should be, for 'systematic construction and metaphysical deduction alike lead to inertness in real life.' (46)

Nevertheless Bonhoeffer still has to suggest specific ways in which, under his 'system', the unity which God gives is given concrete form in his commandment, while avoiding the risks of idealism and positivism. As we well know, he attempts this by means of his concept of *structuring* reality, the basic form of which is the form or structure (*Gestalt*) of Christ. Ethically speaking, 'correspondence with reality' is the same as correspondence with Jesus Christ, or - as Bonhoeffer prefers to describe it - 'conformation with Christ', conceived of initially as taking place in the church. In terms of an ethically responsible life this provides the freedom to relate (or to be 'bound') to God and to one's neighbour. The several ways in which this may be done e.g., deputyship, acceptance of guilt and freedom, venturing decisions, is the subject of extensive treatment by Bonhoeffer in the important section in *Ethics* on 'The Structure of Responsible Life'. (47)

Another important way in which the ethical reality of God's command can be given effect, Bonhoeffer suggests, is through divine mandates, which for Bonhoeffer replaced the traditional Lutheran 'orders of creation'. These have been already much discussed and need no further elaboration here. There is ample justification therefore for James Burtness's comment in his book, *Shaping the Future*, that Bonhoeffer 'is constantly working at the intersection of situations and structures.... The structures for ethical reflection that Bonhoeffer constructs are built on his commitment to time and history as ethical constituents, and to the shaping of the future as the heart of the ethical task.' (48)

Two more examples associated with this particular area under discussion relating to the concrete commandment of God may be briefly mentioned. The first concerns the tension between order and freedom in human activity. As neither ethical absolutism nor ethical situationism are acceptable approaches for Bonhoeffer in seeking the commandment of God, he offers a third way by conceiving of this commandment in terms of 'permission to live as man before God'. This permission is not to be taken as absolute freedom nor licence, since it derives from discipleship and commitment to Christ. God's command is a gracious command, but only in the sense that revealing his will at all is an act of sovereign grace; hence permission entails responsibility - it *commands* freedom, the freedom to obey or disobey God, and thus to live as man *before God*. The permission (in Bonhoeffer's view) is really God's and involves a degree of necessity by defining the area in which God's commandment may be properly heard and obeyed. So the commandment may fittingly be identified as God's will, which allows man the freedom to move confidently along the road in the knowledge that the right decision has already been taken, and is behind him. (49) In this way the dialectic of freedom and obligation in personal life reflects the way in which God has arranged his creation, that is, as a structured reality providing the setting for an 'ordered freedom' which, in the crucified and risen form of Jesus Christ, is passed on to man.

The remaining example in this last area of polarities dealt with dialectically by Bonhoeffer is the relation between law and gospel. In the section 'The Doctrine of the Primus Usus Legis', written as a separate paper but included in the second part of *Ethics*, (50) Bonhoeffer draws attention to the kind of preaching, stemming from the traditional Lutheran distinction between law and gospel, which was largely ineffective because it either concentrated on the law and so preached straight morality, or concerned itself primarily with the gospel and so was purely religious. Bonhoeffer is emphatic that 'this false antithesis of moralizing and religious themes must be replaced by the true distinction between the law and the gospel.' (51)

Bonhoeffer's own solution harks back to his Barthian beginnings,, which familiarized him with the dialectical approach in theology, illustrated by such statements as - 'only he who believes is obedient, and only he who is obedient believes'. (52) In this connection Burtness, supporting the Barthian provenance, refers to Karl Barth's persistent description of the commanding God as a gracious God, and quotes Barth's statement: 'The Law is a form of the Gospel, whose content is Grace.' (53)

Accordingly, in his exposition of the *Primus Usus* (the largely negative and condemnatory function of the law), Bonhoeffer is prepared to say that, since preaching is concerned with the Word of the living God, both law and gospel are contained within it, and that ultimately it is not the preacher but God who distinguishes between them. The distinction between law and gospel, Bonhoeffer believes, derives from the twofold division of reality into sacred and profane spheres, now made one through the coming of Christ.

Bonhoeffer's concept of the justifying Word of God as the ultimate entering into the penultimate, enables him to emphasize both the connection and the distinction between law and gospel, as well as to ensure that there is no precedence of law over gospel nor gospel over law. So as the Christian continues to live in the penultimate while believing the ultimate, law (according to Bonhoeffer) can be seen as containing the gospel and vice-versa. (54) As with the rest of his thinking in *Ethics*, 'in Christ life finds its unity again; the contradiction of "yes" and "no" is indeed present, but it is continually overcome in the concrete action of the man who believes in Christ.' (56)

Following this survey of three areas of contrasting positions - 'act and being', the natural and the unnatural, the ideal and the real - we take up the task of separating out some of the most obvious strengths and weaknesses of Bonhoeffer's approach as it is presented to us in the Ethics. Bearing in mind the point already made about the changing nature of Bonhoeffer's approach in *Ethics*, which to some extent reflects the changing circumstances of his life at the time, (56) we must also have regard to the fact that *Ethics* itself must be seen as a 'staging-post' on a theological journey which lasted for more than two decades, Whether the road from *Sanctorum Communio* to *Letters and Papers*, was a direct route, in terms of development, or suffered diversions, or even re-routing, is still a matter for debate. (57) The position taken here is that this development is more or less continuous - certainly logical - given the nature of the times in which Bonhoeffer lived.

It will be useful, too, to remind ourselves at this stage, of the starting-point adopted by Bonhoeffer for his exploration into ethics; it is in fact traceable to his own christian conviction and the need to work out its implications in an uncertain and turbulent world. God and the world (in Bonhoeffer's view) are somehow to be matched, so that life can be lived in a christian way as God requires it. Since man is unable to become God, God becomes man, so making it possible for man to be man. The purpose of Bonhoeffer's ethical endeavour may therefore be summarized in his own words, as making it possible for 'the reality of God (to)...↲ show itself everywhere to be the ultimate reality.' (58)

From this starting-point we can single out four important leading ideas which may be regarded as strengths in Bonhoeffer's presentation of ethics. The first relates to the theocentric, or christocentric, character of his thought. In an impressively argued book, *Theology and Ethics*, James Gustafson propounds a thesis that the weakness of most traditional western systems of ethics is their anthropological approach. 'Culturally, religiously, theologically, and ethically' (he writes) 'man, the human species, has become the measure of all things; all things have been put in the service of man.' (59) Yet the scientific view of man today is less that of 'grandeur' than that of man being seen as a minute fragment in a universal jigsaw. In view of this, according to Gustafson, it is no longer legitimate to assume that God's principal concern is with safeguarding the interests of human beings; instead it makes better sense to believe that God's primary interest is in creation as a whole. (60)

Nevertheless, most theological systems are designed to serve a human rather than a universal need. For example, in the opinion of Gustafson, even Karl Barth's ethics, which could be regarded as the most theocentric of any in this century, represents the commands of God as principally having to do with meeting the needs of man rather than creation. What is therefore required, in Gustafson's view, is a 'Copernican' revolution which shifts the focus of man, in his dealings with God, from himself to one which places the divine creator centre-stage, and makes the divine interests paramount. Gustafson finds support for this view in H. Richard Niebuhr's conviction that when the world and life are correctly understood from a theocentric perspective, present disorders can be more accurately evaluated, and God's overall purpose accepted as the object of man's confidence and loyalty.

Judged in the light of this change of perspective Bonhoeffer's essentially theocentric approach to ethical discourse must be accounted a strength. Beginning as he does with a concept of reality, totally embraced by God and reconciled to him through the Incarnation, Bonhoeffer ensures that man's plight and his forgiveness are placed in a context which neither humiliates nor exalts him. On the one hand, man's humanity is seen to be derived from God and the work of Christ; on the other, it is seen to be fulfilled only in so far as man makes the appropriate faith-commitment himself. Bonhoeffer's own succinct statement of the importance of the theocentric perspective occurs in a paragraph in which, after rejecting the idea that the reality of the individual or of the world can be starting-points for consideration of christian ethics, declares that the only basis 'is the reality of God as He reveals himself in Jesus Christ.' Bonhoeffer then continues:

> 'It is fair to begin by demanding assent to this proposition of anyone who wishes to concern himself with the problem of a Christian ethic. It poses the ultimate and crucial question of the reality which we mean to reckon with in our lives.... For the question conveys us into the midst of its origin, the reality of the revelation of God in Jesus Christ.' (62)

A second leading idea in the *Ethics* which may be accounted a strength is that of concretion. Heinrich Ott, in *Reality and Faith*, puts the quest for a concrete ethic high on his list of important elements in Bonhoeffer's thought, and instances Bonhoeffer's commitment 'to the way of a situation ethic with content' and 'the concept of the "concrete place", a nexus of experience and responsibility'. (63) These may be said to cover the two points at which the revelation becomes concrete, and in which Bonhoeffer himself was especially interested - the individual and the place. In the case of a concrete place, we have already shown that Bonhoeffer's concern goes back at least to his *Sanctorum Communio*, where the divine revelation is located in the church, and that his insistence on an earth-bound ethic for the individual is traceable to his Barcelona address on a christian ethic delivered in 1929. In both cases Bonhoeffer was very much preoccupied with the idea of earthly reality, and with the problem of living in the world as it is. In an important comment Gerhard Ebeling makes it clear that, for Bonhoeffer, the church was never a mere theoretical possibility at any stage in his life. Both Bonhoeffer's criticism and support spring from his concept of reality which necessitated a concrete, visible entity by which to test the validity of his entire theological position. (64) Similarly, Ebeling suggests, by insisting that the proclamation of the Word has positive and concrete content Bonhoeffer was making it equally plain that 'reality' is 'real' and capable of making its demands upon men in terms of ethical commitment and activity. (65)

In the *Ethics* the chief way in which the concrete reality of God is mediated, both in the church and in ethical behaviour, is through conformation with Christ. Again we are indebted to Ott for his reminder that, 'the thought of conformation includes a strong moment of the personal; it is no longer in the last resort a matter of the realization of ideas and principles, or of abstract duties, virtues and values, but of encounter with a concrete person, of correspondence to him and response to him.' (66) Because Jesus Christ structures all reality and is encountered as a person, according to Ott, content as well as continuity is provided in all situations, and formalism and casuistry are avoided. The strength therefore of Bonhoeffer's notion of concreteness, we believe, follows from its association with a theory of reality which links both earth and heaven and embraces both God and man.

The third leading idea which is a strength in *Ethics* is 'worldliness' i.e., giving prominence to the world as the place where the things of God are manifested and brought into being. Eberhard Bethge tells us that possible titles considered by Bonhoeffer for the *Ethics* included, 'The foundations and structure of a world which is reconciled with God', and also 'The foundations and structure of a united west'. (67) That the plight of the world was to be a major consideration in Bonhoeffer's ethical study is also borne out by the subject matter of the opening chapters entitled 'The Love of God and the Decay of the World' and 'The Church and the World'. (68) Much too of what follows, as we know, takes up the theme of the reality of the world, including specifically the history of the West, which Bonhoeffer believed had fallen away from Christ and which 'as a historical and political form, can be "justified and renewed" only indirectly, through the faith of the

Church.' (69) The explanation for this is that the world, like everything else, is created through Christ, exists in him and finds its true end in him alone. The reality of human existence has a similar basis and justification. So the divine mandates and the penultimate come into their own as the spheres in which christian responsibility is exercised and the process of redemption may begin.

It must be said, however, that too much concentration on worldly concerns was later to bring Bonhoeffer dangerously close to a purely anthropological interpretation of Christianity - by the middle of 1944 he was convinced that he had 'come to know and understand more and more the profound this-worldliness of Christianity.' (70) The question of how far divine transcendence is being interpreted in terms of the world is a familiar one for students of *Letters and Papers*, but in the *Ethics*, as long as the concept of the 'form of Christ' continues to dominate Bonhoeffer's thinking, all is well. Hence, the following passage, in which the church is interpreted in terms of the world, is properly to be found in the context of the chapter 'Ethics as Formation':

> 'The church, then, bears the form which is in truth the proper
> form of all humanity. The image in which she is formed is the
> image of man. What takes place in her takes place as an example
> and substitute for all men.' (71)

It is on this basis too that Bonhoeffer justifies the responsibility which Christians must bear for 'the preparing of the way' (*Wegbereitung*) for what God will do in history - incidentally, providing him with the idea for another possible title for the book as a whole. (72) Bonhoeffer's interest in helping to shape the western world for the benefit of future generations is in no way unrealistic; it is bound up with his belief that the Word of God embraces the reality of the world, and that action in accordance with it should determine its shape.

A fourth strength in Bonhoeffer's ethical approach is his concept of 'responsible action'; this consists in the fact that it describes quite clearly what kind of Christian is required for the purpose of engaging in ethical activity, and who can be trusted with the task of shaping the future. Such a Christian is one who can combine simplicity with wisdom. Simplicity, for Bonhoeffer, means holding fast to God in all circumstances; being single-minded and therefore stable in all one's ways. Wisdom consists in the capacity to see reality as it is, and in the ability to 'recognize the significant in the factual'. Thus, 'to look in freedom at God and at reality, which rests solely upon him, this is to combine simplicity with wisdom.' (73) As we already know, according to Bonhoeffer, the place where God and reality are reconciled 'lies in the midst of history as a divine miracle. It lies in Jesus

Christ, the Reconciler of the World.' (74) The combination of simplicity and wisdom is thus achieved by personal commitment to Jesus Christ, the crucified and resurrected One, who comprises all reality.

Responsible action however includes responsibility for 'proving' the perfect will of God, (75) since Bonhoeffer is quite insistent that the effect of commitment to Christ does not mean that emotion and intuition take over. Observation, reflection, examination and understanding must all play their part in the renewing and transforming of the mind into conformation with Christ. This is the result of divine grace which is renewed every morning. The proving of God's will, in Bonhoeffer's view, must manifest itself in concrete life and action; and this is only possible on the basis of the knowledge of God's will in Jesus Christ. The responsible Christian, he believes, may rest in the assurance that he will receive certain knowledge of God's will, if he is prepared to seek it humbly and in prayer. Then, 'after all this earnest proving, there will also be the freedom to make a real decision and with it the confidence that it is not man but God Himself who, through this proving, gives effect to His will.' (76) Prayerful submission to the judgement of Christ in whom, and through whom, the decision is made is therefore the dynamic which brings about responsible action, as far as Bonhoeffer is concerned. In all this there is a good deal that reflects scriptural and traditional Christian spirituality, and therein lies its strength.

We now turn to the consideration of possible weaknesses in Bonhoeffer's *Ethics*, again concentrating on leading ideas rather than commenting on points in detail. It is first necessary, however, to enter a *caveat*. Many of the usual criticisms of Bonhoeffer's theology tend to be written from the later standpoint of the prison letters, or from the perspective of his writings as a whole, seen as connected or disconnected, as the case may be. Such criticisms generally centre on the number of questions which Bonhoeffer perforce left unanswered, or on the many ambiguities of which he was undoubtedly guilty. (77) Our comments therefore on what are to be regarded as weaknesses in *Ethics* will avoid, as far as possible, such general criticisms, but will concern themselves with what is to be found there and with what must be seen as essential to its approach.

With this in mind, we take up the first of the main weaknesses of *Ethics*, which has to do with the question of its applicability. In a famous sermon Bishop Butler said of morality and religion (linking the two) that it 'must be somewhat plain and easy to be understood: it must appeal to what we call plain common sense, as distinguished from superior capacity and improvement; because it appeals to mankind.' (78) The question must accordingly be asked - how universal in its appeal is Bonhoeffer's approach likely to be? Heinrich Ott has few doubts about this; he sees a definite resemblance, for example, between Bonhoeffer's christological outlook and

Karl Rahner's universalist interpretation of christology. (79) Furthermore Ott also believes that in the world of Eastern thought 'there can be seen a clear trend towards a universalist view of the reality of Jesus Christ.' (80) However, it must be said that for Ott the universal appeal of the ontological Christ rests not simply upon the presentation in *Ethics* but also on what went before and, of course, what follows in *Letters and Papers*, (81) Keith Clements in his book, *Patriotism for Today*, after raising the question whether Bonhoeffer's writings (including *Ethics*) do not leave us with a 'bourgeois, conservative and elitist' impression, concerned more with individual than with corporate action, nevertheless concludes, on balance, that Bonhoeffer is affirming an ethic of solidarity from which much can be learned about patriotism today. (82)

A close examination of the *Ethics* does in fact suggest an approach to ethical discourse and behaviour which conveys the feeling of being over-academic and of limited application. Although the book is given a general title 'Ethics' (*Ethik* being the German title too), Bonhoeffer regularly refers to a 'Christian ethic' in the text, and the arguments deployed rest for their cogency upon particular theological and philosophical assumptions. In addition, in spite of his undoubted concern for the 'christianizing' of the West his treatment of its history tends to be almost exclusively from an individualistic perspective. The purpose of the claim of Christ (according to Bonhoeffer) is to produce men who are real men before God; but little is said about historical institutions, or societies which need to be 'made real before God', and whose effect on the course of history is at least as influential as that of individuals. Whether this omission is a natural one, understandable in view of his protestant background, or whether Bonhoeffer would have wished to remedy it later, must remain a mystery; the intriguing thing is that the means are there to deal with this, namely, in his concept of a corporate reality which is structured by Christ. Although Bonhoeffer himself insisted that the structure of responsible life carried with it the implication that 'no man can altogether escape responsibility, and this means that no man can avoid deputyship' - not even the solitary, 'for his life is lived in deputyship for man as man, for mankind as a whole' (83) - it must be admitted that this kind of universalist remark of itself is insufficient to commend Bonhoeffer's ethical package for acceptance world-wide. A pluralistic and multifaith society would find many of the arguments difficult to swallow. Bonhoeffer's *Ethics*, as we have it, is primarily for the christian believer, and only in an indirect sense could it be said to appeal to members of other faiths, or to secular man.

The next weakness in *Ethics* concerns Bonhoeffer's concept of 'structured' reality. It is no secret, as was pointed out earlier, that Bonhoeffer was deeply indebted to G. W. F. Hegel for his overall view of reality. It is also generally agreed that Bonhoeffer was fully alive to the dangers inherent in Hegel's thinking of identifying God completely with reality, and of subjecting faith to reason. The principal means whereby God structures reality, according to Bonhoeffer, is first through the Incarnation and thereafter through divine mandates, structures of responsible life, and the ultimate-penultimate relationship. The problem which this poses is bound up with the tight-rope which Bonhoeffer tries to walk between ontology and theology. There are occasions in *Ethics* when ontological considerations appear to dominate, and spatial imagery and terminology are frequently used. (84) These tend to be the occasions, too, when the stress is upon incarnation rather than redemption, and when the 'vertical' encounter of God with man in Jesus Christ gives way to the 'horizontal' realisation of his form in human life and creation. Hiroki Funamoto in fact appears to believe that Bonhoeffer, through his concept of the christological structuring of reality, is able to maintain the balance between the 'vertical' and the 'horizontal'. He writes:

> '(The) commandment which comes from God in Jesus Christ has already been fulfilled in the Person of Jesus Christ through His substitutionary work.... For Bonhoeffer ethics is always grounded in the Word of God and the work of Christ and finds its fulfilment in man's participation in the substitutionary work of Christ through the deputyship of being for the other.' (85)

Funamoto's emphasis here is clearly more upon the outside intervention, which brings about salvation, than upon the inner structuring which also effects it. André Dumas, from the opposite angle, insists however that 'since structural and horizontal vocabulary seems, in fact, less suited for speaking about revelation, which is indeed an amazing historical event, constantly renewed eschatologically', Bonhoeffer deliberately adopts a 'forthrightly spatial vocabulary' in order to remove any doubt 'whether an outside event can ever fully make its way into reality.' (86) In other words, for Dumas, Bonhoeffer's use of spatial terms to describe God's revelation in Christ actually safeguards the historicity and actuality of the event. It may conceivably be believed that confusion is here worse confounded. The important thing for our purpose is that there is undoubtedly some confusion at this point. It is difficult to accept that Bonhoeffer wholly succeeds in his intention to reconcile what is basically a Hegelian ontology with Barthian transcendentalism. It is impossible to be certain which has the upper hand in this particular area of *Ethics* - ontology or theology.

That there is substance in this criticism is borne out by the absence in *Ethics* of any clear explanation as to how the church relates to the world, since both are included in the one reality which is structured by Christ and in which his form is being realized. The problem is one and the same as that outlined above. It is no accident therefore that some have seen in the development of Bonhoeffer's later radical thought a tendency for his ontology more and more to take over, and for his theology to merge into humanism. (87) While this viewpoint is by no means incontestable, the prison letters do suggest that Bonhoeffer was continuing to find the problem of the relation of Christ to reality a difficult one, and was moving in the direction of a purely immanentist christology more easily accommodated to a world-come-of-age.

A third leading idea which must be considered a weakness is connected with the way in which Bonhoeffer attempts to deal with concrete formation. Bonhoeffer himself seems to acknowledge this in the section headed 'The Concrete Place', (88) where early on he comments: 'the question of how Christ takes form among us here and now... contains within itself still further difficult questions. What do we mean by "among us", "now" and "here"?' (89) In the paragraph which follows, Bonhoeffer warns us that 'among us', 'now' and 'here', when interpreted simply according to each individual's experience, runs the risk of vagueness and unrestrained individualism. To offset this there are 'collective' as well as 'individual' situations which present us with concrete problems to be considered. These follow from the fact that 'by our history we are set objectively in a definite nexus of experiences, responsibilities and decisions from which we cannot free ourselves again except by an abstraction.' (90) We have already shown that Bonhoeffer's survey of the history of the West (which follows here) regrettably is treated almost exclusively from an individualistic stand-point, and this is accepted too by Heinrich Ott, who regards Bonhoeffer's efforts to deal with the collective situation as a failure. He adds that it should not be impossible for some ethicist 'to say within the framework of a collective situation how Christ is able to take form among us.' (91)

Ott however is among those who believe that time and history are nonetheless vital for Bonhoeffer, as indeed is James Burtness. The latter takes issue with Dumas, who (as we have seen) asserts that Bonhoeffer speaks frequently of Jesus Christ as structure and place, but seldom refers to him as an event in history. By contrast Burtness and Ott, in effect, claim that such words as 'structure' and 'place' in *Ethics* are always controlled by and embedded in time. (92) Akin also to this uncertainty about the concreteness of Christ-formation in time and history, are similar doubts about Bonhoeffer's mandates. The doubts will not be pursued here, beyond noting Karl Barth's well-known anxiety about the number and apparent arbitrariness of the mandates. Barth's hope and expectation was that Bonhoeffer might perhaps be clearer and more concise in another context. (93)

There is little doubt therefore that we have to enquire whether Bonhoeffer in the *Ethics* was completely successful in validating his concept of the concrete - certainly his spatial imagery and idea of Christ-formation were later to recede into the background. The question seems to turn upon the way in which Bonhoeffer's spatial and structural terminology is interpreted. Can it be taken to embrace and include the historical (as Bonhoeffer no doubt intended it to be) - or, as employed within the context of formation, can it only be understood ontologically? Either way, the lack of clarity suggests a weakness.

A fourth weakness is that Bonhoeffer's ethical approach in the *Ethics* is incomplete. This makes it difficult to put him in any specific category. Nevertheless, attempts have been made, especially by American writers, to classify him as a 'relationist', that is to say, one whose ethics are a response to what God has done for us and all mankind. For example, Edward LeRoy Long in his *Survey of Christian Ethics*, which classifies christian ethics into three basic categories - prescriptive, institutional and relational - places Bonhoeffer's approach in the third category. (94) Frederick C. Carney in an opening contribution to the collection of essays in *Norm and Context in Christian Ethics*, after similarly describing three basic positions in Christian ethics - 'virtue, principles and rules' - lists Bonhoeffer under 'virtue'. (95) This is the position which concentrates on the basic attitude of the agent in an endeavour to avoid moral legalism, or the making of merely institutional decisions. The attitude of the agent, by this definition, may be said to derive from an act of commitment on his part, as, for example, to the doctrine of justification by faith.

Again, Bonhoeffer's stress on the given situation has led some to describe him as a 'situationist'. Without a doubt the given situation must be considered as an important ingredient in Bonhoeffer's account of ethical decision-making, but it is not determinative. His insistence on the crucial nature of time and place in this respect must be seen within the context of the thinking in *Ethics* as a whole, taking into account (for example) his framework of Christ-formation, and in particular the concept of deputyship, both Christ's and ours. Other students of Bonhoeffer's ethics - chiefly associated with traditional approaches - describe his ethic as too arbitrary, or too subjective, and at best only prolegomena to the task of ethics proper - a kind of pre-ethics. Certainly it is pertinent to ask whether (like Barth's) his ethics are not almost indistinguishable from his theology. Burtness, who raises this point, describes Bonhoeffer's approach as 'ethical theology' and suggests that he 'perhaps unconsciously, struggled to formulate a theology that is penetrated at every point by ethical concerns and issues and questions.' (96) Ernst Feil accepts this description, and subscribes to the view that 'practice became more important for Bonhoeffer than theory; as a consequence, ethics was strongly integrated into dogmatics'. (97)

The most that can be said is that Bonhoeffer's primary concern was with an ethical ethos or style of life, which could be seen to follow from a commitment to the revelation of God in Jesus Christ and concretely formed in men and in the world. Unfortunately, the links which should connect his concept of Christ-formation with our everyday conduct seem to be woefully inadequate - the need is not met by references to divine mandates, deputyship and the like. Thus there would appear to be some justification for the criticism that what we have in *Ethics* is, generally speaking, not ethics but prolegomena. Bonhoeffer himself would undoubtedly have rejected this suggestion; not simply because there was so much more he had to say but also because, at the heart of his thinking, there was a firm reliance upon the divine initiative of grace which enables both men and creation to be conformed to the likeness of Jesus Christ. Whether in the nature of things this was bound to produce an ethic which is tentative, provisional and on-going is a question which remains highly debatable. As it is, we can express nothing but regret that more specific content and direction were not forthcoming.

FOOTNOTES

(1)   Cited by Dumas, *Dietrich Bonhoeffer: Theologian of Reality*, pp.75-
       6, fn.88.
(2)   See Peters, *Die Präsenz des Politischen*, p.91 and pp.145-51 for the
       view that Bonhoeffer was influenced by the *'pragmatismus'* of William
       James during his stay at Union Theological Seminary 1930-1.
(3)   Cf., 'acquired knowledge cannot be divorced from the existence in
       which it is acquired'. *CD.*, p.43.
(4)   See *E.*, p.62, fn.1.
(5)   'The Challenge of Dietrich Bonhoeffer's Life and Theology' in *World
       Come of Age*, p.28.
(6)   See *LPP.*, 3:8:44, p.378.
(7)   See letter, Phillips, *The Form of Christ in the World*, Appendix 2,
       p.250. Also Bonhoeffer's addresses at Harnack's retirement and funeral,
       DB., p.102.
(8)   *E.*, p.197.
(9)   *Ibid.*, p.365.
(10)   See *ibid.*, pp.193f.
(11)   See *ibid.*, pp.227ff.
(12)   Bethge, *DB.*, (German edition), pp.266ff. Cited in Dumas, op. cit.,
       p.216, fn.3.
(13)   See E., pp.85,88.
(14)   *Ibid.*, p.190.
(15)   See *LPP.*, 30:4:44, 5:5:44, 8:6:44, pp.280,286,329. Also letter in
       Phillips, *The Form of Christ in the World*, Appendix 2, p.251. cf., F.
       Sherman, *Handbook of Christian Theology*, 1974, p.470.
(16)   pp.204-5.
(17)   Letter to P. W. Herrenbrück, *op.cit.*, p.252.
(18)   *AB.*, pp.90f.
(19)   *Ibid.*, p.81, fn.1.
(20)   Cf., F. Nietzsche, *Beyond Good and Evil*, 1973, pp.90ff.
(21)   See *E.*, pp.190, 268, 221.
(22)   *Ibid.*, p.277.
(23)   See *ibid.*, pp.149f.
(24)   Ibid., p.220.
(25)   Letter to P. W. Herrenbrück, *op.cit.*, p.251.
(26)   *LPP.*, 30:5:44, p.282.
(27)   E.g., Ott. *Reality and Faith*, pp.58-61 and Müller *Von Der Kirche
       zur Welt*.
(28)   Jean Bauberot, cited in Dumas, *Dietrich Bonhoeffer: Theologian of*

Reality, p.263, fn.30.

(29) p.14.
(30) *Ibid.*, p.16.
(31) 'The Non-Religious Interpretation of Religious Concepts' in *Word and Faith*, pp.284ff.
(32) *E.*, pp.198-9.
(33) *Reality and Faith*, p.170.
(34) *Ibid.*, especially Chapters 4 & 10.
(35) *Dietrich Bonhoeffer: Theologian of Reality*, p.269.
(36) *Ibid.*, p.270.
(37) *Ibid.*, p.144.
(38) See above, Chapter 5.
(39) *E.*, pp.144-5.
(40) *Ibid.*, pp.133-4.
(41) 'Penultimate and Ultimate in Dietrich Bonhoeffer's Ethics' in *Being and Truth*, 1986, p.387.
(42) See *E.*, pp.150f.
(43) *Ibid.*, p.190 (*Ethik*, pp.202-3).
(44) See *ibid.*, p.201.
(45) E.g., pp.85ff., 270ff.
(46) *Ibid.*, p.276.
(47) pp.224ff.
(48) p.67.
(49) See *E.*, pp.281ff. Cf., Barth: law is the form of the gospel, command is permission, *Church Dogmatics*, 11/2, 1957, pp.583-630.
(50) pp.302-19.
(51) p.316.
(52) *CD.*, p.54.
(53) 'Gospel and Law' in *Community, State and Church*, 1960, cited in *Shaping the Future*, p.112.
(54) Cf., *SP.C.*, pp.43-4.
(55) *E.*, p.221.
(56) See Bethge, *DB*, p.625.
(57) See especially Feil, *The Theology of Dietrich Bonhoeffer*, pp.3-4.
(58) *E.*, p.188.
(59) p.82.
(60) See *ibid.*, especially pp.88ff. cf., St Augustine (*City of God*), 'It is the nature of things considered in itself, without regard for our convenience or inconvenience that gives glory to the Creator.' Cited by H. Oppenheimer in *Looking Before and After*, Collins, 1988, p.118.
(61) *Theology and Ethics*, Vol.1, p.193. See H. Richard Niebuhr, *Radical Monotheism and Western Culture* 1960, pp.48-89.

(62) *E.*, p.190.
(63) p.276.
(64) *In Word and Faith*, p.282.
(65) *Ibid.*, p.284.
(66) pp.277f.
(67) Preface to 1948 edition. *E.*, (1964), p.12.
(68) pp.17-54, 55-63, cf., pp.88ff., 196ff.
(69) p.117.
(70) *LPP.*, 21:7:44, p.369.
(71) p.83.
(72) See *ibid.*, p.12.
(73) *Ibid.*, p.69.
(74) *Ibid.*
(75) Cf., Romans 12:2 (RSV marg.).
(76) *E.*, p.40.
(77) E.g., Godsey, *The Theology of Dietrich Bonhoeffer*, p.279, Ott, *Reality and Faith*, p.286, Dumas, *Dietrich Bonhoeffer: Theologian of Reality*, pp.193, 213, 237.
(78) *The Works of Bishop Butler*, Vol.1. (ed. J.H. Bernard) 1900, Sermon 5, pp.81-2.
(79) *Reality and Faith*, pp.432ff., 372.
(80) *Ibid.*, pp.402ff., 372.
(81) See *LPP.*, 27:7:44, p.373.
(82) pp.137ff.
(83) p.225.
(84) See especially 'Ethics as Formation', pp.64ff.
(85) In *Being and Truth*, *op.cit.*, pp.388-9.
(86) *Dietrich Bonhoeffer: Theologian of Reality*, p.218.
(87) E.g., H. Müller. See Dumas *op.cit.*, pp.248ff.
(88) *E.*, pp.85-8.
(89) *Ibid.*, p.86.
(90) *Ibid.*, p.87.
(91) *Reality and Faith*, p.275.
(92) See Burtness, *Shaping the Future*, pp.59, 67-9, 88, 90.
(93) Letter to P. W. Herrenbrück in *The Form of Christ in the World*, p.251.
(94) See pp.117ff.
(95) See pp.3ff. 'Deciding in the Situation: What is Required?'
(96) *Shaping the Future*, p.25, cf., p.65.
(97) *The Theology of Dietrich Bonhoeffer*, pp.xx and 46.

CHAPTER 8

ETHIC OF REALITY

When Bonhoeffer was arrested at his parents' home in April 1943 the Gestapo found on his desk the notes on which the present Chapter 7 of *Ethics* is based. They were of course unfinished and, although they were afterwards returned, he was not to take up the writing of *Ethics* again. These notes are particularly tantalizing from our point of view in that they take up the theme 'The Ethical and the Christian' (as the chapter heading indicates) and were clearly intended to deal with the practical implications of christian living and acting in the real world. (1) This is precisely the area we are anxious to investigate as being the most relevant to the practice of ethics today. Bonhoeffer does in fact give us a clue to his intentions by suggesting that he is about to examine the working of God's commandment in the mandates, but regrettably this goes no further than a discussion on the mandate of the church. (2)

More to the point however is the question raised by Bonhoeffer at the beginning of the chapter as to whether the 'ethical' and the 'Christian' is a fit subject for discussion at all, particularly in view of his dismissal of moral norms. – either idealistic or positivistic – as authoritative guides to ethical conduct. His conclusion is that it is far from clear what an 'ethic' or an 'ethicist' is; instead Bonhoeffer believes that it is better to begin by saying what they are not:

> 'An ethic cannot be a book in which there is set out how everything in the world actually ought to be but unfortunately is not, and an ethicist cannot be a man who always knows better than others what is to be done. An ethic cannot be a work of reference for moral action which is guaranteed to be unexceptionable, and the ethicist cannot be the competent critic and judge of every human activity. An ethic cannot be a retort in which ethical or Christian human beings are produced, and the ethicist cannot be the embodiment or ideal type of a life which is, on principle, moral.' (3)

In the light of this, any attempt to interpret Bonhoeffer's *Ethics* in the context of christian ethics today faces acute difficulties by way of presenting a clear definition of its approach, or of drawing out the practical implications of what it contains. These difficulties are further increased, as

Tiemo Peters has pointed out, by the fact that *Ethics* has remained a
fragment, not only in the sense that it consists of drafts and incomplete
studies, but also because it does not anticipate or help with the ethical
problems of Peters' own day. In Peters' opinion there is an element of
rigidity (*starr*) in Bonhoeffer's teaching, for example on the mandates,
which is directly attributable to the situation in Nazi Germany in which he
was compelled to think out his ethics, and which prevented him from
confronting wider and more extensive problems. (4)

Allied to this is the question of how far Bonhoeffer's thinking in the
Ethics is complete enough, or sufficiently settled, to provide firm foundations upon which to build today. We know that it is possible to detect
four approaches – even four beginnings – in Bonhoeffer's writing of the
Ethics, (5) and that consequently it cannot be regarded as a systematic
work. While it is hoped that the new critical edition of Bonhoeffer's *Werke*,
now in preparation and asked for by Bethge in his introduction to the
fifth volume of the present edition, will shed further light on the overall
development of Bonhoeffer's thinking, Clifford Green believes that *Ethics*
is the product of a transitional period in the author's life and that his ethical
concepts are lacking in clarity as a result. Had Bonhoeffer survived and
the book been taken up again (Green concludes) it would have had a new
focus and a different orientation. (6)

However, even if we accept that the *Ethics* is a transitional writing, it is
difficult to believe that Bonhoeffer did not regard what had been written
in draft was a work in its own right. That he intended it to be taken seriously
seems to be proved by the immense amount of preparatory reading he
undertook beforehand, (7) and by references to completing his *Ethics* in
the prison correspondence. In the first of these – while admitting that his
ideas were incomplete – Bonhoeffer consoles himself with the thought that
his friend Bethge would probably remember the essentials; in the second
he likens the *Ethics* to a child by which he hopes to be remembered. (8)
It would appear that in view of the seriousness with which Bonhoeffer
himself treated the book, both at the time of writing and later, there is
ample justification for an equally serious treatment of his thinking in *Ethics*
today.

But the case for attempting an evaluation of the *Ethics* against the
background of christian ethics today rests on firmer ground than a mere
plea that we should follow the author's example and take it seriously. In
the first place, although direct comparisons between different periods in
history are almost always misleading (history seldom repeats itself) points
of resemblance nevertheless do occur, particularly at the deeper moral and
spiritual level (how else do we learn from Israel's experience in the Old
Testament?) which make for fruitful comparison. Bonhoeffer's world,

albeit of only four or five decades ago, is no longer our world. We do not have to face the almost total Nietzschean situation of a 'transvaluation of all values' corrupting the moral climate as he did. Nor are we involved in a life or death struggle for national survival as were Germany and other nations in the nineteen-forties. Nevertheless we are not entirely without experience these days of the way in which nihilistic forces can operate, nor of what the rule of terror and subversion can mean. Add to this the ever-present threat of a nuclear holocaust or of global pollution, and we have some of the ingredients for a sense of living in the 'last days' of which Bonhoeffer was so acutely aware.

Bonhoeffer saw this situation in terms of facing 'the void' and interpreted it biblically – as the decisive struggle of the last days and 'the supreme manifestation of all the powers which are opposed to God.' (9) At least one modern student of ethics also describes the modern situation as opening us up to the void, which is characterized as 'meaninglessness, worthlessness and nihilism'. (10) Both writers acknowledge a debt to Nietzsche, but while Bonhoeffer retains his hold on a traditional theistic world-order, Cupitt, the later writer, is convinced that there 'is no moral world-order, no objective purposefulness out there prior to us' and that morality is merely 'a matter of shifting public sentiment.' (11) These two contrasting positions would seem to indicate, broadly speaking, the lines on which the modern debate about moral and ethical issues are likely to be drawn, i.e., between individuals or groups committed to a supernaturalist or metaphysical view of life and those who reject them utterly. Because Bonhoeffer's *Ethics* falls unequivocally into the first category we believe it has much to contribute to christian ethics in our day.

In the second place, while acknowledging that Bonhoeffer's ethical position must be seen as being continually moulded by his response to the Nazi tyranny of his day, we must stress that his deliberate intention was not primarily to respond to a given person or situation but to God. As with Old Testament situations, which he loved to quote, it was not a question of searching in contemporary history for recurrences of centuries' old situations, and of responding to them in like manner, but of letting God be God, and allowing his will to be paramount. Just as in biblical times the individual and the nation responded pragmatically to what was believed to be the Word of God in the time and place where they were, so Bonhoeffer in his own life and times endeavoured to do the same. His ethical concepts arose from this and developed accordingly. God, for Bonhoeffer, could never be an idea or abstraction; he is ultimate reality and 'the claim of this ultimate reality is satisfied only in so far as it is revelation, that is to say, the self-witness of the living God.' (12) From this followed the central importance of the Incarnation and God's concrete commandment, and the conviction that good cannot consist of the realization of ethical ideas, but only 'of the reality of God as the ultimate reality without and within everything that is.' (13)

The case therefore for the continuing relevance of Bonhoeffer's distinctive approach to ethics – tied as it is to history and to place – must finally rest upon the abiding nature of God as reality and the good. To this men are called to respond concretely in whatever age or situation, identifying themselves recognizably with the incarnate Christ in whom the reality of God and the reality of the world are combined. In Bonhoeffer's view the content of ethical decision-making will of necessity vary according to circumstances, but its ethical character will remain constant so long as the endeavour is there to conform to the incarnate, crucified and risen Lord. Hence Bonhoeffer's contention that christian ethics is not, strictly speaking, concerned with ethics nor with ethical systems, but with bringing God to man. By the same token he was prepared to describe Jesus not as an ethical thinker but as one who 'speaks solely of God's way to us and of nothing else.' (14) On the man-ward side, therefore, the emphasis must always be on the response of faith to God's concrete command in Jesus Christ, and the fact that this is always related to a specific time and place. 'God is "always" *God* to us "today" ', he wrote in 1932, and his commandment always concrete to those who obey.' (15)

In practical terms this means two things; first (a point already made in a previous chapter), namely, that Bonhoeffer's *Ethics* has only a limited appeal. (16) That is to say, it cannot be thought of as offering a universal code of ethics which can be recognized by everybody as the relevant answer to the world's moral ills. The *Ethics* is too bound up with christian theological presuppositions, and the need for specific responses to them, for this to happen. Its ultimate vindication must lie in the very nature of Christianity itself, that is, in the belief that a universal and cosmic Christ must eventually be seen to have dominion over the hearts and minds of all peoples and nations, however this truth is finally formulated or expressed. Without a doubt Bonhoeffer thought of the reign of God as being consummated in terms similar to these – as indeed does the New Testament. For practical purposes, however, Bonhoeffer was content to think and work within the parameters of his own personal experience and history. He was a committed Christian, a product of the West, deeply involved in contemporary events, and it is this which endows his ethical thinking with force and authority. Any relevance which Bonhoeffer's theology and ethics (the two – as we have seen – are practically identical) have for us today springs from his engagement with what he himself described as 'reality'. In the words of Ernst Feil:

'Concrete reality, as represented by the concrete real God, the concrete historical incarnation of God's word in Jesus Christ, the concrete empirical church, is in every instance the basis on which (Bonhoeffer's) theology makes its deliberations; the latter are a posteriori, but are nevertheless appropriate on account of that.' (17)

Second, arising out of Bonhoeffer's close identification of ethics with theology, (18) it is futile to treat the *Ethics* as if it were a blueprint directly applicable to each and every ethical problem. Our point is, that just because Bonhoeffer places human life and behaviour so firmly within the setting of God's dealings with mankind and the world, it does provide us with a sure basis for re-thinking christian ethics at the present time. Again we must emphasize our essential agreement with Bonhoeffer's central position that any re-thinking of christian ethics must be anchored in a firm belief in God as reality, at work in nature and history, both as creator and redeemer. For this reason such an ethic must be ready to change and develop as it relates to the historical, sociological and other aspects of the environment in which we live. Hence also we need to hold in tension the elements of continuity and change, present in all life-experience, of which Bonhoeffer himself was so acutely aware. (19)

In sum, therefore, we see the chief relevance of Bonhoeffer's *Ethics* for christian ethical thinking today in his insistence that we are called upon – collectively and individually – to live responsibly before God and our neighbour in the real world. We shall be examining what this means in three specific areas of human behaviour a little later, but at this point we need to remind ourselves of what is implied by this characteristically Bonhoefferian statement.

To begin with, there can be no ambiguity about what constitutes reality; it is God himself who in Jesus Christ has entered into the reality of this world, making of both realities one. 'Living' accordingly results from incorporation into Jesus Christ, by means of which we participate in the divine reality, or the good. The way to goodness – the supreme ethical quest – is thus through a commitment of faith, and to be good, in fact, is to live. Consequently what is important in seeking to become good is to know the will of God as it operates in the reality of this world and in history. Such a knowledge of God's will or commandment comes to us through the incarnate, crucified and risen Christ, so that the Pauline injunction to live and die with Christ is a paramount consideration for the ethicist.

The virtual identification of ethical behaviour with religious experience is therefore inescapable. The coming together of belief and action, man and his neighbour, the sacred and the secular in an all-embracing reality is what Bonhoeffer means by 'responsible living'. Being bound to God and to one's neighbour leaves one free to take part fully in the reality of the life God has given to us to live. 'It is the fact' (Bonhoeffer writes), 'that life is bound to man and to God which sets life in the freedom of a man's own life. Without this bond and without this freedom there is no responsibility. Only when it has become selfless in this obligation does a life stand in the freedom of a man's truly own life and action.' (20)

From this fundamental theological and ethical position of Bonhoeffer's, which we have outlined, flow several corollaries, the first of which points to the need to adopt a new stance or perspective in order to be able to view reality in a new way. This of course is to say no more than what is intended by the customary references to 'conversion' or to seeing things '*sub specie aeternitatis*' – except that in Bonhoeffer's case this stance or perspective is located within reality itself. For this reason, if we fully participate in reality, living itself is a sufficient ethical activity to relieve us of the need continually to strive for the right decision, or to exhaust ourselves in a conflict of responsibilities. (21)

Moreover, because the good is not just a quality of life but the life of Jesus Christ, we live only by responding to the commandment of God which addresses us in Jesus Christ. Life engages with life and this, in our own case, means the totality of life, as it does with Jesus Christ, and includes both the 'yes' and 'no' parts of it. So that partial responses are not enough; our whole life is pledged to Jesus Christ, involving our inadequacies and shortcomings as well as our fulfilments and joys. Thus in words anticipatory of the total response of his own life Bonhoeffer could say: 'The life which confronts us in Jesus Christ, as a 'yes' and 'no' to our life, requires the response of a life which assimilates and unites this 'yes' and this 'no'. (22)

Again, by making such a response the Christian comes to occupy a priestly role – in Bonhoeffer's terminology, a 'deputy' – he represents Christ before men and men before God. Bonhoeffer was clear that 'there is no relation to men without a relation to God, and no relation to God without a relation to men'. Through Christ's incarnation man is accepted, loved, condemned and reconciled in Christ, so that other human beings are as much our life as God is. This conviction provides us with a true basis for our personal and social relationships, and subjects our encounter with men and God to the same 'yes' and 'no' as does our encounter with Christ. (23) The importance of serving Christ through others – even unwittingly – which is at the heart of the Matthean parable of the Great Judgement (Matthew 25: 31–46) was not lost upon Bonhoeffer, for he referred to it frequently; it strengthened his belief that in responding to Jesus Christ we are assuming responsibility for the lives of others as well as ourselves. A similar responsibility, he was convinced, extends to the world of things which also forms part of the total reality unified by Jesus Christ, a point which we shall take up in more detail later.

A remaining corollary of Bonhoeffer's concept of responsible living in the real world is that such Christians combine in themselves two specific virtues – simplicity and wisdom. As we have already indicated, (24) simplicity, in this case, means holding fast to God in all circumstances, particularly in times of uncertainty and turmoil, while wisdom means recognizing reality wherever it is. This combined God-world orientation again may be said to be true of Bonhoeffer himself – he continued to emphasize it in his later writings; (25) indeed it is almost certain he put it to good use to shape his own life and to determine his own destiny. Regarded purely as an ethical ideal it is contradictory and doomed to failure, as Bonhoeffer well knew, but as the command of God in a world at one with God in Jesus Christ it acquires reality and meaning. (26)

In seeking to apply these insights from the *Ethics* to the present situation, which earlier we acknowledged was one of 'moral confusion' (27) we shall refer briefly to three writers who have clear views on where the emphasis in modern ethical thinking should lie. The first in importance, as well as in time, is unquestionably Reinhold Niebuhr whose contribution in this respect is generally recognized. As a christian ethicist his particular emphasis was his insistence on the need to take into account the religious dimension in all ethical problems and to combine it with a realistic acceptance of human self-centredness and sin. It was this approach which led him to question the optimistic liberalism of both secular and religious thinkers of his day. The importance of religion for morality, Niebuhr declared, lay 'in its comprehension of the dimension of depth in life'; by this means it created 'the tension between what is and what ought to be'. (28) It was Niebuhr's opinion that liberal Christianity – inherited from the nineteenth century – had given a false authority to canonical moral codes and standards and under-emphasized the transcendent ideals for which Christianity stood. The Kingdom of God (for him) was always both a possibility in history and an impossible ideal, and it was necessary for clear ethical thinking that this tension should remain. So that, for example, 'the transcendent impossibilities of the Christian ethic of love' should not become 'the immanent and imminent possibilities of an historical process . . . . and the experience of depth in life . . . . completely dissipated by a confident striving along the horizontal line of the immediate stream of history.' (29)

From this assertion of the need for a transcendent dimension as an essential constituent in the approach to moral problems (essential too for Bonhoeffer), we move on to another writer whose chief concern is with their complexity. In a religious article published in *The Times*, John

Habgood, Archbishop of York, drew attention to the dangers inherent in the belief that there are always simple answers to moral questions – especially contemporary ones. In the course of the article he criticized two opposing ethical standpoints – that of moral absolutism, which dispenses dogmatic, authoritarian answers to moral problems, and subjectivism, which relies on human consciousness and current fashion for its authority. Habgood concedes that there is truth in both positions, but – as he observes – since 'moral insights are neither merely given nor merely invented' the search for the right solution is a highly complex one and the result, more often than not, incomplete and subject to correction. (30) Habgood, whose special interests include science, medicine and politics, is only too well aware of the intractable nature of many of the ethical problems which occur in these areas. As with Bonhoeffer, he is out of sympathy both with those who are slaves to moral absolutes and those who become a prey to ethical irresponsibility and indifference. (31)

   A third writer, to whom we have already referred in connection with the contemporary scene, is Don Cupitt who stands at the opposite pole to Reinhold Niebuhr by his rejection of any objective reality beyond the empirical self. There is little doubt that this view reflects the unspoken working assumptions of large numbers of people today, where ethics are concerned, and so may be regarded as representing an influential point of view. Abandoning any belief in God or the soul in the traditional sense, Cupitt opts for an ethic of self-realization which requires us to say Yes to life here and now; such an appetite for life will be liberating and creative. In a revised christian ethics (he writes) 'pride of place must be given to creative, expressive, value-realizing human action . . . . Everybody can *create* and everybody can be God in the sense of being an original, making the rules and creating values.' (32) This focussing upon life and human fulfilment, instead of eternity, must be seen as offering an important corrective to those whose ethical thinking has been too much concerned with what happens beyond the grave. The need to highlight the elements of moral creativity and freedom, arising from a deep involvement in life itself, was indeed one of which Bonhoeffer himself was well aware; it is also one which finds favour among numerous practitioners of ethics today.

   As we have indicated, each of these three leading thoughts, drawn from writers on modern-day ethics, finds a parallel in the thinking of Bonhoeffer's *Ethics*. In the case of Reinhold Niebuhr (whom Bonhoeffer knew) Bonhoeffer saw the need for a religious dimension as essential to morality, and pinned his faith in the christian revelation. With Habgood also, Bonhoeffer was only too well aware of the complex and incomplete nature of much of ethical decision-making, and relied heavily on faith in forming a judgement. In Cupitt's case, the concentration on human life and self-realization as basic ingredients in ethical formation finds corresponding echoes in large sections of the *Ethics*. Moreover each in turn relates closely to Bonhoeffer's overall concern with an ethic of reality. Reinhold Niebuhr's contention that religion is necessary to give essential depth to life and moral issues clearly has to do with the way we think about reality. Habgood's reminder of the intricate nature of ethical problems – particularly those concerned with modern business, politics and medicine – brings us sharply up against the unreality of trying to deal with such problems without adequate professional knowledge and experience; awareness of reality requires an acknowledgement of human fallibility and acceptance of human limitations. Cupitt, by rejecting entirely any supra-natural framework to human existence, limits reality to life here and now, and by so doing affirms his belief in the sole reality of individuals and the value of personal relationships. Bonhoeffer's particular merit is that, using a christocentric concept of reality, he was able to unite both earthly and heavenly realities in a single whole, thereby giving religious depth to a humanism which is truly of this world. By this means too he was able to give added relevance to the doctrine of the Incarnation and the concept of the body of Christ.

Against this background, we turn first to summarize the main features of an 'ethic of reality', derived from Bonhoeffer's *Ethics*, before moving on – by way of illustration – to relate them to three specific areas of ethical concern – the church, society and the world. The principal features of an ethic of reality can be separated out as follows:

1. The concept of reality as one unified by Jesus Christ through his incarnation, crucifixion and resurrection which allows God, the source of reality, to encounter human-kind in history and creation, both as creator and redeemer.
2. The concept of the church as providing in Jesus Christ a recognizable *locus* for the presence of God, offering (in Bonhoeffer's words) not only a pulpit, but the real life of Christ upon earth. (33)
3. The concept of deputyship, which means that the church and human beings are there for others. The church exists for the world and must be open to it, while persons exist for one another. In this way true community comes into being, through the Incarnation, which heals the divisions within reality and reconciles man with man.
4. The concept of conformation, by which Christians are taken up into the reality of Christ, and the church can be seen as a 'section of humanity in which Christ has really taken form'. (34)
5. The concept of responsibility, which is based on correspondence with

reality, which is God, and dependence upon one's neighbour who is also recognized as a responsible agent.

6. The concept of responsible action, which, while bounded by responsibility to God and one's neighbour, allows freedom to engage in ethical activity without knowledge of the outcome, leaving the judgement entirely to God.

7. The concept of the world as the sphere of concrete responsibility, given in Jesus Christ, in which action is more important than theory and the concrete situation contributes to the shaping of the deed.

8. The concept of the ethical man, who combines simplicity with wisdom, understood within the context of the reality of both God and the world.

It is this context of reality, understood as legitimately christian, which we believe most distinguishes Bonhoeffer's ethical approach, and is of most value to christian ethicists today. The need for spiritual renewal among Christians is evident and this renewal is shown in the moral life. Spiritual and moral renewal are brought about by incorporation into the reality of Christ's body, present in the empirical church, and by conformity to the will of God in concrete decision-making with penitence and faith. Given an environment in which conformity with Christ can take place, and a world in which decisions 'in accordance with reality' can be made, ethical behaviour which reflects the dying and rising activity of the incarnate Christ becomes possible. Even so, it has to be recognized that ethical living and ethical choices for the Christians are for the most part undertaken without any clear awareness of the good – living is by faith rather than by sight. This is true, both of the way the Christian occupies his daily life – without undue concern for its ethical aspect – and of his approach to specific problems. This is 'responsible' activity, which applies equally to the way we live and the way we choose. Thus:

> 'because it was *God* who became man, it follows that responsible action, in the consciousness of the human character of its decision, can never itself anticipate the judgement as to whether it is in conformity with its origin, its essence and its goal, but this judgement must be left entirely to God . . . . When the deed is performed with a responsible weighing up of all the personal and objective circumstances and in the awareness that God has become *man* and that it is *God* who has become man, then this deed is delivered up solely to God at the moment of its performance. Ultimate ignorance of one's own good and evil, and with it a complete reliance upon grace, is an essential property of historical action.' (35)

We begin our consideration of three broad areas of ethical concern by looking at the church. Not only was this for Bonhoeffer a starting-point for christian ethics, it was the only mandate to which he was able to give any real consideration himself in connection with its relation to the commandment of God. (36) Because of the Incarnation and the living presence of Christ in the church its members (consisting of all who hear God's Word and keep it) constitute a model community for mankind as a whole. If, as we believe, christian ethics is socially orientated, the church's responsibility for both showing forth and bringing about true community is inescapable. The case however for treating it as a separate area of ethical concern is not clear-cut. On the one hand, not everyone is a member of the empirical church; on the other, the reality of the church embraces humanity, so that every human being is in some ways a participant in it. As we know, Bonhoeffer faced a similar difficulty in seeking to deal with the church as a separate mandate while at the same time recognizing it was involved in the other three. Our case is that the ethical challenges facing members of the church – as members of the church – and the way they are dealt with, are of unique importance and call for consideration as a separate category.

The first point to be made is that the church of which we speak is both visible and hidden – an earthly, empirical body in which Jesus Christ is present as the embodiment of God's reality, but whose boundaries are ill-defined and subject to change. It belongs to the world, in the sense that it has responsibilities to the world, which indeed give it its *raison d'être*. It occupies a space in the world within which conformation to Jesus Christ takes place, and because of this makes possible the conforming of worldly reality to the reality of Christ. It is to be defined therefore in dynamic rather than static terms because of its openness to the world. As part of God's reality, along with the world, continually under judgement itself, yet continually being healed, the church is not to be thought of purely as an 'ark of salvation', nor wholly to be identified with any particular historical form. It is the object of faith which nevertheless has a concrete existence as the divinely appointed place of encounter between God and man.

From a practical point of view therefore the empirical church, wherever located, is to be regarded first and foremost as the community within which men and women are enabled to be conformed to Jesus Christ. It opens up to Christians, by their commitment and involvement, the possibility of practising an ethic of reality which is worldly and community based. The way to this calls for no new aptitudes or techniques, as far as Christians are concerned. It calls instead for participation in the real body of Christ – identification with Christ in his total ministry rather than a simple 'imitation' – involving the whole person in the whole Christ, thought of ontologically or sacramentally as the case may be. Ethical living for the Christian accordingly begins with his incorporation into membership of Christ's body, on the occasion of his baptism, where he is introduced into the pattern of dying and rising with Christ which is the hall-mark of christian commitment.

The specific means whereby the church enables Christians individually and collectively to be conformed to Jesus Christ are well known and need only be referred to briefly. The empirical church provides the opportunity of hearing the commandment of Christ, proclaimed, expounded and discussed in a systematic and authoritative way, which is not available elsewhere. It offers regular access to the real Christ by means of the sacraments, particularly that of the altar, and it affords the opportunity too of sharing in the fellowship-life of the community on which ethically responsible action should be based. These are familiar enough to any committed church-goer, as the appointed means whereby Christians are enabled to die and rise daily with Jesus Christ and be conformed into his likeness.

Equally important, ethically speaking, is that the church as a community should manifest a similar pattern of living. If it is truly open to the world, and prepared to exercise its responsibility to it, its public attitude and moral behaviour will be affected accordingly. If Jesus Christ, its Lord, entered fully into his worldly obligations and worked out his responsibilities in time and space, the same should be true of his body which occupies space in the world. The temptation to escape from worldly reality, especially in times of stress (as Bonhoeffer well knew) is considerable, and continual vigilance is needed to prevent it from becoming an end in itself instead of existing for others. Its primary task is to realise and make plain the unity of earthly and heavenly reality brought about by Christ, and so gather together mankind and all things into one. In this respect, the responsibility of the church, as the redeemed and redeeming community, far exceeds that of the church thought of simply as a collection of individuals. At this point too the ambivalence of the church's role in the 'summoning of the world into the fellowship of this body of Christ, to which in truth it already belongs', (37) becomes most apparent.

Broadly speaking, the church's responsibility to the world parallels that of individual members to each other within the church. First, there is the church's responsibility as a body to proclaim as concretely as possible Christ's commandment to the world. Needless to say, this will be done as much by sacrificial individual and corporate witness as by formal pronouncements. Such responsible action and pronouncements will often need to be the subject of discussion and decision-making in advance if they are to be fully accepted as authoritative declarations of a body conformed to Christ. They will most frequently be effective when they arise from situations 'in life' which create ethical problems requiring responsible christian answers.

Again, the church's responsibility will be exercised in making explicit to a world which equally belongs to Christ its willing acceptance of the world's shame and guilt as well as its need for forgiveness and renewal. Here the community is best seen doing the work of Christ's deputy, through its sacramental life and the identification of individual members with the corpus of mankind. This vicarious aspect of the church's role is not one which is readily understood or acknowledged in the modern world; the ethical implications of representative action by the church and its members, however, are very profound and go to the roots of what is meant by christian responsibility and manifesting the form of Christ.

The third way in which the church discharges its direct responsibility to the world, and which parallels the third responsibility of Christians to each other within the church, is that of sharing fellowship with the world. In much of what has been said already about responsibility within the church and outside, it is evident that no clear distinction can be drawn between ministering to members within and ministering to the world outside. This is particularly true of the church as it seeks to demonstrate its solidarity with the reality of the world which, like itself, has been taken up into Christ. The need for the world to be made aware of the true nature of the church, as a redeemed and redeeming community, is only too apparent; more to the point, a recognition by the world that it shares in the same reality is vital for its own well-being. It is the task of the church to make this plain. Example will probably be more effective than precept in this connection, much of it turning upon the credibility of the church as a 'true community' in its own life and practice. Even so, direct intervention by the church in the form of advice and specific experiments in community living is not ruled out, and these will be the subject of sensitive decisions and prayer of a highly responsible kind. The overall purpose is to awaken 'secular' human beings to the reality of a world which is already Christ's. The inclusion of a religious dimension in the thinking and decision-making of the present-day world is not one which will necessarily commend itself immediately, but it is an essential pre-requisite for being conformed to Christ.

It is clear that what has been said in the foregoing about the church's responsibility to the world depends on the willingness of its members to be conformed to the likeness of Christ, and in so doing to be his deputies in the service of others. Reinhold Niebuhr, from a more protestant stand-point, is nevertheless a representative christian ethicist in pointing to the need for a vital christian faith to shed light on the complex ethical problems of today. With Bonhoeffer we agree that such vitality must begin with the church. Niebuhr's words however are still relevant:

> 'Only a vital Christian faith, renewing its youth in its prophetic origin, is capable of dealing adequately with the moral and social problems of our age; only such a faith can affirm the significance of temporal and mundane existence without capitulating unduly to the relativities of the temporal process. Such a faith alone can point to a source of meaning which transcends all the little universes of value and meaning which "have their day and cease to be" and yet not seek refuge in an eternal world where all history ceases to be significant. Only such a faith can outlast the death of old cultures and the birth of new civilizations, and yet deal in terms of moral responsibility with the world in which cultures and civilizations engage in struggles of death and life.' (38)

The second area of ethical concern which calls for our attention is that of society, roughly defined as embracing the world of institutions and organizations to be found outside the boundaries of the empirical church. While this definition does not correspond exactly to the distinction drawn by Ferdinand Tönnies between community and society (or association), referred to by Bonhoeffer in *Sanctorum Communio* (39) it is sufficient for our purpose in seeking to describe an area in which the need for 'social ethics' looms large. It is with this socio-political dimension in mind that Tiemo Peters, in his study of Bonhoeffer's theology, criticizes Heinrich Ott for not taking Bonhoeffer's interest in a social ethic (*gesellschaftsbezogehe Ethik*) sufficiently into account, and judges that Ernst Feil's exploration of the historical and social categories in Bonhoeffer's theology also does not take us very far. (40) Certainly it must be conceded that there are difficulties in trying to draw out the implications of Bonhoeffer's approach to a social ethic – not merely (as we have already pointed out) because this part of the *Ethics* was left unfinished, (41) but also because in this thinking the distinction between personal and social ethics was often unclear. That Bonhoeffer recognized the need for a socially-orientated ethic is all too evident – the *Ethics* reflects his deep involvement in the political and social events of the time – but his theological presuppositions precluded any sharp differentiation between personal and social reality.

Bonhoeffer's chief objection to a social gospel as such was the risk it entailed of being identified with material progress. In the *Ethics* chapter which deals with 'Personal and Real Ethos' Bonhoeffer criticizes both liberal theologians who were mainly concerned with personal conversion –

and religious-socialist theologians, whose concern was directed towards converting structures. He argues that, while there is undoubtedly a christian responsibility to be exercised towards secular institutions, it is not for the purpose of making them 'christian institutions', but in order to set them free as secular institutions for genuine worldly service. There is no question of subordinating them to the church, for 'under the dominion of Christ they attain to their own true character and become subject to their own innate law'; nor is it a question of allowing them to become autonomous, which is lawlessness and sin, but of giving to the institutions their rightful place in a world created and reconciled by God, since 'under the dominion of Christ they receive their own law and their own liberty.' (42)

In our case it will not be necessary to lay too much stress on the difference between personal and social ethics when applying the concept of an ethics of reality to society. Whether we regard Christians dispersed abroad in society as individuals or collectively, their ethical impact will stem from participating in a Christ-centred reality based on the church. The individual is involved in social ethics through his membership of the church, and the church is involved in social ethics through its members in society. The temptation to subject to evangelistic pressure key individuals or power-based institutions is very great, but is far from being what is really needed. Instead the priority must be the acceptance of the unity of relationship between Christians and others in society, arising from the christocentric nature of reality which we have already described.

A further point must also be made at this stage; it has to do with the concept of discipleship with which a social ethic must clearly be associated. True discipleship – within the setting of total reality – follows from individual decisions which are made responsibly in accordance with God's will. They occur in situations which are interpreted as God-given and which are bound up with a particular time and place. For this reason they are concrete, existential decisions which step by step contribute to both the moral growth of the individual and to social development. John Godsey is correct, we believe to draw attention to the importance which Bonhoeffer attached to the need for obedience, both in the church's internal life and in the life of its members dispersed abroad. He is a less reliable interpreter of Bonhoeffer, however, when he declares that 'within the theology of the Word of God (Bonhoeffer) has introduced what might be called an *imitatio Christi* theology, which means that the community that is established by the hearing of the word must pattern its life after Christ's own life and thus be transformed into his image.' (43) The truth is that conformation to Christ is entirely God's work and not man's and that Bonhoeffer's ethic is concerned more with realization than with imitation. We are at one with Bonhoeffer in believing that christian discipleship is more than a matter of personal following, essential though that is, but also includes incorporation into his body. The ethical and moral consequences which flow from this incorporation turn as much upon who and what one is as upon particular moral choices made in the following of Jesus Christ. Involvement in social issues will therefore be for us – as it was for Bonhoeffer – a question of the quality of the spiritual resources which authenticate our being, and not simply of what we do or say. Others will take note of us that we are 'in Christ'.

In a recent study of the social psychology of Bonhoeffer's discipleship, Kenneth Earl Morris refers to the similarity between the psychological issues of Bonhoeffer's day and our own. Morris is of the opinion that this similarity accounts for the 'continuing resonance of the ethic of discipleship' which is still heard today. He continues:

> 'These issues – the fragmentation of social (and family) soli-
> darity, the concomitant collapse of authority, the ascendancy
> of instrumental reason, the search for a kind of spiritual authen-
> ticity that will lodge in the political community – are live
> dilemmas in our civilization, as they were equally tormenting
> to Bonhoeffer.' (44)

This quotation from Morris's book is helpful in suggesting specific issues in society which are as problematic for us as for Bonhoeffer – the break-up of family solidarity, the flouting of authority and the lack of spiritual authenticity in politics. We can equate these very roughly with the activities covered by Bonhoeffer's mandates since they have a bearing upon the responsibilities of the church, family, work and government. As we know, he argued that these particular institutions 'are divine in that they possess a concrete divine commission and promise which has its foundation and evidence in the revelation.' (45) Thereby Bonhoeffer was able to single out those who experienced these mandates as possessing a spiritual authority over others in society, by this means fulfilling their function as deputies and instruments of his body.

Bonhoeffer's mandates provide us with suitable illustrations of the way in which an ethic of reality can be applied in society today. We have already considered the church; the family, work and government remain to be considered under this head. All three may be described as 'natural' insti-tutions within society, which are also, for the Christian, part of God's creative ordinance for man. All these too are rightly subjected to critical examination in the name of freedom, economic fairness or democracy; all are affected by the fallenness of man and a flawed creation. The need to place such institutions, and those within them, in a context of grace is vital for a proper understanding of the moral issues which surround them. The ethical choices of both parent and child, employer and employee, ruler and ruled, which are continually vitiated by ignorance and egotism, require such a context – available in the church – if they are to be identified as witnessing to an ethic of reality. A principal ingredient of an ethic of reality (as we know) is the freedom to engage in responsible action. John Habgood puts it another way:

> 'To acknowledge the limitations of actions, and to act within a spirit of forgiveness and an awareness of grace, is to be freed from the paralysis engendered by a sense of our own inadequacies; and freed also from the intolerance which refuses to take seriously the convictions of others.' (46)

The ethical problems which well up everywhere in modern society seem to be incapable of resolution – except possibly on a short term basis – without some recognition of the extent to which our power to act is limited by blindness and self-interest and the degree to which our environment is flawed. Without the possibility of redemption (for creation as well as the creature) ethical decision-making is rudderless. It is not surprising therefore that so much well-intentioned ethical advice directed at social institutions and organisations either falls on deaf ears or fails in its objective. The dilemmas of our twentieth-century civilization, to which Kenneth Morris refers, are to be overcome (in our view) only by a recovery of belief in a Christ-centred reality which both illuminates and empowers the ethical actions of the believer. Into this reality, to which Christ gives form in the church, human beings are incorporated sacramentally, and continue to grow in the form of Christ themselves by acting responsibly as his deputies within the body and without.

On the subject of the first of the three specific spheres of social responsibility represented by Bonhoeffer's mandates, there is little doubt that the family (including marriage) is a prime topic for ethical discourse and debate. The facts are only too familiar – they include marital problems, which now reach out beyond issues like separation and divorce to embrace ethical complexities of a biological, medical, psychological and social kind. The nature of the church's contribution as a body to the world outside has already been referred to in general terms – making pronouncements, bearing guilt, manifesting community, all are applicable to problems affecting marriage and the family as elsewhere. Much however will turn upon the attitude and insights of individual Christians as they approach problems in their own families and seek to influence those of others. Here belief in family life as a divinely appointed place in which the commandment of

God is to be concretely heard and concretely obeyed can be of vital importance. The warrant which it gives for the exercise of authority, the opportunity which it affords for training in spirituality, and the guarantee which
it assures of a lasting union are among the most obvious advantages which
this christian understanding of the family brings. The need for serious
ethical reflection on matters relating to the family are not thereby ruled
out; such an understanding, however, will ensure that the reflection takes
place within the framework of an approach which is productive of hope
rather than uncertainty.

With regard to the second of the spheres suggested by Bonhoeffer's
mandates, we use his umbrella term 'work' rather than industry or labour.
Again we see that an ethic of reality has much to contribute to the solution
of the many problems with which work is associated. Human societies are
profoundly affected by changes in methods of work – the industrial and
computer-based revolutions of recent centuries are evidence of this – and
a developing, rather than a static ethic is clearly an advantage in dealing
with these changes. At the same time, there is a general feeling among
human beings that work is not only a social reality, but should also be
regarded as a vocation, that is, in some sense belong to God. Christians
have long recognised this while at the same time succumbing to the temptation to regard some occupations as more vocational than others. Christian
theology too has made much of the belief that the drudgery which is a
familiar accompaniment of work is somehow bound up with the Fall. The
so-called 'protestant work-ethic' conferred on this a stamp of approval
which only in recent years has come to be questioned.

The need to maintain a balance between seeing work as a duty to God
and as ministering to social needs is clearly essential. To accept that one's
place of work is where a concrete demand of God can be heard and obeyed,
is to open up the possibility, not merely of dealing with problems of
authority but also of resolving the tension which exists between serving
God and one's fellow-men. This tension can only be resolved by 'responsible' action (as we have described it) which, imperfect as it is, is taken up
to form part of the on-going redemptive work of the incarnate Christ.

As in the case of the family, the collective responsibility of Christians
through the church will have its appropriate place in contributing to the
ethical problems connected with work. What needs to be fully understood
is that these problems again will need to be the subject of much prior
reflection and professional study. Industrial and technological development, especially, these days gives rise to multifarious ethical problems –
labour relations, nuclear policies, industrial pollutants, defence issues, to
name but a few; the limitations of human knowledge and moral sensitivity
are only too apparent here. The application of an ethic of reality to such

problems will serve to provide a safeguard against the vitiating sins of arrogance and pride.

The sphere of government, regarded by Bonhoeffer as a mandate, is for our purpose to be interpreted broadly to cover political activity of all kinds, whether organised or not. In few other spheres is the temptation to disengage and shirk responsibility so appealing, or the need to engage in compromise so important. Bonhoeffer's own experience as a political activist is particularly helpful in this respect. Most compromise decisions (he remarks) are arrived at by human beings experiencing disunity in the knowledge of good and evil, and troubled consciences result. The responsible Christian however lives his life in the unity of the knowledge of God, and his conscience is no longer divided since it is part of the total reality unified by Christ. (47) His decisions and actions are determined not by the knowledge of good and evil as such, but by the will of God. So 'it is only upon the foundation of the knowledge of the incarnation of Jesus Christ, that conscience can be free in concrete action. The call of Christ alone, when it is responsibly obeyed in the calling, prevails over the compromise and over the conscience which this compromise has rendered insecure.' (48)

An ethic of reality will be especially concerned too, in the political sphere, with ensuring that government institutions, both central and local, are allowed their true autonomy under Christ, and with recognizing (with Bonhoeffer) that 'there is a godlessness which is full of promise', (49) and that this applies to the state as well as to individuals. Where state and church coexist in uneasy tension, as is implied by the doctrine of the two kingdoms, no guarantee of complete autonomy on either side is possible; where the one Christ is accepted as incarnated in both, each is set free to be itself as part of his dominion. The empirical church confines itself to its legitimate responsibilities – which we have already examined – and the state does likewise. In the words of Ernst Feil: 'The relation of church and state cannot be resolved on the basis of principle. One must examine individually every decision of the church to intervene in politics or to refrain from doing so.' (50)

The same careful scrutiny is called for whenever Christians concern themselves with political activity in whatever form; not only thereby is the nature of political authority clarified but the reshaping of political attitudes becomes possible. The whole however turns upon commitment to concrete action by individuals and organised bodies responding in faith to what is believed to be the concrete will of God.

We are aware that in the foregoing we have done no more than set the making of ethical decisions within a theological framework in which discernment of the divine will – the supreme ethical consideration for

Christians – becomes the principal focus of attention. Engagement with the principalities and powers of this world is an engagement with forces of a very uncertain kind in which compromise is essential, carrying with it the possibility of moral risk and danger. John Habgood is right therefore to argue that political action needs to take place within an objective framework of grace since 'the context of grace, however received and known, allows and makes possible – indeed makes necessary – real admissions of ignorance, partiality and the distorting effects of sinful minds.' (51)

   We come to the last of the three main areas of ethical concern in our assessment of Bonhoeffer's *Ethics* and the value which it has for christian ethics today. This is the area of the world – a term we have already employed rather loosely to describe either worldly reality created by God, or worldly reality in contrast to the church. We now use it in a third sense to focus attention upon those aspects of worldly reality which come under the headings of nature (or creation), persons and things. To each of these, human beings are related in some way or other, and this relationship raises ethical questions. Our discussion however will be confined to positions taken up by Bonhoeffer in the *Ethics* and will not, for example, be concerned with the more radical concept of 'worldly Christianity' associated with his prison correspondence. By way of further clarification it is worth adding that neither in the *Ethics* nor in his later letters does Bonhoeffer restrict reality to the secular world. The kind of world-view of Don Cupitt (for example) in which 'God, the self, the cosmos and objective reality, Meaning, Truth and value have been eaten away' (52) is an entirely secular one, and would not have commended itself to Bonhoeffer. Nor do we believe it should commend itself to us. Cupitt's contention however that the media culture ('mediascape') exerts undue influence over the minds and activities of many people – especially the young – today has considerable substance. His view that 'in the mediascape the distinctions between the real and the fictional, the true and the false, the valid and the invalid, real deeds and fantasies – all such distinctions are consumed and lost', if extreme, needs to be heeded. (53) For our purpose, the conclusion that our contemporaries run the risk of losing the sense of reality itself is of the highest importance. But the remedy is not to limit reality to the empirical world which we see around us, but – in the wake of Bonhoeffer – to affirm our christian conviction that worldly reality is reconciled to God in Jesus Christ, by whom, with whom and in whom, the world is judged, forgiven and healed.

   Bonhoeffer was persuaded that 'this indivisible whole, this reality which is founded on God and apprehended in Him, is what the question of good has in view' (i.e., is a matter of ethical concern), also that 'with respect to its origin this indivisible whole is called "creation" ' and that 'with respect to its goal it is called the "kingdom of God".' (54) The aim of christian ethical action (which we have frequently stressed) is to make concrete or real the revelational reality of God in Christ – a key element in Bonhoeffer's approach – and this requires the response of the whole man to the whole of reality, of which the world is already a part. Accordingly ethical behaviour involves active participation in the reality of God and of the world jointly; one cannot be experienced without the other. (55) Where such attempts have been made in history ethical distortion has followed. Bonhoeffer himself (as we know) instanced medieval monasticism – which practised withdrawal from the world – and 'secular Protestantism' – which immersed itself in the world – as examples of this distortion. (56) The importance of his approach is that he attempted to work out an ethic which could combine the claims of both God and the world without separation or confusion. In this his concepts of the ultimate and penultimate, and the mandates, played an integral part. In our view the *sine quâ non* is commitment to a belief in a cosmic reality which has been unified and redeemed by Jesus Christ. Ernst Feil, who also sees Bonhoeffer as taking it upon himself 'to enter into a positive and theologically balanced engagement with the world', goes to the heart of the matter in declaring that 'the fact of God's incarnation alone is the basis for a positive relation to the world and for our services.' In the same context he adds, 'What is important for our study of Bonhoeffer is that it is the name of Jesus Christ which is the source of the Christian's relation to the world and not God and his command of creation.' (57)

A further point arising from this, which we believe to be relevant to christian ethical thinking today, is the realization that both individuals and the church need to relate themselves to the world in a new way. Because the Incarnation brought with it a new beginning for the world, the relation of church and human beings to it is dynamic rather than static, and each is subject to transformation. It is not necessary to agree wholly with Bonhoeffer's statement in *Letters and Papers* that 'the church is the church only when it exists for others', or that 'it is only by living completely in this world that one learns to have faith', (58) in order for this point to be valid – the dynamics of the interplay between persons and institutions is only too well understood these days. In addition, the concept of a church and Christians being changed by the world as well as involved in the business of reshaping the world accords well with the view that ethical and moral insights may change too with education and differing environments.

We now refer briefly, by way of illustration, to a few of the ethical implications of living in the world with respect to nature, persons and things, in the light of our previous remarks. Chief among our present-day ethical concerns with regard to nature is the awareness that the relation between man and creation has become one of exploitation rather than partnership. Man's capacity to explore and conquer his natural environment has paid off handsomely in terms of material comfort and well-being. The cost however is now being reckoned in terms of global pollution and biological destruction – to name the most obvious. The failure to feel any longer 'at home' in the universe is one which can only be overcome by the recovery of a sense of being stewards or deputies in God's creation. Belief in the creation and restoration of all things in Christ is fundamental to this attitude. In the language of Bonhoeffer, life and nature are neither to be treated as ends in themselves or as means to an end, but as aspects of fallen reality in which the crucified and risen Christ is taking form. True worldly living involves a recognition that God through Christ is endeavouring to make himself known as one who wishes to exist not for himself but for us and his creation; acceptance of the responsibility of stewardship follows. To make this truth real and concrete in and through one's ethical choices and behaviour is one of the central purposes of an ethic of reality.

Our next example of 'worldly living' which carries with it ethical implications has to do with human beings as persons, and with inter-personal relations. The unity which is created in Christ between God and the world, between person and person, is manifested most strikingly in the resolving of the tension between the christian and the secular realms. This makes possible the acceptance of natural life – in spite of its flaws – and of other people in spite of their faults. More to the point, this new way of relating to the world produces in the individual a wholeness or 'holiness' which takes the form not of asceticism (although self-denial is not outlawed) nor of self-indulgence (although pleasure-seeking is not condemned) but of integrity and virtue. Such a person, it may be said, represents the ideal of most ethicists today. Herein lies the possibility of a new approach to a modern kind of sanctity which owes more to relatedness and 'being' than to deeds or words. Informing it, however, is conformity to Jesus Christ the unifier of all reality. In this respect we agree with the eminent New Testament scholar who wrote: 'We may fairly say that it is never safe to emphasise the call to holiness as part of Christian teaching, unless the idea of the Holy is understood by constant reference to the Jesus of the Gospels, His example and teaching.' (59)

With regard to inter-personal relations, when the Christian, as a 'real' man before God is willing to recognize others as such, a two-way traffic is able to exist and mutual obligations accepted. Ethical discourse and action are completely transformed as individuals confess themselves members one of another. The biblical warrant for this needs no accentuating; instead we may point to writers, other than Bonhoeffer, who have set this important truth in the context of a christocentric ontology; Teilhard de Chardin and Paul Tillich are among the most distinguished of these. A quotation from

Tillich's *The New Being* is particularly appropriate in this connection. He writes:

> 'The New Creation is the reality in which the separated is reunited. The New Being is manifest in the Christ because in Him the separation never overcame the unity between Him and God, between Him and mankind, between Him and Himself . . . . He represents and mediates the power of the New Being because He represents and mediates the power of an uninterrupted union. Where the New Reality appears, one feels united with God, the ground and meaning of one's existence.' (60)

The modern emphasis is ethical thinking upon wholeness and integrity has much to gain from grounding it in an all-embracing reality which enables not only the thoughts and actions of an individual to be at one, but also the lives of separate individuals to be at unity with each other.

Thirdly, Bonhoeffer in his approach to worldly living in *Ethics* provides us with a rationale for the ethical treatment of things. In a short section following a discussion on deputyship he indicates that humans have an ethical responsibility for the world of things by keeping in mind their essential relation to God and men and the inherent law by which each thing exists. Things form part of the divine reality and their meaningfulness depends upon what God has done for them in Christ. (61) The purpose of an ethic of reality is to make this divine intention evident to all by the exercise of responsibility to all things animate and inanimate. It is perhaps not too fanciful to suggest that these two ways of looking at individual things – their inner law of being and their relation to God and man – parallel the two ethical positions described by John Habgood in *The Times* article quoted earlier. Habgood refers to one as traditionalist – this focusses attention on the givenness of things – the other sees creation as a continuous process, and is descriptive of the liberal position. He observes that traditionalist and liberal positions reflect 'deep differences in belief about what kind of creation it is that God has made and what he is doing in it.' (62) Bonhoeffer's concern was certainly with both, that is to say, with the givenness of the inner being of an entity, and with its potentiality as part of a continuous creative process. The ethicist must take both into account when moral issues affecting things come up for consideration. Again we would stress with Habgood that responsible ethical action in these matters is impossible without the appropriate knowledge, application and technique necessary in each case. As in other fields of ethical exploration, moral insights in the world of things 'have to be won painfully, by reflection on scripture, by attention to tradition, by absorption of the best available knowledge, by a process of trial and error, and by the exercise of creative imagination.' (63) The whole approach must be one of humility and reverence, with certainty by no means guaranteed.

This kind of attitude to the world of things is one which needs to gain general acceptance. An appetite for life, fostered by growth in affluence and health-care, is widespread these days and should be understood for what it is, namely, a divine gift which is also subject to the judgement of God and his forgiving grace. Without a framework of reality, such as Bonhoeffer outlined in *Ethics*, resolution of the ethical problem created by 'worldly living' becomes well-nigh impossible. In the light of it man's relationship with the world of nature, persons and things takes on true meaning and significance.

By now the central proposition in our evaluation of Bonhoeffer's *Ethics* for christian ethics today should have been made clear. This is, that we regard Bonhoeffer's approach to ethical discourse and behaviour by means of a christocentric view of reality as valid. Ethical action is what conforms to this reality and is determined by a realization that we are both bound to God and our neighbour and at the same time free to act concretely in real-life situations. We describe this as an ethic of reality in order to emphasize the importance of ethical action in 'making real' the concrete commandment of God. For Christians this means manifesting the form of Christ in his crucified and risen body, in themselves, in the church and in the world. We believe that this view of a cosmic ethical reality (endorsed by scripture) has much that is positive to offer in the moral confusion which exists today.

FOOTNOTES

(1) *E.*, pp.291f. and editor's fn., p.285.
(2) *Ibid.*, pp.292–302.
(3) *Ibid.*, p.269.
(4) In *Die Präsenz des Politischen*, p.181.
(5) At Chapters 1:3:4 and 6. See *E.*, pp.i–iii.
(6) In a paper presented to a meeting of the International Bonhoeffer Society, Oxford, 1980. Green differs somewhat from Bethge in his dating and arrangement of the manuscripts, e.g., Chapters 1 and 2 (1st approach) mid-March to July, 1940. The 2nd approach includes Chapters 3 and 4 and parts of 6, 1940–1. Chapter 7 is 4th approach.
(7) See list of books in *DB.*, pp.619f.
(8) *LPP.*, 18:11:43, p.129 and 15:12:43, p.163.
(9) *E.*, p.106.
(10) D. Cupitt, *The New Christian Ethics*, p.6 and *Radicals and the Future of the Church*, pp.42ff. cf., *E.*, pp.105ff.
(11) *Radicals and the Future of the Church*, pp.129, 158.
(12) *E.*, p.189.
(13) *Ibid.*, p.194.
(14) *GSV*, p.149.
(15) *NRS.*, p.162 (*GS1*, p.145).
(16) See above, Chapter 7.
(17) *The Theology of Dietrich Bonhoeffer*, p.45.
(18) See above, Chapter 7.
(19) See above, Chapter 1.
(20) *E.*, p.224.
(21) See *ibid.*, p.283.
(22) *Ibid.*, p.222.
(23) *Ibid.*, pp.221–2, cf., section on 'Deputyship' in E.H. Robertson, *Bonhoeffer's Heritage*, pp.45–9.
(24) Above, Chapter 7, cf., *E.*, pp.68ff.
(25) See especially 'After Ten Years', *LPP.*, pp.5ff.
(26) See *E.*, pp.69–70.
(27) Above, Chapter 1.
(28) *An Interpretation of Christian Ethics* (1936), pp.15, 18.
(29) *Ibid.*, p.21.
(30) 'Dangers of Simplifying Morality', October 3rd, 1987. For a similar approach, see R. Gill, *Theology and Social Structure*, pp.106–17. Also B. Mitchell, 'Situation Ethics' in *Norm and Context in Christian Ethics*, p.364.

(31) See *Church and Nation in a Secular Age*, p.184.

(32) *The New Ethics*, p.58.

(33) 'Kirche ist nicht nur Kanzel, sondern Kirche ist realer Leib Christi auf Erden', from an address 'Unser Weg nach dem Zeugnis der Schrifte' given in 1938 and later circulated among Bonhoeffer's students, *GS*11, p.327.

(34) *E.*, p.83.

(35) *Ibid.*, p.234.

(36) See *E.*, p.84 and pp.292ff.

(37) *E.*, p.206.

(38) *An Interpretation of Christian Ethics*, p.44.

(39) See especially pp.55ff. Peter Berger criticizes Bonhoeffer's use of Tönnies' distinction in 'Sociology and Ecclesiology', *The Place of Bonhoeffer*, ed. Martin E. Marty, pp.63f. See also article 'Society' in *A New Dictionary of Christian Ethics*.

(40) *Die Präsenz des Politischen*, p.16 and pp.10–12.

(41) Above, Chapter 7.

(42) *E.*, pp.327–8.

(43) *The Theology of Dietrich Bonhoeffer*, p.280.

(44) *Ethic of Discipleship*, p.132.

(45) *E.*, p.329.

(46) *Church and Nation in a Secular Age*, p.184.

(47) See *E.*, pp.26–37.

(48) *Ibid.*, p.257.

(49) *Ibid.*, p.103.

(50) *The Theology of Dietrich Bonhoeffer*, p.151. Also see p.124.

(51) *Church and Nation in a Secular Age*, p.183.

(52) *Radicals and the Future of the Church*, p.120.

(53) *Ibid.*

(54) *E.*, p.193.

(55) See *ibid.*, p.195. The German 'teilhaben' (*Ethik*, p.208) is better translated 'take part in' to bring out the active sense of 'experience' – the word used in the English text.

(56) See above, Chapter 2.

(57) *The Theology of Dietrich Bonhoeffer*, pp.204 and 83.

(58) 'Outline for a Book', *LPP.*, p.382, and *LPP.*, 21:7:44, p.369.

(59) C.H. Dodd, *The Epistle of Paul to the Romans*, p.191.

(60) P.22. See the appreciative reference to Tillich's 'New Being' in Peter Sedgwick's article 'Justification by Faith', *Theology*, Jan/Feb., 1990, p.8 and quotation from Christos Yannaros, 'What makes someone a Christian is not his private virtue or ideas or convictions, but the fact that he participates organically in the life-giving body of Christ.' H.

Oppenheimer in 'Spirit and Body', *Theology*, March/April, 1990, p.141. fn.21.
(61) See *E.*, pp.235–40.
(62) Above, Chapter 8.
(63) *Ibid.*

ABBREVIATIONS USED

AB	*Act and Being*
C	*Christology*
CF	*Creation and Fall*
DB	*Dietrich Bonhoeffer, Theologian, Christian, Contemporary.*
E	*Ethics*
GS	*Gesammelte Schriften*
IKDB	*I Knew Dietrich Bonhoeffer*
LPP	*Letters and Papers from Prison*
LT	*Life Together*
NRS	*No Rusty Swords* (1965)
SC	*Sanctorum Communio*
Sp.C	*Spiritual Care*
TP	*True Patriotism* (1973)
TWF	*The Way to Freedom* (1966)

SELECT BIBLIOGRAPHY

The basic source material in German for Bonhoeffer's writings is the *Desammelte Schriften* I-IV, edited by Eberhard Bethge, published by Christian Kaiser Verlag, Munich, 1958-74. References are to this edition. The English translation of Bonhoeffer's *Ethics* is that of Neville Horton Smith, Collins Fontana Library, 1964.

A new critical edition, *Dietrich Bonhoeffer Werke*, to comprise 16 volumes is in preparation by Christian Kaiser Verlag. Volumes 1 (*Sanctorum Communio*) and 9 (*Jugend und Studium 1918-1927*) appeared in 1986. The new edition of Ethik, eds., Ernst Feil, Clifford J. Green, Heinz Eduard Todt and Ilse Todt will appear as Volume 6. In all probability this will incorporate a re-arrangement of chapters 2 and 3 (3 preceding 2) in Bethge's 1963 edition, with some minor alterations to the dating of chapter 1 and provenance of other chapters, suggested by Clifford Green. For details see 'The Text of Bonhoeffer's Ethics' by C.J. Green in *New Studies in Bonhoeffer's Ethics*, ed. W.J. Peck, New York: Edwin Mellen Press, 1987. See also J. De Gruchy, Dietrich Bonhoeffer: Witness to Jesus Christ, Collins, 1987.

A comprehensive bibliography of Bonhoeffer material in English by Clifford J. Green and Wayne W. Floyd Jr., *Bonhoeffer Bibliography: Primary and Secondary Sources in English*, was published by The International Bonhoeffer Society in 1986, which also publishes reports of its four-yearly international conferences.

BOOKS BY DIETRICH BONHOEFFER

(For details of German originals and translators, see John De Gruchy, *Dietrich Bonhoeffer, Witness to Jesus Christ*, London: Collins, 1988 ad. loc.).

Sanctorum Communio. A Dogmatic Inquiry into the Sociology of the Church, London: Collins, 1963 (Munich: Chr. Kaiser Verlag, 1960).

Act and Being, London: Collins, 1962 (*Akt und Sein*, Munich: Chr. Kaiser Verlag, 1956).

Creation and Fall. A Theological Interpretation of Genesis 1-3, London: SCM., 1959 (*Schöpfung und Fall*, Munich: Chr. Kaiser Verlag, 1937).

Christology, London: Collins (Fontana), 1971, rev.ed. 1978.

Spiritual Care, Philadelphia: Fortress Press, 1985.

The Cost of Discipleship, London: SCM, 1964 (*Nachfolge*, Munich: Chr. Kaiser Verlag, 1937).

Temptation, London: SCM., 1955 (*Versuchung*, Munich: Chr. Kaiser Verlag, 1953). Combined edition, *Creation and Temptation*. London: SCM., 1966.

Life Together, London: SCM., 1954 (*Gemeinsames Leben*, Munich: Chr. Kaiser Verlag, 1949).

The Psalms. Prayer Book of the Bible, Oxford: SLG Press, 1982 (Das Gebetbuch der Bibel, Bad - Salzuflen: MBK - Verlag, n.d.).

Ethics, London: Collins (Fontana), 1964 (*Ethik*, Munich: Chr. Kaiser Verlag, 1963).

Letters and Papers from Prison, London SCM., 1971 (*Widerstand und Ergebung*, Munich: Chr. Kaiser Verlag, 1970).

VOLUMES OF EXTRACTS FROM THE 'GESAMMELTE SCHRIFTEN'

No Rusty Swords, Letters, Lectures and Notes, 1928-1936 from the Collected Works of Dietrich Bonhoeffer, Vol.1, ed., E.H. Robertson, London: Collins, 1965 (rev.ed. Fontana, 1970) (*GS*I-IV).

The Way to Freedom, Letters, Lectures and Notes, 1935-1939 from the Collected Works of *Dietrich Bonhoeffer*, Volume II, ed., E.H. Robertson, London: Collins, 1966 (Fontana, 1972), (*GS*I-IV)

True Patriotism, Letters, Lectures and Notes, 1939-45, from the Collected Works of Dietrich Bonhoeffer, Volume III, ed., E.H. Robertson, London: Collins, 1973 (*GS*I-V).

Dein Reich komme! (with exposition of 1st Three Commandments), postscript by E. Bethge, Hamburg: Furche - Verlag, 1957. E.T. by E.H. Robertson, *Expository Times* 88 (February 1977) p. 148.

Preface to Bonhoeffer: The Man and two of his Shorter Writings, ed., J.D. Godsey, Philadelphia: Fortress Press, 1965 (contains meditations on the Ten Commandments).

I Loved this People, Dietrich Bonhoeffer, trans. K.R. Crim, London: SPCK, 1966 (collection of small pieces from *GS*11-111 and other works).

Das Wesen der Kirche, Munich: Chr. Kaiser, 1971 (from student notes of Bonhoeffer's lecture 'The Nature of the Church', 1932 ed., by O. Dudzus).

Treue zur Welt (*Meditations*), ed., O. Dudzus, Munich: Chr. Kaiser, 1971.

Prayers from Prison, Prayers and Poems, Dietrich Bonhoeffer, interpreted by J.C. Hampe, London: Collins, 1977 (mostly from *Letters and Papers from Prison* with some additional material).

Fiction from Prison. Gathering up the Past, eds., R. & E. Bethge, C.J. Green, trans. U. Hoffman Philadelphia: Fortress Press, 1981 (*Fragmente aus Tegel*, Munich: Chr. Kaiser Verlag, 1978).

Bonhoeffer for a New Generation, ed., O. Dudzus, London: SCM., 1986 (*Dietrich Bonhoeffer Lesebuch*, Munich: Chr. Kaiser Verlag, 1985. (contains additional untranslated material from the Collected Works). Dudzus has also edited 2 volumes of Bonhoeffer's *Predigten, Auslegungen, Meditationen*, for the same publisher, 1984, 1985).

Meditating on the Word, Dietrich Bonhoeffer, ed., and trans., D.McI. Gracie, Cambridge, MA: Cowley Publications, 1986 (chiefly sermons and meditations on the Psalms from the Collected Works).

A Testament to Freedom: The Essential Writings of Dietrich Bonhoeffer ed., B. Kelly & F. Nelson, New York: Harper & Row, 1990.

SECONDARY BONHOEFFER LITERATURE

Bethge, E. *Dietrich Bonhoeffer. Theologian, Christian, Contemporary.* London: Collins, 1970. (The German original, *Dietrich Bonhoeffer: Theologe - Christ-Zeitgenosse*, Munich: Chr. Kaiser Verlag, 1967, contains appendices and outlines of Bonhoeffer's university lectures omitted from the English version).

Bethge, E. *Bonhoeffer, Exile and Martyr*, ed., J. De Gruchy, London: Collins, 1975.

Bethge, E. *Bonhoeffer. An Illustrated Introduction*, London: Collins (Fount), 1979.

Bethge, E. & R. Gremmels, C. *Dietrich Bonhoeffer: A Life in Pictures*, London: S.C.M., 1986.

Bosanquet, M. *Bonhoeffer, True Patriot*, Oxford: Mowbray, 1978. (formerly, *The Life and Death of Dietrich Bonhoeffer*, London: Hodder & Stoughton, 1968).

Burtness, J. *Shaping The Future. The Ethics of Dietrich Bonhoeffer*, Philadelphia: Fortress Press, 1985.

Clements, K.W. *A Patriotism For Today. Dialogue With Dietrich Bonhoeffer*, Bristol: Bristol Baptist College, 1984.

Day, T.I. *Dietrich Bonhoeffer on Christian Community and Common Sense*, New York: Edwin Mellen Press, 1982.

Green, C.J. *The Sociality of Christ and Humanity: Dietrich Bonhoeffer's*

Early Theology, 1927 - 1933. Missoula, MT; Scholar's Press, 1975.

De Gruchy, J. *Bonhoeffer and South Africa, Theology in Dialogue*, Exeter: Paternoster, 1984.

De Gruchy J. Dietrich Bonhoeffer. *Witness to Jesus Christ*, London: Collins, 1988.

Dumas, A. *Dietrich Bonhoeffer: Theologian of Reality*, London: SCM., 1971.

Feil, E. *The Theology of Dietrich Bonhoeffer*, trans., M. Rumscheidt, Philadelphia: Fortress Press, 1985, (from 3rd rev.edit. of *Die Theologie Dietrich Bonhoeffers, Hermeneutik - Christologie - Weltverstandnis*. Munich: Chr. Kaiser Verlag, 1971. The revised edition deals with T.R. Peters' criticism of the 1971 edition that it lacked concern for the political and social dimensions in Bonhoeffer's thought. Feil emphasizes the unity of Bonhoeffer's approach while insisting on the importance of the interplay of thought and action in his development).

Gill, T. *Memo for a Movie: A Short Life of Dietrich Bonhoeffer*, London: SCM., 1971.

Godsey, J.D. and Kelly G.B. eds. *Ethical Responsibility: Bonhoeffer's Legacy to the Churches*, New York: Edwin Mellen Press, 1981.

Godsey, J.D. Preface to Bonhoeffer: The Man and Two of His Shorter Writings, Philadelphia: Fortress Press, 1965.

Godsey, J.D. *The Theology of Dietrich Bonhoeffer*, London: SCM., 1960.

Gould, W.B. *The Worldly Christian: Bonhoeffer and Discipleship*, Philadelphia: Fortress Press, 1967.

Kelly, G.B. *Liberating Faith: Bonhoeffer's Message for Today*, Minneapolis: Augsburg Publishing House, 1984.

Klassen, A.J. *A Bonhoeffer Legacy*, Grand Rapids: W.J. Eerdmans, 1981.

Kuhns, W. *In Pursuit of Dietrich Bonhoeffer*, London: Burns & Oates, 1967.

Kuske, M. *The Old Testament as the Book of Christ: An Appraisal of Bonhoeffer's Interpretation*, Philadelphia: Westminster Press, 1976.

Leibholz, S. *The Bonhoeffers: Portrait of a Family*, London: Sidgwick & Jackson, 1971.

Lovin, R.W. *Christian Faith and Public Choices: The Social Ethics of Barth, Brunner and Bonhoeffer* Philadelphia: Fortress Press, 1984.

Marty, M. ed., *The Place of Bonhoeffer, Problems and Possibilities in His Thought*, London: SCM., 1963.

Moltmann, J. & Weissbach, J. *Two Studies in the Theology of Bonhoeffer*, New York: Charles Scribner's Sons, 1967.

Morris, K.E. *Bonhoeffer's Ethics of Discipleship: A Study in Social Psychology, Political Thought and Religion*, University Park and London: Pennsylvania State University Press, 1986.

Müller, H. *Von der Kirche zur Welt*, Leipzig: Verlag Keeler und Amelang, 1961.

Ott, H. *Reality and Faith, The Theological Legacy of Dietrich Bonhoeffer*, London: Lutterworth Press, 1971.

Peck, W.J., ed., *New Studies in Bonhoeffer's Ethics*, New York: Edwin Mellen Press, 1987.

Peters, R.P. *Die Präsenz des Politischen in der Theologie Dietrich Bonhoeffers*, Munich: Chr. Kaiser Verlag and Mainz: Matthias - Grünewald - Verlag, 1976. (A Roman Catholic interpretation, stressing the political and social context of Bonhoeffer's thinking).

Phillips, J.A., *The Form of Christ in the World. A Study of Bonhoeffer's Christology*, London: Collins, 1967.

Rasmussen, L. *Dietrich Bonhoeffer: Reality and Resistance*, Nashville: Abingdon, 1972.

Reist, B.A. *The Promise of Bonhoeffer*, Philadelphia: Lippincott, 1969.

Robertson, E.H. *The Shame and the Sacrifice. The Life and Teaching of*

Dietrich Bonhoeffer, London: Hodder & Stoughton, 1987.

Robertson, E.H. *Bonhoeffer's Heritage: The Christian Way in a World Without Religion*, London: Hodder & Stoughton, 1989.

Smith, R.G. ed., *World Come of Age. A Symposium on Dietrich Bonhoeffer*, London: Collins, 1967. (Contains some essays translated from *Die Mündige Welt* I-IV ed., E. Bethge, Munich: Chr. Kaiser Verlag, 1955-63. 5 volumes of *Die Mündige Welt* about Bonhoeffer's thoughts have been published in German).

Vorkink, P. ed., *Bonhoeffer in a World Come of Age*, Philadelphia: Fortress Press, 1968.

Wind, R. *A Spoke in the Wheel: The Life of Dietrich Bonhoeffer*, London: SCM, 1992.

Woelfel, J.W. *Bonhoeffer's Theology. Classical and Revolutionary*, Nashville: Abingdon, 1970.

Zimmerman, Wolf-Dieter & R.G. Smith, eds., *I Knew Dietrich Bonhoeffer. Reminiscences by his Friends*, London: Collins, 1966.

OTHER RELEVANT WORKS

ACCM publications, *A Handbook for Teachers of Christian Ethics in Theological Colleges* (private circulation) London: CACTM, 1964. *Teaching Christian Ethics: An Approach*, London: SCM., 1974.

Aristotle, *The Ethics of Aristotle, The Nichomachean Ethics* (trans. J.A.K. Thomson, rev. by H. Tredennick with Introd. by J. Barnes), Harmondsworth: Penguin, 1976.

Aristotle, *The Politics* (trans. T.A. Sinclair, rev. T.J. Saunders), Harmondsworth: Penguin, 1981.

Baelz, P. *Ethics and Belief*, London: Sheldon Press, 1977.

Barth, K. *The Epistle to the Romans*, (trans. E.C. Hoskyns, 6th ed.), London: OUP, 1932.

Barth, K. *The Word of God and the Word of Man*, London: Hodder & Stoughton, 1935.

Barth, K. *Church Dogmatics*, I-IV, eds., G.W. Bromiley & T.F. Torrance, Edinburgh: T. & T. Clark, 1936-62.

Barth, K. *Dogmatics in Outline*, London: SCM., 1959.

Barth, K. *From Rousseau to Ritschl*, London: SCM., 1959.

Barth, K. *Fragments Grave and Gay*, London: Collins (Fontana), 1971.

Barth, K. *Ethics*, Edinburgh: T. & T. Clark, 1981.

Bell, G.K.A. *The Church and Humanity 1939-1946*, London: Longmans, Green, 1946.

Bentley, J. *Martin Niemöller*, London: Hodder & Stoughton, 1984.

Berger, P. *A Rumour of Angels*, Harmondsworth: Penguin, 1966.

Berger, P. *Invitation to Sociology*, Harmondsworth: Penguin, 1971.

Brooks, P.M. *Seven-Headed Luther. Essays in Commemoration of a Quincentenary 1483-1983*, Oxford: OUP., 1983.

Brunner, E. *The Divine Imperative: A Study in Christian Ethics*, Westminster, 1947.

Buber, M. *I And Thou*, Edinburgh: T. & T. Clark, 1937.

Bullock, A. *Hitler: A Study in Tyranny*, Harmondsworth: Penguin, 1962.

Butler, J. *The Works of Bishop Butler* Vol.1, ed. J.H. Bernard, London: Macmillan, 1900.

Castle, E.B. *Ancient Education and Today*, Harmondsworth: Penguin, 1961.

Cave, S. *The Christian Way. A Study of New Testament Ethics in Relation to Present Problems*, London: Nisbet, 1949.

Cupitt, D. *The World to Come*, London: SCM., 1982.

Cupitt, D. *Only Human*, London: SCM., 1985.

Cupitt, D. *The Sea of Faith. Christianity in Change*, London: BBC, 1985.

Cupitt, D. *Life Lines*, London: SCM., 1986.

Cupitt, D. *The New Christian Ethics*, London: SCM., 1988.

Cupitt, D. *Radicals and the Future of the Church*, London: 1989.

de Chardin, T. *The Phenomenon of Man*, London: Collins (Fontana), 1959.

de Chardin, T. *Le Milieu Divin*, London: Collins (Fontana), 1964.

Devlin, P. *The Enforcement of Morals*, Oxford: OUP., 1965.

Dodd, C.H. *The Epistle of Paul to the Romans*, (Moffat New Testament Commentary), London: Hodder & Stoughton, 1932.

Ebeling, G. *Word and Faith*, London: SCM., 1963.

Ebeling, G, *The Nature of Faith*, London: Collins (Fontana), 1966.

Ebeling, G. *Luther, An Introduction to his Thought*, London: Collins, 1970.

Eliot, T.S. *The Idea of a Christian Society and Other Writings*, London: Faber & Faber, 1982.

Ellul, J. *The New Demons*, London and Oxford: Mowbrays, 1975.

Ewing, A.C. *Ethics*, London: EUP., 1967.

Fackenheim, E. *The Religious Dimension in Hegel's Thought*, Bloomington and London: Indiana University Press, 1967.

Fairweather, I.C.M. & McDonald, J.I.H. *The Quest for Christian Ethics*, Edinburgh: Handsel Press, 1984.

Fletcher, J. *Situation Ethics*, London: SCM., 1966.

Frankena, W. *Ethics*, Englewood Cliffs: Prentice-Hall, 1973.

Gill, R. *Theology and Social Structure*, London and Oxford: Mowbrays, 1977.

Gustafson, J. *Theology and Ethics*, Vol. 1, Oxford: Basil Blackwell, 1981.

Habgood, J. *A Working Faith*, London: Darton, Longman & Todd, 1980.

Habgood, J. *Church and Nation in a Secular Age*, London: Darton, Longman & Todd, 1983.

Hare, R.M. *The Language of Morals*, Oxford: OUP., 1964.

Hare, R.M. *Freedom and Reason*, Oxford: OUP., 1965.

Hart, H.L.A. *The Concept of Law*, Oxford: Clarendon Press, 1961.

Hart, H.L.A. *Law, Liberty and Morality*, Oxford: OUP., 1968.

Hauerwas, S. *The Peaceable Kingdom. A Primer in Christian Ethics*, London: SCM., 1984.

Hebblethwaite, B. *The Ocean of Truth: A Defence of Objective Theism*, Cambridge: CUP., 1988.

Hirst, P.H. *Moral Education in a Secular Society*, London: Hodder & Stoughton, 1974.

Holmes A.F. *Ethics. Approaching Moral Decisions*, Downers Grove and Leicester: Inter Varsity Press, 1984.

Houlden, J.L. *Ethics and the New Testament*, Harmondsworth: Penguin, 1973.

Houlgate, S. *Hegel, Nietzsche and the Criticism of Metaphysics*, Cambridge: CUP., 1986.

Hudson, W.D. *Modern Moral Philosophy*, London: Macmillan, 1981.

Inge, D.R. *Christian Ethics and Modern Problems*, London: Hodder & Stoughton, 1930.

Jacques, J. *The Right and the Wrong*, London: SPCK., 1965.

Jeffreys, M.V.C. *Education Christian or Pagan*, London: ULP., 1946.

Jeffreys, M.V.C. *Personal Values in the Modern World*, Harmondsworth: Penguin, 1962.

Kee, A. *The Way of Transcendence. Christian Faith without Belief in God*, Harmondsworth, Penguin, 1971.

Kee, A. & Long, E.T. eds., *Being and Truth. Essays in Honour of John Macquarrie*, London: SCM., 1986.

Kegley, C.W. *The Theology of Rudolf Bultmann*, London. SCM., 1966.

Kierkegaard, S. *The Journals 1834-1854, Selections*, London: Collins (Fontana) 1958.

Kirk, K. *Some Principles of Moral Theology. And their Application*, London: Longmans, Green, 1920.

Kirk, K. *The Vision of God. The Christian Doctrine of the Summum Bonum*, London: Longmans, Green, 1931.

Küng, H. *Does God Exist? An Answer for Today*, London: Collins (Fount, 1980.

Küng, H. *Global Responsibility: In Search of a New World Ethic*, E.T., J. Bowden, London: SCM, 1991.

Leff, G. *Medieval Thought*, Harmondsworth: Penguin, 1958.

Lehmann, P. *Ethics in a Christian Context*, London: SCM, 1963.

Lillie, W. *An Introduction to Ethics*, London: Methuen, 1961.

Long, E. LeRoy. *A Survey of Christian Ethics*, Oxford: 1967.

MacIntyre, A. *A Short History of Ethics*, London: Routledge & Kegan Paul, 1967.

MacIntyre, A. *After Virtue. A Study of Moral Theory*, London: Duckworth, 1981.

Mackie, J.L. *Ethics: Inventing Right and Wrong*, Harmondsworth: Penguin, 1977.

Mackinnon, D.M. *The Problem of Metaphysics*, Cambridge: CUP., 1974.

Mackintosh, H.R. *Types of Modern Theology*, London: Nisbet, 1937.

Macquarrie, J. *Extentialism. An Introduction Guide and Assessment*, Harmondsworth: Penguin, 1973.

Macquarrie, J. *Twentieth Century Religious Thought. The Frontiers of Philosophy and Theology 1900-1980*, London: SCM., 1981.

Macquarrie, J. & Childress, J. eds., *A New Dictionary of Christian Ethics*, London: SCM., 1986.

Manvell, R. & Fraenkel, H. *The July Plot*, London: Pan Books, 1966.

Marty M. & Peerman, D.G. eds., *A Handbook of Christian Theologians*, New York & London: Meridian, 1974.

Masterson, P. *Atheism and Alienation. A Study of the Philosophical Sources of Contemporary Atheism*, Harmondsworth: Penguin, 1973.

Mehta, V. *The New Theologian*, Harmondsworth: Penguin, 1968.

Mitchell, B. *Law, Morality and Religion in a Secular Society*, London: OUP., 1967.

Mitchell, B. *Morality: Religious and Secular*, Oxford: Clarendon Press, 1985.

Richardson, A. *The Bible in the Age of Science*, London: SCM., 1961.

Richardson, A. *Religion in Contemporary Debate*, London: SCM., 1965.

Robertson, E.H. *Christians against Hitler*, London: SCM., 1962.

Robinson, J.A.T. *The Body: A Study in Pauline Theology*, London: SCM., 1952.

Rupp, E.G. *The Righteousness of God*, London: Hodder & Stoughton,

1953.

Schilling, S.P. *Contemporary Continental Theologians*, London: SCM., 1966.

Scholder, K. *The Churches and the Third Reich* (2 vols.), E.T., J. Bowden, London: SCM, 1968.

Shirer, W.L. *The Rise and Fall of the Third Reich*, London: Pan Books, 1964.

Sidgwick, H. *Outlines of the History of Ethics for English Readers*, London: Macmillan, 1896.

Snook, I.A. *Concepts of Indoctrination: Philosophical Essays*, London: Routledge & Kegan Paul, 1972.

Sorley, W.R. *Moral Values and the Idea of God*, London: CUP., 1924.

Sutherland, S. *God, Jesus and Belief*, Oxford: Basil Blackwell, 1984.

Theology, London: SPCK., Vol.xciii (Jan/Feb and March/April 1990), Nos.751 and 752.

Tillich, P. *The Courage to Be*, London: Nisbet, 1952.

Tillich, P. *The New Being*, London: SCM., 1963.

Trevor-Roper, H.R. *The Last Days of Hitler*, London: Pan Books, 1952.

Urmson, J. ed., *The Concise Encyclopedia of Western Philosophy and Philosophers*, London: Hutchinson, 1975.

Warnock, G.J. *Contemporary Moral Philosophy*, London: Macmillan, 1967.

Warnock, G.J. *The Object of Morality*, London: Methuen, 1971.

Warnock, M. *Ethics Since 1900*, London: OUP., 1966.

Williams, B. *Ethics and the Limits of Philosophy*, London: Collins (Fontana), 1985.

Wilson, B. *Religion in Secular Society: A Sociological Comment*, Harmondsworth: Penguin, 1969.

Mortimer, R.C. *The Elements of Moral Theology*, London: A. & C. Black, 1947.

Murdoch, I. *The Sovereignty of Good*, London: Routledge & Kegan Paul, 1970.

Neill, S. *Men of Unity*, London: SCM., 1960.

Newbigin, L. *Honest Religion for Secular Men*, London: SCM., 1966.

Niebuhr, H. Richard, *The Responsible Self*, San Francisco: Harper & Row, 1963.

Niebuhr Reinhold, *An Interpretation of Christian Ethics*, London: SCM., 1936.

Niebuhr Reinhold, *Nature and Destiny of Man*, 2 vols. London: Nisbet, 1943.

Niebuhr Reinhold. *Moral Man and Immoral Society*, London: SCM., 1963.

Nietzsche, F. *Thus Spoke Zarathustra: A Book for Everyone and No One*, Harmondsworth: Penguin, 1969.

Nietzsche, F. *Beyond Good and Evil: Prelude to a Philosophy of the Future*, Harmondsworth: Penguin, 1973.

Nowell-Smith, P.H. *Ethics*, Harmondsworth: Penguin, 1954.

Oldham, J.H. *Real Life is Meeting*, London: Sheldon Press, 1942.

Oppenheimer, H. *Looking Before and After*, London: Collins (Fount), 1988.

Outka, G.H. & Ramsey, P. eds., *Norm and Context in Christian Ethics*, London: SCM., 1969.

Osborn, A.R. *Christian Ethics*, London: OUP., 1940.

Passmore, J. *A Hundred Years of Philosophy*, Harmondsworth, Penguin,

1968

Paton, H.J. *The Moral Law: Kant's Groundwork of the Metaphysic of Morals*, London: Hutchinson, 1948.

Plato, *The Republic* (trans. D.Lee, rev.ed.) Harmondsworth: Penguin, 1974).

Plato, *The Laws* (trans. T.J. Saunders, rev.ed.) Harmondsworth: Penguin, 1975.

Ramsey, I.T. *Religious Language. An Empirical Placing of Theological Phrases*, London: SCM., 1967.

Raphael, D. *Moral Philosophy*, Oxford, OUP, 1981.

Reardon, B. *Hegel's Philosophy of Religion*, London: Macmillan, 1977.

Wilson, J., Williams, N., Sugarman, B. *Introduction to Moral Education*, Harmondsworth: Penguin, 1967.

Wright, D. *The Psychology of Moral Behaviour*, Harmondsworth: Penguin, 1971.

INDEX

References in footnotes are indicated as f followed by the chapter number followed by the footnote itself.